D0722687

# PETER PAN'S
## FIRST XI

*Also by Kevin Telfer*

The Remarkable Story of
Great Ormond Street Hospital

# PETER PAN'S FIRST XI

## THE EXTRAORDINARY STORY OF
## J. M. BARRIE'S CRICKET TEAM

## KEVIN TELFER

SCEPTRE

First published in Great Britain in 2010 by Sceptre
An imprint of Hodder & Stoughton
An Hachette UK company

1

Copyright © Kevin Telfer 2010

The right of Kevin Telfer to be identified as the Author
of the Work has been asserted by him in accordance with the
Copyright, Designs and Patents Act 1988.

All rights reserved. No part of this publication may be
reproduced, stored in a retrieval system, or transmitted, in any form
or by any means without the prior written permission of the publisher, nor
be otherwise circulated in any form of binding or cover other than that
in which it is published and without a similar condition being imposed
on the subsequent purchaser.

A CIP catalogue record for this title is
available from the British Library.

Hardback ISBN 978 0 340 91945 3
Trade Paperback ISBN 978 0 340 91965 1

Typeset in Janson Text by Palimpsest Book Production Limited,
Grangemouth, Stirlingshire

Printed and bound by Clays Ltd, St Ives plc

Hodder & Stoughton policy is to use papers that are natural, renewable
and recyclable products and made from wood grown in sustainable forests.
The logging and manufacturing processes are expected to conform to
the environmental regulations of the country of origin.

Hodder & Stoughton Ltd
338 Euston Road
London NW1 3BH

www.hodder.co.uk

For Bridget

# CONTENTS

# INTRODUCTION

'I tend to think that cricket is the greatest thing that God created on earth,' said the dramatist Harold Pinter. J. M. Barrie, the hero of this book, agreed, saying that 'it was an idea of the gods.' He declared that 'cricket is the only game they [the gods] play themselves.' These two writers, among the most successful dramatists of their respective eras, illustrate the enduring relationship of cricket with literature. Pinter suggested that it is the opportunity for narrative, character development and the amount of drama within a game of cricket that makes it appeal to writers so much. 'Drama happens in big cricket matches. But also in small cricket matches,' he said. 'When we play, my club, each thing that happens is dramatic: the gasps that follow a miss at slip, the anger of an lbw decision that is turned down. It is the same thing wherever you play, really.' One of Barrie's cricketing friends was of the same mind: E. W. Hornung, creator of Raffles, the gentleman cricketer and thief, wrote of 'the unfolding drama of a cricket match on a hot summer afternoon'.

Barrie's team, the exotically named Allahakbarries, represent the pinnacle of this curious correlation between the cricket bat and the writer's pen. Indeed, if you were to draw a Venn diagram with each circle representing a well-known writer from the last years of the nineteenth century and the first years of the twentieth, the greatest area of convergence between them all would be the Allahakbarries Cricket Club.

Imagine the most improbable of all cricket teams in which the inventors of some of the most famous fictional characters in the English language – Sherlock Holmes, Peter Pan, Jeeves and Winnie-the-Pooh – all played. A team which had links with some of the game's most celebrated cricketers, including W. G. Grace and Donald Bradman. And a team which as well as authors and journalists included African explorers, a big-game hunter, cartoonists, artists, politicians, lawyers, editors, scholars, professional soldiers, publishers, actors, the occasional first-class cricketer, an international footballer and a missionary. Some of them, in those days of renaissance men and talented dilettantes, managed to combine many of these different roles. This collection of extraordinary individuals was what made the Allahakbarries unique.

The most astonishing figure of them all is J. M. Barrie, the mercurial little Scottish playwright and novelist and the energetic captain of his team. He is the main reason for this account of the Allahakbarries being more fascinating than any story of an invented amateur Edwardian cricket team could ever be: no writer could make up a character as compelling, complex, strange and contradictory as Barrie, nor as simultaneously funny and tragic. 'J. M. [Barrie] has a fatal touch for those he loves,' observed D. H. Lawrence in a letter to Barrie's ex-wife. 'They die.'

Of the vast amount of writing he produced in his lifetime, *Peter Pan* is the only work of Barrie's that remains generally well known, but the story of Barrie's inspiration for *Peter Pan* has more recently become celebrated too. It was told in the Hollywood film *Finding Neverland* in 2004 and in far greater depth (and accuracy) in Andrew Birkin's *J. M. Barrie and the Lost Boys*.

Barrie's relationship with the real lost boys, the Llewelyn Davies brothers, also forms a part of this book, but it is Barrie's constant and fanatical love of playing games, and cricket in particular, which is at its heart.

The Allahakbarries are a reminder of what A. A. Milne called 'a world in which imaginative youth could be happy without feeling ashamed of its happiness.' This book therefore documents not only the adventures of a most unusual cricket team, but also how these adventures give a compelling insight into the era in which they played.

§ I §

# OPENERS COME TO THE CREASE

# 1

## THE CRICKETING SCOT
## WHO WOULDN'T GROW UP

BARRIE (CAPT.)
An incomparable Captain. The life and soul of his
side. A treat to see him tossing the penny. Once took
a wicket.

J. M. Barrie, Allahakbarries C.C.

> Was ever set so huge a heart
> Within so small a frame?
> So much of tenderness and grace
> Confined in such a slender space.
> Harry Graham, 'J. M. Barrie'

---

If there had been no J. M. Barrie there would not have been
anything quite as entertaining, ludicrous or, indeed, as terrible
at cricket as the Allahakbarries Cricket Club. For Barrie was
the captain, the wit, the instigator, the Machiavellian schemer,
scorer, writer-in-residence, anarchist and organiser of this improvised team of writers and other friends and acquaintances. The
team even has his name strangely but ingeniously embedded
within a well-known Muslim phrase as their title, by way of
tribute, acknowledgement and recognition of ownership. For the
Allahakbarries were his team and they would have been nothing

without him. But could the author of *Peter Pan* have lived without them? Biographers of this spellbinding and strangely charismatic man have largely dismissed the Allahakbarries as a fun, even delightful, but relatively inconsequential part of Barrie's life. However, this ignores the fact that play was of the utmost importance to him – more important for a large part of his life than anything else, in fact; even his writing. For Barrie there was nothing more essential in life than playing games and having fun with friends. 'How good of you to write me about my play,' he wrote to Madame de Navarro, his cricketing 'enemy', after she had been to the theatre in London to see Barrie's *The Little Minister* in 1897, 'and how heartily glad I am that you liked it. Still on the whole, I own, I should prefer to be complimented on my "play" at Broadway. That after all is life.' The play that he most wants to be complimented on is his play at cricket and Barrie would certainly have swapped places with one of his many cricketing heroes if that had been possible.

It is difficult to understand now just how popular he was as a writer during his lifetime, so much has his reputation diminished after his death, and was already declining by the end of his life. Yet he was the most commercially and critically successful British writer of his generation, not just with *Peter Pan*, but also through a large number of other plays as well as novels and journalism.

Barrie first privately printed a booklet for his team of Allahakbarries in 1893. This was a time when he was becoming recognised as one of the most talented writers in Britain, but it appears that he hadn't yet learnt to take himself too seriously. The final pages of the book included a number of 'Hints To the Team by their Captain'. The first of these hints was: 'Don't practise on opponent's ground before match begins. This can only give them confidence.' Another was: 'Should you hit the ball, run at once. Don't stop to cheer.' Some years later he wrote to the captain of an opposing team: 'As one captain speaking to another, I would beg you not to let your team see that you are hopeless

8

of their winning. It will only demoralise them still further.' His communications about his cricket club were full of this kind of gleeful nonsense. Has there ever been a captain quite like him?

Captains are usually identified early on in their playing careers, in whatever sport. When someone new enters a team they are first judged on whether they can play the game. But once that hurdle has been negotiated, the next question may be: 'Is he captain material?' Most often, the question does not even have to be asked because captains, like all leaders in life, have a tendency to identify themselves as such, without being picked or chosen. Clearly this was the case with Barrie.

Not many cricket captains can have looked like him. His team was also far from typical – and every team reflects their captain. Physically he was not the sort of man that other men look up to. Captains need to be sturdy and physically charismatic, like W. G. Grace, for example, or even Captain Hook. But Barrie was a weedy fellow a little over five feet tall. In fact, as a onetime member of the Allahakbarries during the late 1890s, Philip Comyns Carr, pointed out, 'If you had met Barrie, a cricketer was about the last thing that you would have imagined him to be. For he was small, frail and sensitive, rather awkward in his movements, and there was nothing athletic in his appearance. And yet cricket was his great enthusiasm.' Jerome K. Jerome said that 'he was a great cricketer, at heart.' Yet despite his extensive playing career with his own side, and links with many of the leading players during his lifetime, from C. B. Fry and 'Plum' Warner to Donald Bradman, Barrie has remained on the very peripheries of the annals of cricket, just as he has come to take up a place on the periphery of literature. And, of course, he was Scottish, something that Barrie himself recognised as a handicap. 'No Scot really knows anything about cricket', he confided to his audience, which included the Australian test team, in a speech in 1934.

Captains also need to be able to rouse and inspire their teams with strong leadership yet despite his success as a writer Barrie was often a shy and withdrawn man. As the legal guardian of five children, he gave in to almost their every whim. He never had his own children and was plagued by rumours of impotency throughout his life: 'The boy who would never go up', according to one wit quoted by Andrew Birkin. He was not a man's man. Or, at least, not at first sight.

But Barrie certainly defined himself as a man's man and archetypal masculine characters such as soldiers, explorers and sportsmen were unquestionably drawn to him. When he lay waiting for death in the Antarctic, polar explorer Robert Falcon Scott addressed one of his last letters to Barrie, writing that 'I never met a man in my life whom I admired and loved more than you but I never could show you how much your friendship meant to me – for you had much to give and I nothing.' Arthur Conan Doyle, six feet tall, broad-shouldered, barrel-chested and described by one member of the Allahakbarries as 'the colossus' of the team, wrote that there was nothing small about Barrie except for his body. Explorers of the African interior, hunters and soldiers as well as numerous writers, artists, politicians and even first-class cricketers all allowed themselves to be directed, captained and often made fun of by the wryly humorous little Scot in the Allahakbarries' games.

So this small man possessed a more commanding presence than his physical frame might suggest. And he had other qualities as a captain and cricketer. He had courage and cunning in equal measure. He brought his own irrepressible brand of humour to the game, as well as the most boyish enthusiasm possible. J. M. Barrie was successful over a long period of time in persuading an extensive coterie of his friends, many of great fame and reputation, to turn out in games that ranged from the theatrical to the absurd, and often both at the same time. He badgered them, made jokes about them, issued commands and drummed up excitement in frantically scribbled letters. Matches, in fact, were not so much played as staged, with Barrie directing the proceedings. Perhaps it is no surprise, then, that he used the cricket team to implicitly promote the myth of Peter Pan among his friends and transform unwitting grown men into boys, temporarily at least; to turn a cricket pitch into a kind of Neverland (the fantasy island where Peter Pan lives) and whole weekends away in the country into boyish adventures. Philip Comyns Carr wrote that 'It is true that [cricket] was typically a schoolboy's enthusiasm; and in this it was also in line with another part that he was acting, that of his own Peter Pan, the boy who would not grow up. I should be exaggerating if I said that he wore a striped elastic belt with a snake clasp to hold up his flannels; but I am almost inclined to believe it, so much did his cricket suggest the schoolboy.'

There can have been few men in history, certainly not successful ones at least, who have been more dedicated to the idea – and the practice – of play than Barrie. It is one of the great themes of his work and the one true occupation of his most famous character, Peter Pan, who is in constant rebellion against what he sees as the dull routine of adult society. Barrie's own devotion to play started as a child and it is there that the story of the Allahakbarries truly begins. For Barrie everything important began in childhood and indeed, according to him, 'Nothing that happens after we are twelve matters very much.'

––––––––

James Matthew Barrie was born in Kirriemuir, a small town just north of Dundee between the coastal lowlands of Scotland's east coast and the great mountain wilderness of the Cairngorms on 9 May 1860. The natural world was a powerful source of fascination for Barrie throughout his life. He was the second youngest of eight children, though two more siblings had died in infancy. He was known as Jamie by his parents, though as an adult he was known to various people by many different names, including JMB, Jimmy and even Sir Jazz Band Barrie. He invented many more names for himself as writer's pseudonyms, including Gavin Ogilvy, James Anon, M'Connachie and Hippomenes. These separate identities gave Barrie the opportunity to explore the various aspects of his complex personality, though he almost always wrote about them all in the third person, which suggests that he was never entirely comfortable in his own skin.

The family was not wealthy, but they did not struggle to eat. His father, David Barrie, was a weaver. Both he and Barrie's mother, Margaret Ogilvy, were religious. Margaret had been a follower of a fundamentalist Calvinist sect known as the Auld Lichts (old lights), though, as was customary, she took on her husband's faith when they married. Nonetheless she remained committed to many of the more severely puritan religious traditions of her early years, which had included the absence of music and hymns. Barrie himself showed no interest in music throughout his life; indeed, certainly for a writer at least, he was capable of what could be thought of as genuine philistinism, preferring to play games than read poetry, listen to music, visit art galleries, or speak another language. Years later Edward Elgar had lunch with Barrie and, knowing his aversion to music, said to one of the other guests that 'After lunch . . . we'll bind Barrie to a chair and put him to death to slow music.' Theatregoing too was seen by the Auld Lichts as another rung on the ladder to damnation, yet that did not dissuade Barrie from becoming a dramatist.

Barrie's father, David, was a member of the relatively more moderate Free Church of Scotland. Barrie made little mention of his own religious views during his lifetime, either for or against the church, and his lack of obvious religious commitment suggests that he was agnostic in practice. But the Auld Lichts served him well at the start of his career, as the source of a number of early articles and his first three novels, all set in a semi-fictionalised Kirriemuir which he called Thrums. These stories were based on his mother's recollections of growing up. Drawing so closely from either his own personal experience or the experience of those near to him, was a theme that continued throughout his life as a writer. So much so, in fact, that at times it seemed hard to draw the line between his writing and his experience; between truth and fiction. He became adept at transforming a personal experience into an account that mixed fantasy and reality. 'That man would make copy from his grandmother's bones', said one critic of Barrie while Barrie himself admitted in his notes that 'literary man can't dislike anyone he gets copy out of.' This deliberate intermingling of fact and fiction sometimes resulted in private jokes appearing in Barrie's writing for public consumption, but it also obscured the boundaries between what was real and what was invented and suggests, along with a great deal else, that Barrie was a fantasist, an escapist, who used writing to try to evade what Samuel Johnson called 'the pain of being a man'. Or perhaps it is an admission that all writing is in some sense fiction, a process of selecting certain facts to turn into a digestible and entertaining narrative for readers. After all, fiction has to come from somewhere. In later life Barrie wrote of himself that 'facts were never pleasing to him. He acquired them with reluctance and got rid of them with relief.' And this applies as much to Barrie's accounts of cricket as to any of his other writing.

It was growing up in Kirriemuir that Barrie first learnt to play cricket, as he remarks in a letter from 1899 to an opposition captain who he was arranging to meet in his home town. 'I promise to avoid showing you the spot where I learned a certain game which I will not mention by name, though it is a spot you can not help regarding with a profound and melancholy instinct.'

Why does he not mention cricket by name? Because the Allahakbarries had just that summer defeated his friend's team: that's why the spot may have aroused a 'profound and melancholy instinct'. But there might be another reason for this as well, for the cricket pitch in Kirriemuir occupies a wild and windswept position just above the cemetery at the top of Kirrie Hill. There are remarkable views from the top of the hill: northwards to the southernmost reaches of the high Cairngorm Mountains and the wilds of Glen Clova, covered in snow through the winter months; and south to arable farmland, the valley of Strathmore and the more gentle contours of the Sidlaw Hills. This is where Barrie watched his first proper games of cricket, games that inspired the comment in his memoir, *The Greenwood Hat*, that 'Cricket had been my joy since I first saw it played in infancy by valiant performers in my native parts'. Many years later, in 1930, Barrie paid tribute to this fact when he presented the town with a cricket pavilion and a *camera obscura*, built on the ground where he first watched and played the game. 'Our site on the Hill is as grand as Broad Ha'penny, the cradle of cricket,' Barrie said that day, 'and the outlook is one of the fairest in our land.'

Barrie watched and played cricket here as a boy with his home-made bat. The wickets were made of iron and could not be sent flying, for they were the gates of the cemetery itself. He played in early childhood wearing his jacket inside-out in order to distinguish to himself that he was undoubtedly a 'member of the club'. Cricket was one among many games and physical activities that Barrie indulged in as a child. These also included Scottish games such as spyo, smuggle bools and kick-bonnety, but he was particularly keen at marbles and he wrote in his diary when he was eighteen: 'Grow up & have to give up marbles – awful thought.' He also enjoyed ice-skating, football, fishing and long walks – often travelling vast distances. He had an early love of adventure and fantasy stories too, from tales of pirates in so-called penny dreadfuls, to adventure stories such as *Coral Island* by R. M. Ballantyne, which remained one of his favourite books the whole of his life ('Ballantyne was for long my man' he later wrote in a preface to an edition of the book). Islands, also, continued to exert a powerful fascination for Barrie into adulthood, combined with a powerful need for self-sufficiency as though he himself were marooned on one. And here in Kirriemuir outdoor re-enactments with friends of imagined adventures, and amateur dramatics performed in the family's wash-house, also provided the opportunity for play, for fantasy, and the development of the playwright's instinct for staging drama. He later remembered 'our escapades in a certain Dumfries garden, which is enchanted land to me'. Barrie's first proper play, in fact, was performed when he was still at school at Dumfries Academy. It was called *Bandelero the Bandit*. Reflecting on the play in later life, Barrie wrote that 'No page of it remains, but though it played for less than half an hour it contained all the most striking scenes that boy had lapped up from his corner seat'. A local clergyman denounced the play as being grossly immoral, and the story was reported in a number of newspapers. It gave Barrie his first taste of fame. And perhaps it was this as much as anything that set the seal on his ambition. By the time he was eighteen he wanted more than anything to be a writer, with only the rather more remote and fantastical possibilities of being a pirate or an explorer to compete against it. And it was arguably not so far from his father's own profession as it seemed: Barrie became as proficient at weaving stories, thread by thread, as his father no doubt was at weaving at the loom.

In a later echo of his terror at the idea of having to give up marbles, Barrie wrote in *Margaret Ogilvy* that 'The horror of my boyhood was that I knew a time would come when I also must give up the games.' But in later life Barrie actually found even more games to play; as well as cricket he was also fond of croquet, and particularly a more anarchic form of this game, called golf croquet, as well as badminton, shuffleboard, billiards and many other games that Barrie invented himself such as egg-cap and capey-dykey.

The most memorable moment of Barrie's childhood, though, and perhaps the most important too, was the death of his brother, David, when Barrie was six. He died in an ice-skating accident the day before he turned fourteen. Until that day David had been the great hope of the family. He was tall, intelligent and athletic.

Many of Barrie's biographers have speculated that David's death was the single event that first inspired the story of Peter Pan. Andrew Birkin, in his astonishingly detailed and poignant book, *J. M. Barrie and the Lost Boys*, is one of them. 'If Margaret Ogilvy drew a measure of comfort from the notion that David, in dying a boy, would remain a boy forever, Barrie drew inspiration. It would be another thirty-three years before that inspiration emerged in the shape of Peter Pan, but here was the germ, rooted in his mind and soul from the age of six.' This was exaggerated, no doubt, by the fact that Barrie attempted to impersonate his dead brother in order to cheer up his grieving mother. He wrote that he had

> an intense desire . . . to become so like him that even my mother should not see the difference, and many and artful were the questions I put to that end. Then I practised in secret, but after a whole week had passed I was still rather like myself. He had such a cheery way of whistling, she had told me, it had always brightened her at work to hear him whistling, and when he whistled he stood with his legs apart, and his hands in the pockets of his knickerbockers. I decided to trust to this, so one day after I had learned his whistle (every boy of enter-prise invents a whistle of his own) from boys who had been his comrades, I secretly put on a suit of his clothes . . . and thus disguised I slipped, unknown to the others, into my mother's room. Quaking, I doubt not, yet so pleased, I stood still until she saw me, and then – how it must have hurt her! 'Listen!' I cried in a glow of triumph, and I stretched my legs wide apart and plunged my hands into the pockets of my knickerbockers, and began to whistle.

Some biographers have suggested that David's death also caused the condition of psychogenic dwarfism in Barrie. Situations of severe stress in childhood can trigger this condition, and David's death and his mother's subsequent grieving may have been enough to do so with Barrie. Whether this is true or not, it was certainly the case that Barrie would in another sense be the boy who would never grow up – for he never made it much above five feet tall. His height was something that troubled him a great deal. In *The Little Minister*, Barrie wrote about himself through the character of Gavin Ogilvy. '"It's a pity I'm so little, mother," he said with a sigh. "You're no' what I would call a particularly long man," Margaret said, "but you're just the height I like." . . . Though even Margaret was not aware of it, Gavin's shortness had grieved him all his life.' Barrie also felt later that his height had been a great factor in his decision to become a writer. 'Six feet three inches . . . If I had really grown to this it would have made a great difference in my life. I would not have bothered turning out reels of printed matter. My one aim would have been to become a favourite of the ladies which between you and me has always been my sorrowful ambition.' Instead, Barrie realised that 'Ladies have decided that he is of no account'.

Barrie himself later speculated that perhaps he was the real-life embodiment of Peter Pan, the boy who would not grow up, as much as any real boy he claimed to have inspired his most famous story. There's no doubt that there is a very large streak of boyishness that inspired and ran through his cricket team, and which manifested itself in Barrie's love of games and occasional pranks. It was a ceremony of his as an adult, for example, to play the 'stamp game' whenever his friends moved to a new house, whereby he would stick a licked stamp onto the ceiling with the help of a coin. But how much was this a part being played by Barrie – a desire to escape the extremely adult identity of the writer who almost by definition has made the study of human nature his subject?

The concept of the eternal boy was certainly not one that Barrie invented in 1904 with *Peter Pan*, for the 1880s and 1890s were already awash with images of everlasting youth, such as Oscar Wilde's *The Picture of Dorian Gray*, published in 1891.

Jackie Wullschläger, in her book, *Inventing Wonderland: The Lives of Lewis Carroll, Edward Lear, J.M. Barrie, Kenneth Grahame and A.A. Milne*, argues that in a century dominated by changes in the perception of children, the 1880s and 1890s in particular were dominated by images of boys and male youth. 'Barrie was five when *Alice* appeared in 1865,' she writes, 'and by the time he began to write, the famous icons of childhood tended to be boys rather than girls. Millais's portrait of his grandson in *Bubbles*, reproduced in homes across the country in the Pears Soap advertisement, and Little Lord Fauntleroy, the best-selling do-gooder in the velvet suit and the Vandyke collar, were the crazes of the 1880s, and *Treasure Island*, *Kidnapped* and *Huckleberry Finn* were all giving the boys' adventure story new success.'

She defines Barrie and the other authors in her book as 'fantasy writers', who had 'appeared from nowhere yet could have come at no other time. For each was not only childlike, but born into a society which made a cult of childhood. The Victorian icons that gained wide popularity reveal this. All were images of eternal youth: Dickens's Little Nell, Wilde's Dorian Gray, the girl in Millais's Cherry Ripe . . . The Edwardians, in a playful society headed by a playboy king, were as fixated on children's pursuits.'

But there were plenty of 'grown-up boys' around too, examples of what the cricket writer Eric Midwinter, in his book *Quill on Willow*, calls 'permanent adolescence'. Midwinter suggests that W. G. Grace, the man who completely dominated cricket from the 1870s to the 1900s, and was certainly not a physical specimen of eternal boyhood with his broad shoulders and large beard, was nonetheless a perfect example of this arrested psychological development. Bernard Darwin listed a number of reasons for suggesting this: 'he had all the schoolboy's love for elementary and boisterous jokes; his distaste for learning; his desperate and undisguised keenness; his guilelessness and his guile; his occasional pettishness and pettiness; his endless power of recovering good spirits.' According to the sports historian Richard Holt, 'Grace never grew up and this was his secret. He was the greatest of all the "boy-men" of the age.' He did not, however, fit into the more dandified image of the youth that began to be seen in fictional characters such as Dorian Gray in the 1890s.

THE "LEVIATHAN BAT,"

*Or Many-Centuried Marvel of the Modern (Cricket) World, in his high-soaring, top-scoring, Summer-day Flight. (Dr. William Gilbert Grace.)*

When Barrie had reached thirteen – the age his brother David was when he died – he went to Dumfries Academy where he played football for the school. It is here also that there are the first records of Barrie's cricket. He first appeared in 1875, aged fifteen, batting right-handed at number eleven, but over the years he was promoted up through the order to number three. More notable than that, though, is the fact that Barrie was also having some success at left-arm bowling for his school – dismissing the last four batsmen of Hutton Hall Academy in June 1877, according to a report in the *Dumfries and Galloway Standard and Advertiser*. But despite Barrie's efforts, his team were soundly thrashed by seventy-two runs by Hutton Hall, with Barrie only making a single run, and only one member of his team making it into double figures. It was a valuable lesson in learning to live with cricketing mediocrity; performances such as these were commonplace once he took up his captaincy of the Allahakbarries.

The following year, in 1878, Barrie left Dumfries Academy and made his way to university in Edinburgh. He had not yet acquired the gregarious nature that meant in later years he was able to assemble cricket teams from his friends and throw week-long summer garden parties. Indeed, he was a lonely figure at university, described by one fellow student as being 'shy and diffident . . . attracting but little observation, but himself observing all and measuring up men and treasuring impressions'. A member of Barrie's future cricket team was studying medicine at the same time and also, it seems, 'measuring up men and treasuring impressions'.

Arthur Conan Doyle, born in 1859, a year older than Barrie, was at Edinburgh between 1876 and 1881 where he found the inspiration for his most famous character: Sherlock Holmes. One of Conan Doyle's professors, Dr Joseph Bell, liked to explain his deductive reasoning to his students, often based on remarkably little apparent evidence, and this trait, along with others such as Bell's wiry physique, provided the basis for Holmes. Conan Doyle acknowledged the debt in his dedication in *The Adventures of Sherlock Holmes*: 'To my old teacher Dr Joseph Bell MD'. Barrie and Conan Doyle did not meet while they were at university; their first meeting was ten years after Conan Doyle graduated, on the cricket pitch in 1891, as both of them were achieving enormous success as writers.

These two men, both major figures in this tale, were brought up on a diet of imperialist success as the British Empire continued to expand during the mid to late nineteenth century. Britain was the most prosperous and powerful country in the world, despite the increasing economic power of Germany and the United States as the twentieth century approached. In 1882, Britain occupied Egypt, which gave them control over the important Suez Canal, providing easier access to their most prized colonial possession: India. And from the 1880s Britain was also heavily involved in the 'scramble for Africa' south of the Sahara, which saw them take control of a number of African territories. Barrie was never an explorer himself, other than in the realms of the mind, and nor was he a proto-imperialist; he made as little mention of politics in his life as he did religion. Yet his cricket team, with explorers, soldiers and politicians as well as writers, and redolent of the leisure time afforded to the successful upper classes of the wealthiest country in the world, was nonetheless linked with empire and imperialism. Indeed, cricket itself became the ultimate sporting statement of the British Empire, a stamp just as much as railways and tea drinking, which was indelibly impressed on Britain's territories across the globe; not just a game but a mark of Englishness. After all, surely only a nation fighting its battles in far-off places could afford to spend days on end playing cricket safe in the knowledge that if there was danger it was certainly not imminent. Richard Holt writes in *Sport and the British* that in the late nineteenth century 'Sport was never seen as purely playful; it was a national institution and beneficial for Britain. Team games, in particular, were "a good thing". The thrust of much of the sports propaganda of the later nineteenth century proceeded along predictably patriotic lines, becoming ever more fervent as the British Empire spread through Africa and Asia. Wherever the British went, the gospel of sport went with them. "The Englishman carries his cricket bat with him as naturally as his gun-case and his india-rubber bath", remarked *Blackwood's Magazine* in 1892.'

When Barrie graduated from Edinburgh with his MA in 1882 all he had apart from his degree was ambition, and, no doubt, as he describes in *The Greenwood Hat*, 'a certain grimness about not being beaten': he was as determined as ever to become a writer. And within a year he had his first real opportunity when he applied for and was offered the post of leader-writer for the *Nottingham Journal* on a salary of three pounds a week. There was no real editor of the newspaper; instead a foreman-compositor, sub-editor and reporters worked together to create enough content for the paper to be printed in the early hours of each morning. The paper was owned by two wealthy brothers who had little to do with its day-to-day running and so it was the foreman-compositor, a man called Penny, who effectively ran the operation, dividing content into two types – news and 'tripe', tripe being virtually anything that did not fit into the former category. The small lad from Scotland was there to write a leader column and to supply all the tripe, and he was given free rein to write on whatever subjects he chose. In fact, over the next year-and-a-half, Barrie produced an astonishing amount of copy on all kinds of themes, including cricket.

His account of 'A rural cricket match', which appeared in the paper on 2 July 1883, when Barrie was twenty-three, under the pseudonym of Hippomenes, is the first major piece of writing of Barrie's on the subject of cricket. It describes the encounter between the fictional villages of Slowcum Podger and Mudcombe, though we assume that it is based on a real game between two villages that Barrie had been to see himself. It was most likely a game that he had stumbled across while on one of his habitual long country walks one Saturday – his only day off in the week. Though it is not as polished as his work subsequently became, the piece has humour, absurdity, sharp insight and elements in which the description prefigures the whole enterprise of founding his own team, and writing about them. 'For years I had thought of it,' he said in a speech to students at Dundee University in 1922 about the founding of the Allahakbarries.

Barrie writes in the preamble to his description of the game that 'cricket, like angling, makes a man very circumspect about what he says. You can as implicitly believe the cricketer who tells a story of how he (in the old days again) never ran for anything less than a four, as you can trust the angler when he swears that had it not been for the treacherous state of the bank he would have landed a salmon weighing forty-two pounds and a half.' Barrie develops a number of sketched characters who all have comic names: Slipper is the skipper of Slowcum Podger, for example. He wins the toss 'and means to send his men in first.'

> Of course Swiper and Blocker are to go in first, that is the recognised thing in Slowcum Podger, and equally, of course, they do not get their pads on before Skipper has given them a number of those 'tips' which would be as useful as they are freely presented if they were ever acted on, which, it is hardly necessary to say, they never are. Blocker is a safe man, but the great difficulty about Swiper is that he too often gets bowled before he has time to settle down.

But Swiper does not have one of his better days and is caught and bowled in the third over of the innings: 'Swiper retires covered with ignominy. How transitory a thing is popularity!' The captain, Slipper, 'looks Swiper over contemptuously from head to foot and turns from him as if he knew him not.' But Slipper was also destined for embarrassment as 'Slinger has taken his off stump first ball. Looking like a collar with all the starch taken out of it, the discomfited captain retires with affected indifference, and, when he reaches the pavilion, ironically takes off his cap in acknowledgement of the applause no one offers to give.'

This light-hearted sketch has some similarity in mood, though not quite the same level of absurdity, as Barrie's later writings about his own team. But Barrie did not appear to consciously model himself on Slowcum Podger's unsuccessful captain, who walked to the wickets in a 'proud not to say haughty manner'.

Barrie found time to send pieces to London publications as well as turning out an enormous amount of copy for the journal. And in August 1884 he scored his first success when an article of his was published in the *Pall Mall Gazette*. Things at the *Nottingham*

*Journal*, though, were not going so well. The paper was making a loss and the owners looked for ways to save money. They realised they could buy syndicated leader columns for much less than they were paying Barrie to write them, so they decided to let him go and in October 1884 Barrie made the long journey back north to Kirriemuir. It was the end of his first and last 'proper' employment: for the rest of his life he played off his own bat.

Better news followed soon after. In November, an article that he had called 'Auld Licht Idylls', based on stories that his mother had told him about growing up in Kirriemuir, was published in the *St James' Gazette*. The editor, Frederick Greenwood, liked the piece, though he changed the title to 'An Auld Licht Community'. Barrie sent more pieces to Greenwood and other editors on a number of different subjects, but he soon received a rejected piece by return from Greenwood with a note scribbled on the back: 'But I liked that Scotch thing – any more of those?'

Barrie soon made sure that there were. And so began a whole series of Auld Licht articles, starting with 'An Auld Licht Funeral' and 'An Auld Licht Courtship'. He enlisted his mother to remember more stories and by March 1885 Greenwood had published a number of Barrie's articles. Barrie tells in the third person the story of 'James Anon', his journalistic pseudonym, in *The Greenwood Hat*, a collection of early articles 'tied together with a string of memories which the re-reading of them had evoked'. It was in March that he wrote to Greenwood to ask him whether he should come to London.

> I did not ask for a place on the paper, and indeed, except for that year at Nottingham I have been a 'free-lance' all my days. I did, however, promise to abide by his decision. It came promptly, telling me to stay where I was till he saw more of my work. So, to put it bluntly, I set off for London next week, on the night of March 28, 1885.

Barrie writes about that long journey to London 'in that soft autumn light that seventy looks back on twenty-five', and describes his alter ego of James Anon.

> He is gauche and inarticulate, and as thin as a pencil but not so long (and is going to be thinner). Expression, an uncomfortable blank. Wears thick boots (with nails in them), which he will polish specially for social functions. Carries on his person a silver watch bought for him by his father from a pedlar on his fourteenth birthday (that was a day). Carries it still, No. 57841. Has no complete dress-suit in his wooden box, but can look every inch as if attired in such when backed against a wall. Manners, full of nails like his boots.

This is the picture of our captain. A small and slender man with piercing greyish blue eyes. A socially awkward and shy creature who shrank from the noise and commotion of London yet paradoxically turned into one of the city's most seemingly gregarious and well-connected men. Cynthia Asquith, his secretary after the First World War wrote in her book on Barrie that 'It soon struck me that for a reputed recluse Barrie had an astonishing number of devoted friends'. Barrie was all alone in London in those first months, yet surrounded by the city's ever-growing throng of humanity; it was by now the most populous city in the world. In *The Greenwood Hat* he writes that 'He wished too that he knew some other Anons.' But his loneliness was also an asset of sorts: he had nobody to distract him from his work. And he worked phenomenally hard at striving to become a successful writer from his humble lodgings first in Guildford Street, not far from where Dickens used to live, and then Grenville Street; both in Bloomsbury, both close to Great Ormond Street Hospital. Forty-five years later he donated the rights to *Peter Pan* to the hospital, but for now he did well to earn enough money to buy food and pay his rent.

> He was in that Grenville Street house . . . off and on for years, sometimes in its finest apartments (all according to the state of his finances), but at first he had a room not much larger than a piano case; it was merely the end of a passage, and was only able to call itself a room because it had a door. It looked on to a blank wall, two or three yards away, with a dank tree between him and the wall. When he stood on the window ledge, as he sometimes did for company, he could count the leaves on the tree.

Barrie extended his repertoire as a writer as he bombarded editors with stories. He crafted amusing and idiosyncratic articles about obscure subjects like 'On Folding a Map', 'On Running After One's Hat' and 'A Rag of Paper' and took on the persona of a large cast of characters in his writing including a doctor, a sandwich-board man, a member of parliament and a cat. Whether he realised it or not, he was clearly beginning to move beyond mere journalism and into the world of literature by creating elaborate little fictions. He published his first novel, *Better Dead*, in 1887 though he had to pay for the privilege and the result was not a success. But over the next two years, from 1885 to 1887, through a combination of talent and hard work, he became extraordinarily successful as a freelance journalist, and had contributed to most of the significant publications there were, including the *National Observer* which regularly contained contributions from writers including Rudyard Kipling and Thomas Hardy. 'The most precious possession I ever had,' he later wrote, 'was my joy in hard work.'

Barrie's reputation grew and he began to earn the respect and friendship of a number of editors including William Nicholl of the *British Weekly* and W. E. Henley of the *National Observer* (whose daughter inspired the name and the character of Wendy in *Peter Pan* by calling Barrie her 'friendy', though unable to pronounce the 'r' properly it came out as 'fwendy'). And of course there was Greenwood, who had started it all. 'I dare not say how much I love Mr Greenwood,' said Barrie in a speech in 1907. 'He invented me. I owe almost everything to him.' Barrie further acknowledged the helping hand given to him at the very beginning of his career by Frederick Greenwood when he named his autobiographical volume *The Greenwood Hat*. He writes, somewhat apocryphally according to at least one of Barrie's biographers, and, as usual when writing about himself, in the third person, that he bought the top hat in order to impress Greenwood, and presumably other editors as well: 'He understood that without a silk hat he could not advance upon a lordly editor, and from first to last it was used entirely for this purpose every few weeks.'

It was undoubtedly on one such occasion that Greenwood told Barrie that the novelist George Meredith had complimented one of Barrie's articles. Meredith was highly regarded at the time and Barrie was certainly a fan: 'He was royalty at its most august to Anon'. Greenwood arranged an introduction and Barrie set off by train to see the esteemed author at his home in Boxhill in Surrey, though he reveals that it was actually not the first time that he'd been. The other attempt had not been a success. On his 'very first railway journey on coming to London' Barrie sat on a grassy bank outside Flint Cottage – he calls it 'the shrine'. But when he saw Meredith advancing down the garden path he ran away.

> If the Hat was with him it must have been in his hand; he could not have run with it on his head. Meredith knew of this affair afterwards, and also of the store I set by the Hat, which made him throw back his head and laugh uproariously. He always insisted afterwards that I was wearing the Hat on that pilgrimage.

After Greenwood's introduction, though, Meredith became a good friend and a companion on walks through the Surrey countryside.

Did cricket become a social accoutrement for Barrie, rather like the hat? A way for this man from a relatively humble background in rural Scotland to fit in with the intellectual classes in London? Philip Comyns Carr certainly seemed to think so. 'He was always acting a part, always representing himself as something at once more cunning and also more simple than he really was. I do not know whether Barrie ever had the opportunity to learn cricket in his boyhood, either at the village school of Kirriemuir or at the Dumfries Academy; but I like to think that he had not, and that his enthusiasm for the game only began when he came to England and began to study the part of a member of the English middle class.' Of course, we know that Barrie did indeed learn cricket as a boy and played at his school, but that does not discount the possibility that cricket also offered an opportunity for Barrie to fit into an unfamiliar social milieu. Barrie's team came to represent not just their captain's own quirky personality, but a far wider sense of what it meant to be English in the late Victorian and Edwardian years; almost a caricature of it, in fact: Englishness through a strange Scottish writer's eyes.

# 2

## THE WRONG SIDE OF THE BAT:
## THE BIRTH OF THE ALLAHAKBARRIES

The Allahakbarries played a few matches yearly for several
summers, that first one being the most ignominious.
On the glorious hill-top at Albury where they were
overwhelmed that day by Shere, Anon rashly allowed
practice bowling, and one of the first balls sent down
(by Bernard Partridge) loosened two teeth in the head
of the prospective wicket-keeper, who was thus debarred
from taking any further part in the game.

J. M. Barrie, *The Greenwood Hat*

L ife was getting less lonely for Barrie as he began to make the
acquaintance of his 'openers', the first members of his team.
In London in 1885, a few months after he had arrived in the
capital, he began sharing rooms with his friend T. L. Gilmour.
The two first met while Barrie was working in Nottingham and
in 1885 Barrie discovered that Gilmour was living close by on
Southampton Row, also in Bloomsbury.

Thomas Lennox Gilmour, a fellow Scot by heritage and also
educated at the University of Edinburgh, but raised in
Lincolnshire, was an occasional journalist and also private
secretary to Liberal politician Lord Rosebery. He was a sturdy,
solid chap, and a remarkably loyal one too, 'a burly, simple,

*Gilmour's portrait of Barrie*

warm-hearted, lovable man' according to Cynthia Asquith. Gilmour and Barrie were friends for the rest of their lives and the two of them were the only two who played in both the first and last of the Allahakbarries games. But a semi-professional relationship soon developed between the two of them as well: Gilmour became Barrie's banker, and later a kind of informal business manager.

Barrie managed without a bank account altogether for some time and got Gilmour to cash cheques for him. He eventually gave in, though with much distrust, to Gilmour's insistence that a bank account was a necessary part of modern life. So much of Barrie's life found its way into print that it's unsurprising to find an article about this episode, called 'From St Pancras to the Bank.' Barrie began 'searching my envelopes, boxes, drawers, pockets and other likely places for cheques, of which I had a number, though all for small amounts. I had intentionally hidden them here and there, for one must be careful with cheques.' Barrie often wasn't careful with cheques, though, which caused him regret some years later, after he was embezzled by his theatrical agent and fellow Allahakbarrie Addison Bright. Gilmour, who in the article is called Gilray, helps him to arrange the bank account. 'As we set off on our singular adventure my mentor may be conceived striding a little in front of me and occasionally looking behind him.'

They are shown into a small room in the bank. 'Then I saw that Gilray was introducing me to the bankers. Bankers are of medium height, slightly but firmly built, forty or forty-one years of age, and stand in an easy attitude, with nothing about them to suggest their vocation save that they keep their hands in their trouser-pockets.'

Barrie and Gilmour went on holiday together in the summer of 1886, renting a houseboat on the Thames at Cookham in Berkshire, and the following year repeated the experiment on the same river at Hampton. It was a popular leisure activity at the time and presaged Jerome's famous account of idling on the Thames published a couple of years later. Frequent escapes to the country were always an important feature of Barrie's life. Gilmour was his constant companion on these trips in the early days, but soon another man, Henry Breton – or H. B. – Marriott-Watson also accompanied them on walks out of London. Marriott-Watson was a large New Zealander who, like Barrie, was trying to establish himself as a writer of both journalism and fiction. The three of them also watched cricket together, particularly at Lord's, the self-designated 'home of cricket'.

> Anon was not long in London before he found his way to Lord's. The most charming sight he saw there was at an Eton and Harrow match. Among the dense crowd moving slowly round the ground stood a babe, an Etonian 'scug', more properly attired than any other mortal may hope to be, but a-weary and asleep. In this sleep he stood, buffeted this way and that, but tile, socks, rosette, cane hooked on arm and all continued to function correctly – the perfect little gentleman. [. . .] Anon went alone to Lord's at first and did not dare speak to any one, but by his second year he was accompanied by friends, such as Gilmour, already darkly referred to and to be more fully exposed presently, and Marriott-Watson with whom Anon afterwards wrote a play.

The 1880s are now seen, in cricket terms, as the interval between what has become known as the middle age of cricket – 'the era of top-hats and braces, of roundarm bowling and murderously rough wickets' – and the golden age of cricket, the era between 1890 and 1914 when cavalier batsmen in particular thrived on the best cricket pitches there had ever been and the game became by far the most popular in England. 1890 was also the first year of the county championship, which featured nine counties for the first five years and which in that first year was won by Surrey. And it was also the year that the famous pavilion at Lord's was built, though even after it was erected, Barrie preferred to sit on the turf, or the 'sward' as he called it. He never actually played at the great ground, though many of his Allahakbarries team did, both for Authors' teams and some, including Arthur Conan Doyle, in first-class games. Before 1890, cricket had been far less organised and wickets remained unpredictable. But at least three of the great names of the golden age were already playing when Barrie was watching games at Lord's: W. G. Grace, Arthur Shrewsbury and A. E. Stoddart. Andrew Ernest Stoddart was in fact based at Lord's where he played for Middlesex County Cricket Club, making his debut in 1885, so it's likely that Barrie saw him play a number of times there. Less likely is that Barrie saw Stoddart compile what was the highest score ever at the time: 485, for Hampstead against the Stoics on 4 August 1886. It was said that the night before this epic innings, which he completed in just 370 minutes, Stoddart was up playing poker all night, and that after his innings he played tennis in the evening and went to a dinner party later.

––––––––––

Barrie's circle of friends had grown considerably by 1887 and many of them played a part in his team. They included Jerome K. Jerome, who was a year older than Barrie, and who was also striving to make his way as a journalist. Jerome's background was one of poverty and childhood tragedy as both his parents had died while he was growing up in east London; his father when he was twelve and his mother when he was fifteen. He wrote in his autobiography that about the East End of London there is a menace, a haunting terror that it is to be found nowhere else. The awful silence of its weary streets. The ashen faces, with their lifeless eyes that rise out of the shadows and are lost. It was these surroundings in which I passed my childhood that gave me, I suppose, my melancholy, brooding disposition.

Jerome, like Barrie, also had a brother who had died when he was six. But unlike Barrie he had not had a university education, though since about the age of ten he had been determined to become a writer. It was an ambition that was cemented when he claims to have seen and spoken to Charles Dickens, the most famous living writer in the world at the time, while walking through Victoria Park in east London.

He went to school until the age of fourteen in Lisson Grove, very close to Lord's cricket ground, commuting all the way back and forth across London every day, a journey of almost two hours each way. And at the age of fourteen he started working as a clerk for the London and North Western Rail Company at Euston Station.

It was the first of a number of jobs. For some time he was an actor in a touring theatre company but had to return to London penniless after unscrupulous managers failed to pay his and other actors' wages. He was for some time destitute on the streets in London, before scratching a living as a so-called 'penny-a-liner' journalist, filing bits of copy on all kinds of events – fires, crimes, elopements and suicides – happening all over London. It did not pay well, but he quickly managed to earn ten shillings a week doing it – enough to rent a room. He then did a number of jobs as a secretary for various individuals and firms, writing more and more in his spare time. After many attempts, in 1885 some of his articles were at last accepted by publications such as *The Play*, who gave him five pounds for serial rights to his essays. Jerome's writing bureau that be bought with the money became his desk for the rest of his life.

In that same year, Jerome and his friend George Wingrave moved from their shared rooms just off Tottenham Court Road, closer to Barrie and Gilmour near the British Museum, in Tavistock Place. Around this time, Jerome sent the first of his 'Idle Thoughts' essays to F. W. Robinson, the editor of *Home Chimes* magazine. Robinson liked it and commissioned a whole series of articles at a guinea a time and the following year *The Idle Thoughts of an Idle Fellow: A Book for an Idle Holiday* was published. Other contributors to *Home Chimes* at this time included Mark Twain, Algernon Charles Swinburne and J. M. Barrie.

A friendship developed between Jerome and Barrie. They had some superficial similarities in style: they both had a good instinct for comedy and were considered quirky and idiosyncratic by their peers, though in very different ways. They were also both outsiders in the literary world and lovers of theatre. Jerome introduced Barrie to his friends who included the artist Bernard Partridge and Barrie's future theatre agent Addison Bright.

There's no doubt that the two writers influenced one another as well. Barrie's own holidays on a boat on the Thames in 1886 and 1887 preceded Jerome's writing on the subject of 'messing about in boats'. Jerome took his honeymoon on the Thames, and a trip up the river with two of his friends in 1889 formed the basis of his most famous work, *Three Men in a Boat*.

Jerome's love of male companionship, fine wine and cigar-smoking, now that he had the means to afford such extravagances, undoubtedly helped to inspire Barrie's own hymns to camaraderie and tobacco in a series of articles for the *St James' Gazette*, and later published by Hodder and Stoughton as *My Lady Nicotine*. Certainly, Jerome and his friends were among a group of men that Barrie was beginning, for the first time in his adult life, to engage with socially, after the lonely years of university and the start of his time in London. According to Benny Green in an introduction to *Three Men in a Boat*, 'They present a picture of a forgotten kind of bachelor life, with peace and stability stretching out from it in all directions, with its simple and innocent pleasures, its evenings by firesides, its holidays on houseboats, its nine-penny cigars and its tobacco and nine shillings a pound.'

There is also a more thorough sense in which Barrie and Jerome shared sympathetic views which also found expression in cricket, and in particular the Allahakbarries. Jerome's *Three Men in a Boat* is a pastoral work about escape from the city. At the start of chapter six he writes 'It was a glorious morning, late spring or early summer, as you care to take it, when the dainty sheen of grass and leaf is

blushing to deeper green'. His articles, book and editorship in the guise of the Idler are all about inhabiting a space that is a retreat from the fast-paced life of a society dedicated to making money and progress. 'Idling always has been my strong point,' he writes in *The Idle Thoughts of an Idle Fellow*. 'I take no credit to myself in the matter – it is a gift. Few possess it. There are plenty of lazy people and plenty of slow-coaches, but a genuine idler is a rarity.' Jerome makes it clear that his idling is very much a rebellion against the urgency of industrial society and that, at least in part, is where the enjoyment of idling lies. 'It is impossible to enjoy idling thoroughly unless one has plenty of work to do. There is no fun in doing nothing when you have nothing to do. Wasting time is merely an occupation then, and a most exhausting one. Idleness, like kisses, to be sweet must be stolen.'

Cricket is also a pastoral, generally slow-paced pursuit that rebels against the modern veneration of doing things quickly. It is a game that even in the instant information, hyper-paced world of the early twenty-first century can still be played for five days and end in a draw. And Barrie, in his most famous work, *Peter Pan*, has a pastoral character as his hero and a rural Neverland full of games and companionship in which time does not play by the same rules as in late Victorian and early Edwardian society. According to Wullschläger, Peter Pan 'became a natural and pervasive Edwardian god: a playful, wild outdoor hero who never ages, combining in one image the delights of rural and childhood retreat.' For Barrie cricket represented the exact same thing: rural and childhood retreat.

Peter wants to escape from what he sees as being the drudgery of adult life, as seen in this exchange between him and Wendy.

'Would you send me to school?' he inquired craftily.
'Yes.'
'And then to an office?'
'I suppose so.'
'Soon I should be a man?'
'Very soon.'
'I don't want to go to school and learn solemn things,' he told her passionately . . . keep back, lady, no one is going to catch me and make me a man.'

By the end of 1886 another friend and crucial member of the Allahakbarries team was also in town; crucial in the main for it was he who helped to inspire the name of the team. His name was Joseph Thomson. Thomson, a geologist, naturalist and Scot, was an altogether different explorer than Jerome, an explorer who had been far further than the outer reaches of the Thames, and almost as far as Neverland; his previous journey in 1885 had been to Nigeria. Thomson's gazelle is named after him. And though he was only twenty-eight at the time, he had already explored large parts of Africa and written a number of books about his adventures. Barrie had first met him in 1881 when Thomson had returned from the epic Tanganyika expedition – his first – which he had lead for most of the way at the tender age of twenty-one after the death of the original expedition leader early on the trip. Thomson wrote an account of the trip in *The Central African Lakes and Back*. He was the first of a number of explorers and adventurers that Barrie befriended in his life. The two men shared the same literary taste too, with a deep love of adventure stories by authors including R. M. Ballantyne and Sir Walter Scott.

The bachelors were massing at the start of 1887, the first of Queen Victoria's Jubilee years, celebrating the fiftieth anniversary of her coronation, but even more importantly the year that marked the beginning of the illustrious Allahakbarries Cricket Club.

Barrie had been in the habit of going on long walks since his childhood and now in 1886 and 1887, in his mid to late twenties, he often headed into the countryside with two of his London friends: Gilmour and Marriott-Watson. Walking had become a favoured pastime of London's intellectual classes in the 1880s, in part because of the renown of the Sunday Tramps, a rambling club made

*Joseph Thomson in Africa*

37

up of some of London's leading brains from academia, literature, law and other areas of life, who often walked twenty to twenty-five miles at a time. They were led by the author and critic Leslie Stephen, who is said to have set a ferocious pace at the front of the group between 1879 and 1891. There are superficial similarities between this group of walkers and Barrie's cricket team with their male camaraderie and love of the outdoors, though the Tramps were rather more serious than the Allahakbarries. The *Oxford Dictionary of National Biography* notes that 'the trips were characterised by plain living, hard walking, and very little idle chatter.' The same could not be said of Allahakbarries' cricketing weekends in the country, which were characterised by silly games, drinking, feasts and plenty of idle chatter. Barrie's friend George Meredith had in fact invited the Tramps to stop off for lunch at his house at Box Hill near Dorking and was elected an honorary 'tramp' himself. And it was Meredith, a keen walker and a lover of nature, who most likely inspired the choice of Shere as the location of the first of the Allahakbarries games, by either walking the nine miles or so there from his house with Barrie, or telling him the way. When Barrie spent much of the summer living in the village a few years later, in 1892, he often walked in the opposite direction to see Meredith at Box Hill.

Barrie describes in his book of memoirs *The Greenwood Hat* how he, along with his two companions, decided to start the cricket team when they were out of London on one of their walks together.

Sometimes the three of them went for long tramps in Surrey, oftenmost to lovely Shere, in which village, 'over the butcher's shop,' Meredith told me he had written one of his novels. On these occasions they talked so much cricket that it began to be felt upon them that they were hidden adepts at the game, and an ambition came over them to unveil. This was strengthened by the elderly appearance of the Shere team, whom they decided to challenge after letting them grow one year older.

Barrie's memoirs are not always entirely reliable, but it is probable that this resolution to play a game against Shere took place in 1886 and the game itself was arranged for September the following year. Barrie was appointed captain, 'by chicanery it is said by the survivors', he adds, and he had more than a year to bring together a team. He 'thought there would be no difficulty in getting a stout XI together, literary men being such authorities on the willow.' But he had to work much harder to assemble a team than he thought, and he was wildly wrong in his assertion that they would be in any sense 'stout'.

It may have been Meredith who introduced Barrie to Shere, a village near Guildford in Surrey, but ever since the railway was opened with the nearest station less than a mile away at Gomshall, in 1849, it had become an increasingly popular destination for Londoners. By the later part of the century tourists, and artists in particular, were drawn to the village by the beautiful surrounding landscape of woods, hills and sandy heathland. Up until then it had been an extremely tranquil village, inhabited mainly by agricultural workers – blacksmiths, wheelwrights, saddlers, coopers, millers and maltsters – and a few major landowners. And it remained a peaceful place in the 1880s, though with a growing population and more newcomers arriving there all the time, a trend that continued for the next few decades.

Shere is well known still for being a beautiful English village. The clear, shallow, gravel-bottomed Tillingbourne stream runs right through its centre past the old butcher's shop, now called Lavender Cottage (the same place where Barrie reports that Meredith wrote a novel). On the bridge next to Lavender Cottage there is usually a paddling of ducks on the water close to where weeping willows brush the water with their gracefully drooping branches. The duck is a type of bird closely connected with cricket, and became especially connected with the Allahakbarries due to their lack of skill in the game. Indeed, if the team had wanted a mascot it surely would have been a duck, for whenever they turned out there was a raft of feathered, quacking fowl in their wake.

*An indispensable part of their luggage?*

One of Barrie's first mentors in London, William Robertson Nicoll, the editor of the *British Weekly*, also loved Shere. He visited it first on Barrie's recommendation, and took holidays there regularly from 1890. He stayed at Anchor Cottage whenever he was in the village, the same rooms Barrie took when he was there playing cricket. Nicoll described Shere as a kind of rural paradise. 'Here,' he wrote, 'there are on every side liberal abundant moors, lovely lanes, deep woods, quiet, quaint villages and other features innumerable which gladden you at every turn. The restfulness, the charm of the place sink into one. It is so lovely London is dull in comparison.' In his autobiography, Jerome also commented on the bucolic nature of Shere. 'It was a little old world village in those days. There was lonely country round it: wide stretching heaths, where the road would dwindle to a cart track and finally disappear. One might drive for miles before meeting a living soul of whom to ask the way: and ten to one he didn't know.'

Shere set the tone for the other rural locations that were the backdrop for outings of the Allahakbarries. The team only actually played in London on a handful of occasions, at Denmark Hill in south London and at Kensington Gardens. Kensington Gardens were not really of London anyway, for the gardens were mythologised by Barrie as a kind of fantasy-land in *The Little White Bird*, published in 1902, where the character of Peter Pan made his first appearance in a magical and enchanted Arcadia, rather than part of a grubby, smoky and overcrowded metropolis. In *The Little White Bird*, Peter lives on the island in the middle of the Serpentine and sometimes rows across to Kensington Gardens in his boat made of a bird's nest. And on the frontispiece to *The Little White Bird* there is a 'child's map' of Kensington Gardens with cricket prominently featured on it: the cricket pitches are marked in large letters with ducks on the round pond just above, and in the corner of the gardens there is a curious sentence: 'cricket is called crickets here'.

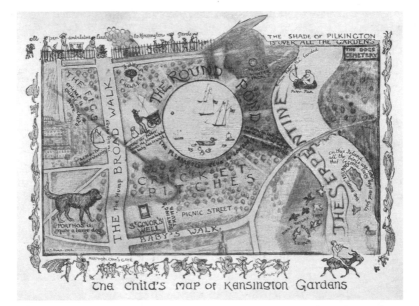

The child's map of Kensington Gardens

41

But the setting of Allahakbarries games in these idylls is symbolic of Barrie's wider preoccupation both with a return to nature, and of finding a pastoral paradise. Because for Barrie cricket was far more than just a game, it was also a symbol of opposition to the modern urban values of dour progress, profit margins and colonial expansion. For others, cricket was able to be assimilated into these categories, so that in fact it became a sporting hymn to imperialism and even warfare. But cricket for him, at least in those early days, was about a return to the pastoral way of life, a way of life that at the end of the nineteenth century seemed to be endangered by industry, urbanisation and population growth. 'Is cricket politics? Go to!' he once remarked in a speech. What, after all, resembles pasture more than a cricket pitch? It was a romantic view and in many senses an inaccurate one for cricket had its origins in commerce and gambling as much as a rustic delight in games, but Barrie was more interested in what it symbolised to him now, at the end of the nineteenth century – a green belt against the advancing wave of bricks and chimneys. 'We played in the old style', confirms Conan Doyle in his autobiography, 'caring little about the game and a good deal about a jolly time and pleasant scenery.'

Barrie was greatly influenced by Thomas Hardy, a great chronicler of rural life, who was a friend of Meredith's and became friends with Barrie too. Hardy's pastoral novel *The Woodlanders* was published in 1887 and Barrie returned to the pastoral theme again and again in his work: the division of urban and rural life and the return of man to nature. Barrie was far from being alone in developing the pastoral theme – in the mid to late nineteenth century it preoccupied major novelists including Eliot, Hardy and Meredith. Pastoral works have, since the Greeks and the Romans, tended to have play at their heart and they are also nostalgic for a golden age in which man and nature are in perfect harmony, though Barrie's naming of 'Neverland' suggests that he realised that this fantasy was a futile exercise. It can literally never be so. The naming of Peter Pan as a character is at the centre of this theme, too. Pan is the Greek god of nature and pasture. He is also connected with paganism, fertility, music and play and has the hindquarters, legs and horns of a goat. In the map of Kensington Gardens in *The Little White Bird* Peter is playing pan pipes and riding on the back of a goat, illustrating his connection with the god. The untrammelled, irresponsible nature of Pan fascinated the Victorians, who in general valued respectability and moral restraint. Barrie did not make Peter look like the goat-god but he wanted Peter to have some of Pan's aura, and he uses his character not just to represent youth but also to represent youthful society – a relatively carefree state of mankind in opposition to the hard-working industrial society with little time for games. 'Proud and insolent youth,' says Hook to Peter. 'Dark and sinister man,' answers Peter. Peter represents the love of play; Hook the love of money. There were also a number of other authors writing about the character of Pan. In Kenneth Grahame's *The Wind in the Willows*, Pan appears in chapter 7, 'The Piper at the Gates of Dawn', while Barrie's fellow Allahakbarrie Maurice Hewlett wrote a play called *Pan and the Young Shepherd* in 1898.

But as well as being a rural idyll, Shere also has something quintessentially English about it too, like many of the other villages where the Allahakbarries played. Like cricket itself. An editorial in *The Times* in 1920 stated that 'cricket has probably had a greater share than any other of our national sports in making England what it is.' In fact, the whole Allahakbarries enterprise has the sense of being almost a parody of English-ness, with so many clichés of English national identity of the type that might have appeared in a *Monty Python* sketch: white flannels, striped blazers and straw boaters worn by eccentric writers playing cricket together. Cricket and pretty villages are wedded together in the mythology of English national conscious-ness because as well as representing a form of Englishness they also represent continuity – a link with a reassuring past, which creates the illusion that time has stood still – the fantasy at the heart of *Peter Pan*. A German writer, Paul Cohen-Portheim, wrote in 1930 that 'English sport, English art, English society are all rooted in that peaceful green-tufted countryside with its gently undulating hills and lofty copses, its flocks and herds and pale scudding clouds . . . and nature is human, hospitable and amiable.'

The irony behind all this stuff about Englishness, of course, is that many of the Allahakbarries weren't English, starting with the captain, which further suggests the possibility that Barrie was acting out a part with his team, as Philip Comyns Carr suggested: the part of the upper middle-class Englishman. Marriott-Watson, a New Zealander, and Joseph Thomson, another Scot, were included in the team that Barrie put together in 1887 to play the village of Shere. And there was even a French-American among them.

Paul du Chaillu was a renowned traveller and anthropologist, and an acquaintance of Thomson, the other explorer in the team. Barrie refers to du Chaillu as being 'of gorilla fame' as he was the first white man in modern times to see gorillas, and pygmies too, on expeditions in the 1850s and 1860s. He was born in 1835 and was therefore considerably older than Barrie – a fifty-two-year-old man in 1887. In the seventies and eighties, his work was mainly on the early societies of northern Europe and he produced two major works from his studies: *The Land of the Midnight Sun* in 1881 and *The Viking Age* in 1889. One of Barrie's first biographers, Denis Mackail, who also played in the last of the Allahakbarries games in 1913, described du Chaillu as 'quite one of the ugliest men there has ever been, and as his English was as extraordinary as his appearance, it was often impossible to understand what he was trying to say.' Nonetheless, Barrie persuaded him to come and play cricket.

He also managed to cajole one of Jerome's friends, Bernard

Partridge, to come along, at least according to Barrie's own account. Partridge was one of the regulars in the team over the next decade and more, and later he formed the main link that brought in more players from the satirical journal *Punch*. In Barrie's stories throughout the history of the team, Partridge is always at the heart of the fun, both for his wild bowling and the way in which he used his pads when batting. But Mackail is not so sure that Partridge was a member of the team on its first appearance in 1887 and certainly thinks that Jerome did not make it either. He writes that:

> In the stern search for accuracy, and with *The Greenwood Hat* once more as a dangerously doubtful guide, it seems impossible now to be quite certain whether, as some say, there were two matches this season, or if the second, in which, according to Barrie, they impressed a couple of strangers at the last moment, and triumphed – took place in the following year. A haze conceals too much of these earliest outings, but on the whole it looks as if neither Bernard Partridge nor Jerome K. Jerome was actually implicated in the first of all.

However, Barrie does specifically mention Partridge bowling a ball which 'loosened two teeth in the head of the prospective wicket-keeper'. But it is true that Barrie is not always the most reliable of narrators: as another of Barrie's biographers, W. A. Darlington, put it, Barrie was 'supreme in his own domain, which lies between the world of fact and the world of fancy'. In *The Greenwood Hat* there are a number of apparent errors in

*Bernard Partridge, self-portrait*

his account of the team: he says, for example, that he 'twice made books about the Broadway Week' yet only one was produced; the other was about cricket at Shere. So who should we believe? Unless it can be proved otherwise, we are forced to accept the word of the captain of the team, for he was not only captain but writer-in-residence, scorer and archivist rolled into one. And Barrie's version may not always be the most truthful, but it is invariably the most entertaining, which is what this story, as well as Barrie's cricket team, is all about. As far as the Allahakbarries go, Barrie's word is, more or less, law.

Bernard Partridge was a handsome man, a year younger than Barrie. He was born in 1861 and was the son of Professor Richard Partridge, FRS, president of the Royal College of Surgeons, and nephew of John Partridge (1790–1872), portrait-painter extraordinary to Queen Victoria. Like Conan Doyle, he was educated at Stonyhurst College, and they were just two years apart at the school. He was one of *Punch*'s longest serving cartoonists, working at the magazine from between 1891 until his death in 1945. But in the 1880s, before his career in illustration had begun, he had been working as a stained-glass designer and as a decorator of church interiors, as well as doing some acting under the stage name of Bernard Gould. Indeed, he appeared in a play in the title role of Richard Savage, which was a one-off collaboration between Barrie and Marriott-Watson in 1891. He also collaborated with another of the early members of the Allahakbarries, illustrating a book called *On the Stage – and Off*, a series of essays about the theatre land by Jerome that described a very different world to the one that would soon become dominated by Wilde, Bernard Shaw and Barrie. But at this time, in 1887, these three had yet to have a single play performed in a major theatre between them.

According to Barrie's later reminiscences, it appears that Augustine Birrell was also selected for the first of the Allahakbarries games, though once again Mackail suggests that the two did not meet until 1890, three years later. Barrie's version is the more appealing of the two because he implicates Birrell in a funny story on the train on the way to the match.

Birrell was a tall and gangly man with large hands and keen, intelligent eyes, though these attributes did him little good as a cricketer, it seems. In a photograph that appears in *The Greenwood Hat* he is standing at the crease in an extremely awkward and unusual stance with the bat grounded and slanted backwards toward the wicket, and with Gilmour waiting expectantly behind the stumps. The novelist A. E. W. Mason stands close by with his hands in front of him. Birrell was ten years older than Barrie and during his lifetime he had careers as a barrister, a journalist and critic, academic and politician. In the late 1880s, after having already established a career in the law and published a book of essays, he was trying to be elected as a liberal Member of Parliament, unsuccessfully contesting parliamentary seats in Liverpool in 1885 and Widnes in 1886. He was eventually elected in 1889, as the MP for West Fife, where he remained until 1900. Barrie made fun of Birrell's cricket incessantly for much of the rest of his life, writing to the opposing captain Madame de Navarro in 1899, for example, to reassure her that Birrell 'is the M. P. and can't play at all. He is a Frank Millet and to prove it I am willing to play Millet and give you Birrell if you like.'

The game against Shere took place in September 1887 and it was not until they were in the train from Waterloo on the way down to Shere, that Barrie realised with horror the full extent of his players' ignorance of cricket. The explorers in particular struggled to grasp the fundamentals: Thomson even turned up at Waterloo station wearing pyjamas. Then there were difficulties in understanding how to use the most rudimentary equipment for cricket – the bat, for example. Barrie afterwards identified Birrell as the culprit who did not know which side of the bat to hit the ball with. He tells the story himself of the journey on the train, in the third person, as ever:

On the eventful today, however, he found out in the railway compartment by which they advanced upon Shere that he had to coach more than one of his players in the finesse of the game: which was the side of the bat you hit with, for instance. In so far as was feasible they also practised in the train.

In a later conversation related by Cynthia Asquith, who was by then Barrie's secretary, with another of the Allahakbarries, the writer Charles Whibley, Barrie 'exchanged reminiscences of that engaging fancy cricketer, Augustine Birrell, who, Barrie said, had required a little coaching in the finesse of the game – for instance which was the side of the bat you hit with, and what to do when the umpire shouted "Over".' Birrell was not the only one to struggle with this aspect of cricket, though. Mackail says that 'neither of the explorers had ever handled a bat before, and there was widespread confusion as to how it should be employed'. But the presence of the adventurers among the team was a crucial factor in its development, for it was they who helped to transform it from being a loose conglomeration of eleven literary types, to the Allahakbarries, a name redolent of what was seen as the exoticism of the Orient. Barrie relates how the team got its name on the train to Shere:

> Two of the team were African travellers of renown, Paul du Chaillu of gorilla fame and the much-loved Joseph Thomson of Masailand. When a name for the team was being discussed, Anon, now grown despondent, asked these two what was the 'African' for 'Heaven help us', and they gave him 'Allahakbar'. So they decided to call themselves the Allahakbars, afterwards changing with complimentary intention to the Allahakbarries.

Of course, 'Allahakbar' does not mean 'Heaven help us'; it actually means 'God is great' – *Allahu Akhbar*. But as Barrie would certainly agree, and as an ancient journalistic adage decrees, you should never let the facts stand in the way of a good story. In his speech at University College, Dundee (then a part of St Andrews University), Barrie suggests that du Chaillu was actually responsible for supplying the name. 'I asked an African traveller', he said, 'and who, by the way, constantly ran away at the end of each over and had to be brought back for another – I asked him what was the Moorish for "Heaven help us"?' That in this instance it was du Chaillu and not Thomson that Barrie was referring to is revealed by his report of du Chaillu's behaviour at the end of each over, which is elaborated on further in *The Greenwood Hat*: 'There were many other painful incidents, among them the conduct of du Chaillu, who stole away every few minutes and had to be pursued and brought back in custody'. This is presumably because when the umpire said 'over' the Frenchman assumed that the game had finished.

Despite the avowed provenance of 'Allahakbar' as being 'African', the reality is that it is Islamic and therefore from any Muslim part of the world, which at the time mainly meant north Africa, the middle East, India and Indonesia. These were all places that had been influenced in different ways by colonialism; in fact, most Muslim countries had been occupied by the nineteenth century by non-Muslim European powers, particularly Britain, France and the Netherlands. In late-nineteenth-century Britain there was a deeply ingrained fascination for what was seen as the exoticism of these countries, which were often loosely grouped together, certainly from Egypt eastwards, as constituting 'the Orient'. This fascination is seen in Oscar Wilde's fairy tales, *The Happy Prince and Other Tales*, for example, which was published in 1888 and contains many colourful images of Egypt in the title story ('the tomb of the great King . . . wrapped in yellow linen and embalmed in spices'). A popular ten-volume edition of the *Nights of Arabia*, full of eroticism, magic and romance, was published in Britain between 1885 and 1888. In Britain the Orient became a place which symbolised fantasy, which makes the name of the team all the more apposite, though the Allahakbarries were far from being Wildean aesthetes themselves. Barrie, though, certainly wanted his enterprise to have a whiff of the exotic about it.

In that same train carriage Marriott-Watson is supposed to have repeated, 'gamely', the mantra that 'intellect always tells in the end' in an attempt to bolster his own flagging confidence: surely such a distinguished set of intelligent young men would prevail over the country folk of Shere? It was an eventful journey, for all this took place in just forty-five minutes from Waterloo before they arrived at Gomshall station and were transported by horse-drawn wagonettes to the ground, not in the village of Shere itself but on 'the glorious hill-top of Albury' which is just over a mile south-west of Shere. The pitch at Albury is set on sandy heathland and surrounded by trees; it is an extremely idyllic spot, though for the Allahakbarries that day it was to be anything but. The captain let his bowlers practise. But Partridge injured the wicket-keeper who could no longer take part in the match, leaving the Allahakbarries at an even greater disadvantage. Barrie then won the toss and put Shere in first, 'and indeed he took the field to teach the Allahakbarries the game, first telling them what to do when the umpire said "Over".' No doubt there was a breathless hush, even among the babbling Allahakbarries, broken only by birdsong, before the umpire called out 'play' and the first ball was bowled. Barrie writes that

> Unfortunately Shere had a horribly competent left-hander who at once set about smiting the bowling, and as this entailed constant changes in the field besides those ordered by the umpire the less gifted of the Allahakbarries decided that their captain knew no more about the rules than themselves.

The 'horribly competent left hander' was almost certainly the landlord of The White Horse Inn at the centre of Shere, a man called Dickie Askew, who was also a keen amateur artist. 'What is a literary "slating" compared to being hit for four fours in an over?' wrote Barrie the following year in a way which suggests that he knew the answer from bitter personal experience, probably from Askew smashing him all over the ground (note that at the time there were just four balls in an over, which was changed to five in 1889 and the present six balls in 1900).

Shere hit a very large total ('It is immaterial now how many runs Shere made, but the score was a goodly one') and in reply, the Allahakbarries struggled to score anything. There is one remaining scorebook of the Allahakbarries and though it is listed as containing the scores of games that the team played in between 1899 and 1903, it probably actually records this very first match, the opponents being listed as 'Shere Fire Brigade'. Nonetheless, the scoring is shabby and incomplete, and the best indication of what happened comes from Barrie's own, rather unreliable and no doubt embellished, anecdotes about the game. In the scorebook, for example, Birrell is not listed, yet that does not entirely discount his participation, and anecdotally he was certainly meant to be there. We can be certain, though, that Marriott-Watson opened the batting and the Allahakbarries were curious to see whether his maxim that 'intellect always tells in the end' would turn out to be true. They thought that it might be when they saw him hit his first ball hard and were preparing to cheer, but then noted that he was immediately caught at point by the local curate. Barrie says that he made two; Gilmour 'swears he made five' and in total the team made the grand total of eleven (a figure which is backed up by the scorebook). Both Thomson and du Chaillu were out without scoring. Many times throughout his life Barrie related one incident in particular from this first match, when he was joined out in the middle by 'a man of a rare scholastic turn,' as he put it in a speech at Dundee. Despite his non-appearance in the scorebook, it is likely that this man was Augustine Birrell. Barrie relates the story of what happened next in *The Greenwood Hat*:

One man who partnered him was somewhat pedantic and before taking centre (as they were all instructed to do) signed to Anon that he had a secret to confide. It proved to be 'Should I strike the ball to however small an extent I shall run with considerable velocity.' He did not have to run.

It is a story that also made it into W. G. Grace's *Cricketing Reminiscences* in 1899, though he told it in rather a different way to Barrie, saying that Barrie had been the wicket-keeper and the batsman was on the opposing side.

It is unclear whether it was also on this occasion that Birrell broke one of Barrie's bats. Barrie told of how 'Augustine Birrell once hit so hard that he smashed the bat of Anon, which had been kindly lent to him, and instead of grieving he called out gloriously, "Fetch me some more bats."' Barrie is characteristically uncaring about where or when this event may have taken place – he was happy just to weave it into the mythology of his team, which built up over time until he had an enormous repetoire of stories to tell about the Allahakbarries.

The Allahakbarries' innings was so short that Barrie reports that Shere went in again, but when the formidable pub landlord, Askew, came out to the centre once more, the Allahakbarries had decided they had seen enough. 'The way we finished it,' said Barrie, 'was by saying to the innkeeper that we all wanted to come and dine at his inn. And so he went away and we got him out.' They dined at Askew's pub, The White Horse, which was a raucous evening with du Chaillu particularly keen to boast of his exploits on the field of play. The team returned to London by train, either later that night or the following day.

In their first game, then, the Allahakbarries had been soundly thrashed. On paper they'd been not just beaten but humiliated. Barrie, however, disagreed: 'The general feeling was that the eleven had been beaten but not disgraced'. Strangely their morale was not dented at all. 'We were a good deal elated by that first match of ours, and our spirits began to run very high,' said Barrie later. And it's true that things could only get better: although they were to get beaten many more times, they were never to be quite as thoroughly trounced and made to look such rank amateurs as on this first occasion.

Barrie revelled in the camaraderie and playful nature of the enterprise. It reflects the fact that in just two years of hard work and success in London, Barrie's character had at least in part been transformed from that train journey from Scotland when he first arrived, when he was 'gauche and inarticulate' and wore 'an uncomfortable blank' as his expression. Then he could hear 'the hopes and fears that are thumping inside him.' But now he was a man in his element, confident, happy and surrounded by friends. He no longer seemed to fear being thought of as ridiculous. He was also determined to gain far more enjoyment from his cricket team. Did his team know this at the time? Probably not, but as Mackail writes,

> if any of them supposed that he had exhausted this form of pleasure, or would spare them if he wanted them on the next occasion, they were profoundly mistaken. He had taken ten grown-up men, with some of whom he was on anything but intimate terms, had changed them into boys again for one whole, long day, and had been their acknowledged and undisputed chief. This was happiness, and time, for once, must certainly bring it again.

It was the beginning of a series of matches against Shere. Marriott-Watson later moved to the village and remained there for the rest of his life. The first match was short, and because of this there is little evidence to assess the relative merits or otherwise of the players, though Gilmour continued to boast about his five runs for a long time. The other members of the team were not great players, and some, like Birrell and Partridge, continued to be the butt of Barrie's jokes about cricket throughout the history of the club, and beyond. Jerome wrote that

> I was never any good at cricket myself. I had no chance of learning games as a boy, and cricket is not a thing you can pick up at any time. As for Barrie himself, he was evidently very knowledgeable about cricket, but had distinct shortcomings on the pitch. He was, however, especially proud of his slow, left-handed bowling, which he famously thought was the slowest there had ever been.

Barrie reported that after delivering the ball, he would go and sit on the turf at mid-off, and wait for it to reach the other end – 'which it sometimes did!' He also made the joke that if he didn't like the look of a ball he could easily go and fetch it before it reached the other batsman and bowl it again. 'My better class of bowling is slow', he once said. 'Its whole cunning lies in this – it makes me laugh to read in the papers about people being slow bowlers – they don't know what slow bowling is. You go on flourishing and flourishing, preparing for the ball more and more widely, and when you finish the ball is about half-way down, but pursuing its relentless way to the wicket.'

Nonetheless, some were impressed by the Scot's lobs: Conan Doyle, for example, said that 'Barrie was no novice. He bowled an insidious left-hand good-length ball coming from leg which was always likely to get a wicket.' Barrie may have been shielded somewhat by the great emphasis on off-side play at this time in cricketing history, which meant that great heaves to the leg-side were not seen as being good form. W. G. Grace's brother, E. M. Grace, who was even more competitive than the notoriously cut-throat W. G., was a man without moral scruples on the cricket field, and his gamesmanship ushered in a new era of competitiveness in cricket, though off-side batting was still seen as being more proper than hitting to the leg-side. A story of one of E. M. Grace's early appearances illustrates the point. Grace had pulled a ball from outside the off-stump to the square leg boundary and in response, the bowler shouted out 'That's not cricket.' 'It may not be cricket,' replied the batsman, 'but it's four runs.'

Barrie was capable of taking wickets, and continued to score the occasional success, and now and again take a surprising haul. He even had a couple of good innings with the bat in his career, though this was even more surprising than his triumphs with the ball. He batted right-handed, and though he seldom scored many runs, onlookers were impressed by his courage in the face of the bowling. His biographer, Mackail, relates that:

> He hardly troubled to dodge. His calm was spectacular, and no violent or unexpected blow was ever seen to disturb it. It was the others who gasped, yelled, or shuddered, but never Barrie. Indomitable; there can be no other epithet to sum up the cricketing spirit in that small and fragile frame.

The courage required from batsmen, particularly in those days of little protective padding and far more unpredictable wickets than in the modern era, was one of the reasons why they especially came to be seen as some of the great heroes and role models of the 1890s and 1900s. Bowlers, meanwhile, were not nearly so worshipped. As Barrie wrote in a humorous piece in 1888, 'The feelings of a bowler, how seldom are they considered'. No, it was the batsmen who were the heroes – and probably have been ever since. The pitches at the time meant that balls were far more prone to behave in unexpected ways and leap up to injure batsmen, though at this time the improvement in first-class grounds, at least, was also dramatic and was a further reason why batsmen became increasingly exulted – it was getting much easier at the highest level of the game to make big scores and perform heroic deeds. In 1887 the era of dashing and heroic amateur batsmen such as Jackson, Fry, Ranjitsinhji, MacClaren and Stoddart, was just beginning, emulating the wider obsession throughout society over the following twenty-five years with handsome and athletic boys and young men. Cricket was also fast becoming the most popular of all sports in an era in which sport as a whole became a far more prominent part of society. The improved transport system helped, particularly the introduction of a railway network across the country, which allowed the Allahakbarries to get to games in Worcestershire just as easily as those in Surrey. But Britain had also become immensely wealthy and the upper classes had more leisure time than ever before. With legislation in the 1870s that brought a shorter working week and meant that Saturday afternoon was free, as well as the introduction of bank holidays, it meant that the working classes had more time on their hands too, though significantly less than the upper classes, of course. But the attendance figures from this era of cricket were enormous. In 1904, for example, seventy-nine thousand people saw Yorkshire against Lancashire and in 1906, more than eighty thousand watched Surrey play Yorkshire. Of course, with crowds like these, and the feats of cricketers reported in the newspapers, many players became national figures, even idols.

Sport also became more institutionalised and commercial in nature during this time. In his book *Edwardians at Play*, Brian Dobbs, writing in the 1970s, argued that 'Sport, as we know it, was born in that quarter of a century' between 1890 and 1914. The Allahakbarries were a long way from representing this increasingly serious form of sport. They were amateurs in the truest sense, and played for the joy of the game, and for the love of play. Their games were often disorganised and occasionally, like their first outing at Shere, rather shambolic, but that was all part of the fun. In fact, the Allahakbarries represented a conscious rebellion against the rationalisation of sport and Barrie in particular dreaded the idea of taking it all too seriously. 'We never cared whether we won or lost', said Barrie, 'We played the game.'

But there was an element of amateurism with the Allahakbarries that some contemporary purists objected to; in particular the idea that Barrie's cricket team was actually just an elaborate joke and his team wasn't treating the game seriously enough. Philip Carr, in his introduction to the 1950 edition of the *Allahakbarries Book of Broadway Cricket 1899* argues that this is precisely what the team was. He writes that Barrie 'would have given much to be good at [cricket]; but he was far less than good. So what did he do? Give up playing cricket? Never! He just turned cricket into a joke.'

There's a distinction to be made between sport and play. It is intuitive to think of sport as being a form of play, largely because of the language used to describe participation in sport – 'playing cricket', for example. But at the end of the nineteenth century sport in England began to acquire the characteristics of work more than those of play. Organised sport is like work because it is task oriented and generally involves physical exertion, preparation, has a formal structure, organisation and a serious purpose. Play, on the other hand, is all about leisure, diversion and fun with no other aim than enjoyment. Joking is a legitimate part of play, but is often frowned upon in sport, an altogether more serious pursuit. The Victorians and Edwardians had an ambivalent attitude to leisure, as work had come to be valued far more than play, yet due to the wealth of the country there was more leisure time than ever before. Proverbs such as 'the devil makes work for idle hands' are emblematic of the Victorian philosophy towards leisure. In the industrialised era sport began to be taken far more seriously, and sporting organisations took on the same structures as businesses, ultimately becoming a multi-billion pound industry. According to Richard Holt, in his essay, 'Cricket and Englishness: The Batsman as Hero', 'Cricket was a form of highly organised competition in which the rules of play and its etiquette were elevated into a new civic ideal of vigour, integrity and flair.' Cricket was being transformed into not only a more serious and commercial game, but also one loaded with 'British values' and 'saturated with expansionist imperial and Darwinist concerns': it was being politicised. Yet there were still amateurs at the highest level, as well as teams including the Allahakbarries at a rather lower level, who rebelled against the notion of cricket as anything other than a game to be played for the fun of playing.

Throughout this period, first-class cricketers were divided into two types: amateurs and professionals, often also called gentlemen and players. Amateurs, or gentlemen, were wealthier men who played cricket as a pastime, but not to earn money, or at least not in theory (W. G. Grace was the most notable of the 'shamateurs', who made lots of money out of the game yet continued to call themselves amateurs). Amateurs often played for a few seasons in their early twenties, as an interlude between school and the rest of their adult lives, before properly starting their careers. There were lots of jobs around in Britain's wealthy economy for these young men once they had completed their stint at the wicket and they were often supported by money from their families too. It meant that it was relatively easy for talented amateurs to pursue the game at the highest level. Professionals, or players, by contrast, were from the lower social orders and were paid to play, and often did so for as long as they could: it was their livelihood. They were the workhorses of the county teams, while it was the amateurs who generally provided the flair. There were exceptions, of course, but the majority of amateurs were there to bat, and be heroes.

The background to this age of exciting amateur batsmen was the increase of cricket coaching within public schools, which began at the end of the 1880s to produce a number of batsmen whose play was characterised by adventure, wristy off-side drives and cuts and a belief in playing an aesthetically pleasing and aggressive form of the game. These amateur batsmen, far more

AMATEURS AND PROFESSIONALS.

*Caddie (visiting).* WHAT KIND O' PLAYER IS HE?" *Caddie (engaged).* "'IM? HE JUST PLAYS AS IF IT WAS FOR PLEESURE!"

than their cricketing forerunners even, including W. G. Grace, were the Peter Pans of the cricket world, who were enjoying the game for its own sake rather than necessarily the winning of it. This was about playing the game in its true spirit, as they saw it, probably to do with their youth as much as their amateur status. As Patrick Morrah, in *The Golden Age of Cricket*, writes:

> These young cricketers personified the era that was now beginning. They possessed a dash and *insouciance* that had been lacking in even the best among their predecessors. They were true amateurs; they played cricket because they liked playing cricket; they went their own way and they cared neither for averages nor for public criticism.

The division of dashing amateurs and workaday professionals enforced the existing social distinctions in late Victorian and Edwardian English society. Richard Holt writes that 'In cricket the classes and the masses seemed by mutual consent to occupy their rightful respective places whilst the Empire was strengthened by sporting contacts. Professionals might provide muscle and consistency but amateurs were supposed to have the flair, the sense of command, the wider vision and aesthetic appreciation.' Cricket united the social classes, and it became universally followed. It seems remarkable from the modern perspective that amateurs and professionals could play side by side at the same level of the game, and the fact that a number of members of the Allahakbarries, though not any of those who played in the first game at Shere, could also play first-class games as amateurs as well as representing such occasional sides.

But county sides were not the only teams that amateur cricketers could play for. There were gentlemen's sides, some of which still exist, and since 1845 there had also been a wandering, or nomadic, side without their own ground called I Zingari, Italian for 'the gypsies', which may have been one of the models for the Allahakbarries. They were a more serious outfit than the Allahakbarries, though, founded by a group of old Harrovians, with a motto, 'out of darkness, through fire, into light', represented by their club colours of black, red and gold. There were other wandering sides too, such as the Free Foresters and the Eton Ramblers. These sides formed the foundation of country house cricket, which became extremely popular at private houses in the 1890s and 1900s. These were beginning to be more decadent days towards the end of the century, encouraged by the fun-loving Edward, Prince of Wales who famously loved racing as well as other sports, and the socialising that went with them. Patrick Morrah writes in *The Golden Age of Cricket* that in country house cricket

> the social aspect was paramount. The company was carefully selected; the entertainment was lavish. Lovely ladies graced the scene. Cricket in the sun on beautiful grounds, punctuated by champagne lunches and strawberry teas, was followed at night by dancing, revelry and more champagne until the small hours of the morning.

So this first outing to Shere from the Allahakbarries, at the very start of what became known as a glorious age for amateur cricket, was a rather restrained occasion by contrast with some of the pomp and splendour of country house cricket weekends.

Barrie and his gang returned to London. Barrie was eager to see his first novel, *Better Dead*, appear in print, which he did in November 1887 after he had paid twenty-five pounds to Swan Sonnenschein, Lowrey, and Co. of Paternoster Square to publish it. It was a so-called 'shilling shocker' with a murderous plot yet also full of humorous sketches of contemporary figures. One of them, Lord Randolph Churchill, wrote to Barrie to tell him how much he had enjoyed the book, but Barrie was later rather ashamed of it and when asked what he thought of *Better Dead* he referred the questioner to its title. He went home to Kirriemuir for Christmas that year, buoyed not only by having his name on a book for the first time, but also by a commission from the editor William Nicoll: he had persuaded Hodder and Stoughton to print a volume of Barrie's Auld Licht articles from the *St James' Gazette* with the simple title of *Auld Licht Idylls*. Barrie spent Christmas and New Year hard at work on this next book, which he was determined to turn into a success.

When he returned to London his time sharing bachelor's rooms with his friend, Gilmour, was coming to an end as Gilmour had got engaged to Miss Elizabeth Keltie, only daughter of John Scott Keltie, another Scotchman, and at the time librarian to the Royal Geographical Society. He was an influential figure at the society over a long period, most notably a number of years later during the polar expeditions of Shackleton and Scott. The introduction to Elizabeth had come through Joseph Thomson and in 1888 Barrie met many more explorers and adventurers as he and Gilmour went to the Keltie's house in Highgate almost every Sunday. Mackail relates that Barrie used the opportunity not just for conversation, but also to 'challenge the whole party at various indoor games. His skill at tiddlywinks was outstanding. He was amazing and unequalled at throwing cards into a hat. He conjured a little, too, at which there was more laughter and admiration. All this, one may say, was to show the company that even if he couldn't lead expeditions to the equator, he still had gifts of his own. He chose his own ground – as he always did – and he beat the lot.'

Barrie's confidence was growing and his skills as a captain, too, as he developed a more masterful side of his personality. His team were growing in stature as well: Marriott-Watson had his first novel published in 1888, Gilmour was to be married that year and Barrie continued his meteoric rise as a writer. But could they translate these successes off the pitch into success on it in 1888?

# 3

## WHITE FIGURES ON REASONABLE
## TERMS: THE FIRST GAMES

Scrupulous attention to the laws, and as far as possible
to the customs, but a game within a game for the captain
at any rate. To see his friends making fools of themselves
under his orders. To frighten them beforehand, laugh at
them afterwards, but never to let them off. A very few
stood back, and were too proud or self-conscious to
oblige in this way. But a surprising number of surprising
characters did their worst and utmost over and over again,
and were rewarded with fun at the time and memories
afterwards.

Denis Mackail, *The story of J.M.B.*

---

The Allahakbarries had not had an auspicious start but they
were full of determination at the start of 1888 to avenge their
defeat at the hands of Shere. The details of this and the next few
games are rather murky, yet it seems that 'the eleven eminent
men' improbably prevailed against the villagers in only their
second game. The only account of the 1888 game, in fact, comes
from the pen of the less than reliable captain of the team. Barrie
was strangely obsessed with cows at this time, a fact that he recog-
nises in his memoirs *The Greenwood Hat* where he writes that
'Anon had conceived an esteem for the cow, the placid divinity

who chews the cud of life equally, ever the same, yesterday, today and tomorrow, judging man more by the way he offers her grass than by his personal attractions.' And in his brief and sketchy account of the 1888 game Captain Barrie also brings a bovine theme to proceedings when he boasts that

> The next time the Allahakbarries played Shere they won because they arrived two men short. They scoured the country in a wagonette, seeking to complete their team, and took with them, despite his protests, an artist whom they found in a field painting cows. They were still more fortunate in finding a soldier sitting with two ladies outside a pub. He agreed to accompany them if they would take the ladies also, and all three were taken. This unknown was the Allahakbarrie who carried the team that day to victory, and the last they saw of him he was sitting outside another pub with another two ladies.

From this scant evidence it seems that the Allahakbarries broke their collective duck only a year after they had been trounced by Shere. Yes, they had a little outside help, but the win nonetheless left their captain feeling optimistic about many future victories. There is no clue as to the identity of the mysterious soldier and the artist who played for the team that day and no hint as to what the scores were either. In fact, there is only Barrie's word to attest to the fact that the game took place at all, and it remains a shadowy episode in the history of the side.

The incentives for many of the younger men in the Allahakbarries to stay in London at this time were clear. Barrie was on the verge of becoming one of the most famous writers in England, Jerome was having success with his first books and in 1889 *Three Men in a Boat* was published and became hugely successful, despite a number of negative and rather snooty critical notices, which complained in particular of its colloquial language. Marriott-Watson had his first novel, *Marahuna*, published in 1888 and was also getting pieces printed in a number of prestigious journals. He soon after became the literary editor of the *St James' Gazette*. Gilmour got married on 24 November, and on the eve of the wedding he met with his male acquaintances, and most of the Allahakbarries team, including Barrie, Thomson, du Chaillu and Marriott-Watson, as well as the bride's father, at the Holborn Restaurant. It was also his last night sharing lodgings with Barrie, who for the next few years lived on his own.

But Barrie was mocking his reputation for shyness by continuing to expand his social and professional circle. And this meant more cricketers for his side. W. E. Henley was the latest editor to fall under his spell, and they soon became friends as well as professional acquaintances, though Henley did not play cricket, at least partly because one of his feet had been amputated as a youth due to tuberculosis, just one of his many health problems. However, Henley's daughter Margaret appeared in the first of the Allahakbarries books as the 'Captain's Girl'. Henley edited the *Scots Observer* and then the *National Observer* and many famous writers appeared on the pages of these two publications including Robert Louis Stevenson, Thomas Hardy, Rudyard Kipling, H. G. Wells and W. B. Yeats as well as Barrie and Marriott-Watson. According to Mackail, 'To be one of "Henley's young men" in those days was in itself an accolade.'

Barrie was beginning to move in the highest circles of literary London. And he recruited from the *Observer* an additional member for his team: the assistant editor, Charles Whibley. Whibley, just a few months older than Barrie, was a highly conservative man, an advocate of population control who wrote a column expounding his conservative views and in particular his opposition to state education. Barrie, on the other hand, if he had stood for parliament, would most likely have stood as a Liberal, and two of his greatest friends, A. E. W. Mason and Augustine Birrell, were Liberal politicians. Yet Whibley and Barrie became friends for the rest of their lives, perhaps because Whibley was, according to Mackail, 'one of the most glorious, inspiriting, and much-loved companions that the world has known.' Barrie later wrote of Whibley's batting, in the first of the Allahakbarries books, that he 'hits blooming hard, blooming high, and blooming seldom', and elsewhere that he 'threw unerringly in the wrong direction'. He also listed the *National Observer* office as one of the Allahakbarries practice grounds, along with 20 St John's Wood Road: Lord's Cricket Ground.

At the end of 1888 Marriott-Watson and Barrie started writing a play together, which turned out, like some other of Barrie's writing collaborations as opposed to his solo efforts, as something of a failure. It was called *Richard Savage*, and was based on the life of the notoriously badly behaved eighteenth century poet. When it did eventually get performed, at the Criterion Theatre in 1891, it was its one and only performance.

Barrie, though, was so hard at work that he had many other projects on the go at the same time. There is an irony here. For a man so outwardly dedicated to play, Barrie was also intensely devoted to hard work. 'I do not know when it came to me – not very early, because I was an idler at school, and read all the wrong books at college. But I fell in love with hard work one fine May morning.'

At the start of 1889 Barrie published another book, called *An Edinburgh Eleven*, which had originally been a series of papers in the *British Weekly*, edited by William Robertson Nicoll. Despite the cricketing title, it was not at all a book about cricket, but instead character sketches of eleven luminaries from Edinburgh, which included his friend Joseph Thomson, Robert Louis Stevenson (who he corresponded with at length in the South Pacific but never actually met) and one of his old professors David Masson. Barrie later told the story in a letter to Nicoll that although the book was not about cricket, many were fooled by the title into thinking that it was, including the most famous cricketer of all. He wrote:

Do you remember how, in the early life of the British Weekly, I wrote some papers for you on Scottish worthies, which were afterwards published as a little volume under the title 'An Edinburgh Eleven'? And how Dr W. G. Grace came across it and tossed it aside on discovering that not one of my eleven could bat or bowl?

Barrie did, however, write many pieces that were about cricket, though none of them serious, and on 11 May 1889, two days after Barrie turned twenty-nine, he put the Allahakbarries in print for the first time in the *Edinburgh Evening Dispatch*. These Allahakbarries were not easily recognisable at first as Barrie had disguised the team, but his report clearly refers to the first two games that the Allahakbarries played at Shere. Instead of Shere, Barrie calls the village 'Stoke-in-the-Ditch' and instead of the Allahakbarries he calls his team 'Celebrities at Home'. He rarely wasted a story and if there was anything from real life that he could turn into copy then he would do so, as is the case here. He writes: 'The home team was a local eleven, captained by the innkeeper, and the visitors were all from London.' The innkeeper was that same 'horribly competent left-hander', Dickie Askew, the landlord of The White Horse in Shere, that you will remember from the first game. Barrie goes on:

> The whole affair was a joke, got up by a barrister (and Member of Parliament), who has been employed in the Parnell Commission, and is something of a humorist. The scene of the match was the village I call Stoke-in-the-Ditch, because it is a favourite resort of artists, two of whom were in the team.

The barrister and MP that Barrie mentions here is Augustine Birrell, who fits all the criteria listed in the article, and was noted as something of a humorist, with a characteristic style of writing, which came to be called 'Birrelling'. For this story, Barrie makes

Birrell the captain of the side, rather than him. But he does not give the real names of any of his team because, he writes, 'It would be unfair to give the names of the celebrities, as several of them stipulated for secrecy, and all played under assumed names.' The aliases were all of a ridiculous kind. Birrell, for instance, became Sir Walter Raleigh (ironically, Barrie later played informal cricket with a real Sir Walter Raleigh after the First World War), while Joseph Thomson was Alan Quatermain and Paul du Chaillu, Peter Boulanger. Barrie listed the team in full and made a pithy note under each of their names as to their various qualities or otherwise. This was a device he used both in print and in speech on a number of occasions. Thomson, for example, is said to have 'captained a team in Africa, and scored heavily against the Zulus' – a reference to his extensive travels in Africa. Du Chaillu, meanwhile, whose alias Peter Boulanger probably comes from Georges Ernest Boulanger, a notorious French general of the 1880s, was 'Said to be good in the field, but never tested so far.' It's not certain which of the Allahakbarries 'Lord Fauntleroy' was meant to be, but according to Barrie he was a 'good change bowler. Generally goes in last man, and has been known to carry his bat.'

*General Georges Ernest Boulanger*

Clearly the whole thing is a great in-joke with his team-mates, and there is a real sense in which, unknown to the readers of the *Edinburgh Evening Dispatch*, the true audience of this piece is meant to be the Allahakbarries alone. But it is also telling that he is now calling the team 'Celebrities at Home'. Another joke, of course, but it is a further demonstration of how Barrie felt that not just his star was on the rise, but also those of his friends.

The account tells the story of the game in similar terms to those that Barrie described the first Allahakbarries game at Shere. And the closeness of the two tales supports the idea that Barrie's 'true' stories about his cricket side are indistinguishable from the fictional ones; that the truth is always hidden somewhere amongst embellishments, exaggeration and humour.

> The Celebrities won the toss, and immediately decided to send their opponents in, their argument being that they themselves would look less idiotic in the field than at the bat. By this time the captain was probably the only man in the eleven who did not wish that he was back in London. He had some trouble in setting his field, partly because he did not know the technical terms, and partly because it had got out among them that long-on was the safest place to stand at. No less than seven men insisted on standing at long-on.

As in the 1887 game against Shere, the local side made a good total – 100 for four – and the Celebrities in reply were decimated, scoring just thirteen, of which seven were byes. This compares to the eleven that Barrie reports they scored in the first match at Shere. The story of their innings reveals Barrie's likely alias as being John Ward, 'a terrific punisher of loose bowling'. Barrie relates how, 'To the admiration and envy of his side, John Ward (a journalist) stepped out boldly to a leg ball and cut it past point. For this he scored two amid tremendous applause.' The impression is that this is a further joke for the benefit of his colleagues, and it is true – he really did score two runs in that first game.

The whole piece is written in that gleeful style of comfortable farce that Barrie loved, and which appeared again in his two small books about the Allahakbarries team. This is a kind of rehearsal for those books, privately printed for his friends, but all the more amusing to them because it was a private joke being played out in public. 'I heard yesterday that a society paper is very anxious to get the real names of the eleven', writes Barrie at the end of the article.

Barrie's second book set in his thinly disguised home town of Kirriemuir, *The Window in Thrums*, was also published in May 1889 and this more than anything that he had published before made a name for him as a serious writer of fiction. Robert Louis Stevenson later wrote to Henry James from the South Pacific to show his appreciation:

> Hurry up with another book of stories. I am reduced to two of my contemporaries, you and Barrie – O, and Kipling – you and Barrie and Kipling are now my muses Three. And with Kipling, as you know, there are reservations to be made . . . But Barrie is a beauty, *The Little Minister* and *The Window in Thrums*, eh? Stuff in that young man; but he must see and not be too funny. Genius is in him, but there's a journalist at his elbow – there's the risk.

*The Window in Thrums* extended Barrie's range so that his readers could see that the Scot was more than just a teller of funny stories; he could elicit a whole range of emotional reactions through his prose. Actually, he was a master at it.

There was no cricket for the Allahakbarries in the summer of 1889, and his article about the 'Celebrities at Home' was a kind of apology to his team for this as well as a joke, for Barrie had other plans – he was leaving British shores for the first time. He and his friend Joseph Thomson, back from his latest expedition to Africa, decided to tour Europe for a month. They went to the Alps – Lake Constance, the Austrian Tyrol, the Stelvio Pass, Lake Como and Lucerne – and eventually made their way to Paris. But Barrie did not like the experience very much, in particular the fact that he was not in control of the trip and was undoubtedly subordinate to his experienced travelling friend. He missed what is evidently one of the pleasures of captaincy, and of writing

The Thrums

This dellightful little creature is very retiring and knows a intervuve diveckly by his stelthy treds. When he hears one he runs like litening and gets under the sofer-cushions or inside the peyanno or crawls in under the slates till it is all over. He use to live in a old licht-house once. He is a marvelus mixture of the most commical humour and the most lewtyul paythoss. He is a regoular 'Ramsgitsingey at cricket. He was to have gone to Orstrafia with Mr Stodert but they thought it was better for the Empire that he should not. You should see him snick them among the slippers (I hope that is right.) When he goes in to bat the fielders all come close up to him Just to take hints in batting.

too: the feeling of being in control. With captaincy, indeed with the whole Allahakbarries adventure, Barrie was the force that drove it all, that organised each new match, and brought each new player into the team, and then set down through his narratives the events that had taken place – as he had seen them. He combined the instinct of the writer – to select information, direct characters and control meaning – with the instinct of the captain to be in charge of his players. So much so, indeed, that the Allahakbarries became characters in his cricketing cameos, all subordinated to the writer's whim.

Barrie did not stay in London after returning from his expedition, but returned to Kirriemuir instead to stay with his family for the next six months. He worked harder than ever, particularly on *The Little Minister*, which was the third of the novels about Thrums, the semi-fictionalised Kirriemuir of his mother's youth. And he watched with amusement as tourists arrived there to try and find the actual 'window in Thrums' that referred to the title of the second novel in this series – and to seek him out, too. Real fame and celebrity had come to Barrie in 1889, even in this small town in east Scotland.

Barrie returned to London in 1890 and made preparations for another match against Shere in the summer. Throughout the nineties, Barrie and Gilmour met in the first months of each year and decided who to pick for the team, though Barrie said that he was guided by two particular, though very simple, principles in his decision: 'With regard to the married men, it was because I liked their wives, and with regard to the single men, it was for the oddity of their personal appearance.' According to many cricket historians this summer marked the true beginning of the golden age of cricket, though predictably none of them cite the Allahakbarries game of that year as being the single event that triggered this age! In fact, it is a rather vague definition of the start of an era, and the date is generally chosen because it was the beginning of the County Championship. The end extended to a far more easily identifiable point in history: the start of the First World War in 1914. This definition of the era, though, is a controversial one; indeed the cricket writer Derek Birley calls it a 'hackneyed description'. There's no doubt that for people looking back on the late Victorian and Edwardian years immediately after the First World War, there was enormous nostalgia – and not just for cricket. People remembered the summers as being perpetually sunny: 'As usual in those summers before the war, the weather behaved so perfectly that both lunch and tea could be eaten out of doors', one writer recalled in the 1930s. And in the post-war years the cricket was romanticised in particular by the famous cricket writer Neville Cardus, who went to matches at Lord's with Barrie in the 1920s. Cardus's purple prose was significant in defining the years between 1890 and 1914 as being distinctly golden. But cricket at the time, for all its attacking batsmanship, and charismatic figures, was also changing very quickly and subject to violent criticism that it was boring and that the laws needed to be changed to make it less so. It was certainly not the settled era of perfect cricket that the epitaph of 'golden age' marks it out to be. Brian Dobbs makes a similar point in his book *Edwardians at Play:*

> Sir Neville Cardus once wrote of '. . . hot days in an England of forgotten peace and plenty', and those words might serve as an example of the way the era has frequently been treated. What, if we are to be honest, we must not forget, is that although the sun shone, it also went behind the clouds as often and as maddeningly as today, that the 'peace' was tempered by an aggressive and restless desire for war among a vocal and significant minority, and that the 'plenty' was not shared out among the many, but jealously guarded by the few.

In the spring of 1890 Barrie published his paean to bachelor life, *My Lady Nicotine*, a collection of articles along far simpler lines than his efforts from Thrums. They were humorous and farcical in a similar bent to his writings about the 'Celebrities at Home' cricket match, and introduced the legendary tobacco: the Arcadia Mixture. The material was all assiduously collected from real-life experience, which included at this time the friendship of an ever-increasing number of bachelors. Gilmour and Marriott-Watson, thinly disguised, played significant roles in the stories.

> Darkness comes, and with it the porter to light our stair gas. He vanishes into his box. Already the Inn is so quiet that the tap of a pipe on a windowsill startles all the sparrows in the quadrangle. The men on my stair emerge from their holes. Scrymgeour, in a dressing gown, pushes open the door of the boudoir on the first floor and climbs lazily. The sentimental

face and the clay with a crack in it are Marriott's. Gilray, who has been rehearsing his part in the new original comedy from the Icelandic, ceases muttering and feels his way along the dark lobby. Jimmy pins a notice on his door 'Called away on business,' and crosses to me. Soon we are all in the old room again, Jimmy on the hearthrug, Marriott in the cane-chair; the curtains are pinned together with a pen-nib, and the five of us are smoking the Arcadia Mixture.

For Barrie, arcadia was as much about the companionship of other men and the apparent spaciousness of their futures ahead of them as the tobacco that he smoked with his friends. Smoking, like cricket, seemed to make time slow down or even stand still, and this relief from the headlong rush to death, the one certainty of life, reassured Barrie considerably.

More cricketers were being added to Barrie's collection at this time, too. They included the portrait artist Charles Furse, who was the sometime wicket-keeper for the Allahakbarries. 'You should have seen Charles Furse as wicket-keeper,' wrote Barrie, 'but you would have to be quick about it as Anon had so soon to try someone else.' There was also the journalist Henry Massingham, known as H. W. and born the same year as Barrie. He became the editor of radical newspaper *The Star* in the summer of 1890.

It's unclear what happened in the match against Shere in June 1890, though they certainly played. It is most likely that the Allahakbarries lost, though no record or account survives of the game. In July that year Barrie made his escape to a far more remote location than the Surrey countryside when he rented a cottage in Glen Clova, a Highland valley north of Kirriemuir and just south of the mighty Cairngorm massif. He took his family with him, who were both proud and horrified at the extravagance. Barrie spent his time walking, fishing and writing before returning to London again, later in the summer.

MR. PUNCH KEEPS HIS EYE ON CRICKET.

THEN (1841)    and    NOW (1891).

In 1891 the Allahakbarries finally became a true force to be reckoned with. For it was this year that Arthur Conan Doyle, Barrie's most dependable 'ringer', joined their increasingly swollen ranks to contribute more with bat and ball on his own than all the other Allahakbarries combined. But before the cricket this season, Barrie was busy with Marriott-Watson and the cast of *Richard Savage*, rehearsing his first ever play on a proper theatre stage – The Criterion on Piccadilly Circus. The play had its first performance on the afternoon of 16 April 1891. It was not a success. Despite the negative reactions, though, and the fact that this was the play's only performance, it did not dissuade Barrie from further involvement with the theatre: he was addicted to writing plays for the rest of his life. Just over a month later, in fact, on Saturday, 30 May, Barrie's second play, titled *Ibsen's Ghost*, was performed at Toole's Theatre in Covent Garden, this time rewarded with highly complimentary reviews – a 'clever little parody' according to *The Times*.

It was a great way for Barrie to go into the game against Shere, full of confidence and with the added bonus of having the creator of Sherlock Holmes, 'the most perfect reasoning and

observing machine that the world has ever seen', alongside him
to solve the puzzle of how to turn winning cricket matches into
a habit.

Arthur Ignatius Conan Doyle was born in 1859, making him
a year older than Barrie. The two had followed each other
around a bit: they were both Scots, though Conan Doyle's family
background was almost entirely Irish, both had gone to the
University of Edinburgh and both headed south soon after. Both
were writers too, of course, but Conan Doyle had also had a
career as a GP by the early nineties, after seven years in practice in Southsea, Portsmouth. And in many respects Barrie and
Conan Doyle could hardly have been more different, especially
in terms of their respective physiques – Conan Doyle was a bear
of a man, standing more than six feet tall and fluctuating in weight
between fifteen and sixteen stone, whereas Barrie was a foot
shorter and probably not far from being half his weight, at least
in 1891 – he filled out somewhat in later years. Barrie's moustache looked as though a boy was hidden beneath it; Conan
Doyle's was a grand masculine accoutrement. Conan Doyle's
stature and ability at cricket, as well as his medical qualifications,
drew occasional comparisons with W. G. Grace; from Albert
Kinross, for example, who played under Doyle for an authors'
team. 'Conan Doyle was our captain, and in some ways he
reminded me of W. G. He hadn't the beard, but he was much
the same make of a man, solid, four-square, and an "all-rounder".'
But despite his apparent solidity, he was like Barrie a quirky,
unconventional man too, something which was expressed particularly in his spiritualist beliefs. His interest in spiritualism at this
time was still in its early stages, though it was an interest which
continued to develop throughout his life.

Conan Doyle was still enjoying his first flush of real success
as a writer, almost entirely as a consequence of his most famous
character, Sherlock Holmes. Although Holmes was mainly based
on Conan Doyle's old professor at Edinburgh, there is speculation

that the name 'Sherlock' was derived from the names of two Nottinghamshire cricketers of the 1880s: Frank Shacklock and Mordecai Sherwin. Shacklock was a fast bowler who took almost 500 wickets in his first-class career while Sherwin bagged more than 600 catches behind the stumps; thus a common sight on scorecards of the time was 'bowled Shacklock, caught Sherwin.' From there to Sherlock is a relatively small step and it is a plausible enough theory, though there is no hard evidence to prove that it is true. Conan Doyle shared the dubious honour of being most famous for inventing a single fictional character with a number of other Allahakbarries. But Holmes also became so ubiquitous that many other members of the team wrote about him too, including Barrie, Wodehouse and Milne. And despite the fact that the first Holmes story, *A Study in Scarlet*, was published in 1887 and that it was only with the second, *The Sign of the Four*, published in February 1890, that he achieved major recognition, Conan Doyle was already anxious to kill Holmes off by 1892. In April of that year he wrote, 'I am in the middle of the last Holmes story, after which the gentleman vanishes, never never to reappear. I am weary of his name.'

At first, Holmes's appearance in *A Study in Scarlet* was meant to be a one-off. It may have remained that way were it not for a remarkable meeting that spawned the second Holmes story as well as one of the most notorious works of the late nineteenth century. At the end of August in 1889 Conan Doyle was invited to the Langham Hotel in Portland Place to meet Joseph Marshall Stoddart (no relation to the cricketer), the managing editor of American journal *Lippincott's Monthly Magazine*. He was in London trying to set up a British version of his publication, which specialised in printing complete, full-length novels. Conan Doyle was not the only author at this meeting; Oscar Wilde was there as well, along with an Irish journalist and MP called Thomas Patrick Gill. Conan Doyle was impressed by Wilde, and he later wrote that 'his conversation left an indelible impression upon my mind'. But the tangible consequence of the evening was that Stoddart commissioned Wilde to write the story that was published as *The Picture of Dorian Gray*, and Conan Doyle to write the second of the Sherlock Holmes stories: *The Sign of the Four*.

Dorian Gray and Sherlock Holmes have few immediately obvious similarities, but critic Jackie Wullschläger suggests that both of them are examples of a classic character type from the 1890s – the narcissistic, *fin-de-siècle* dandy. Dorian Gray was another example of someone who did not want to grow old, though he is a young man rather than a boy like Peter Pan. He maintains his youth while his portrait grows old. Holmes, on the other hand, uses drugs when he hasn't got a case to keep his mind occupied, and his justification reveals the same spirit of the dandy, the narcissist and the aesthete that was to be found in other characters of the age.

> What else is there to live for? Stand at the window here. Was ever such a dreary, dismal, unprofitable world? See how the yellow fog swirls down the street and drifts across the dun-coloured houses. What could be more hopelessly prosaic and material? What is the use of having powers, Doctor, when one has no field upon which to exert them? Crime is commonplace, existence is commonplace, and no qualities save those that are commonplace have any function upon earth.

There is a curious tension in Holmes between the rational scientist and romantic aesthete, a tension which mirrored that in Conan Doyle himself, a trained scientist with a belief in spiritualism. It was a tension that Conan Doyle recognised too, for although Holmes appeared to have little time for sentiment, Conan Doyle himself described the stories as being in the tradition of the 'fairy kingdom of romance'. Barrie noticed the curious character of Holmes before he met Conan Doyle for the first time, and he wrote a gentle parody of the great detective which appeared in the *Speaker*.

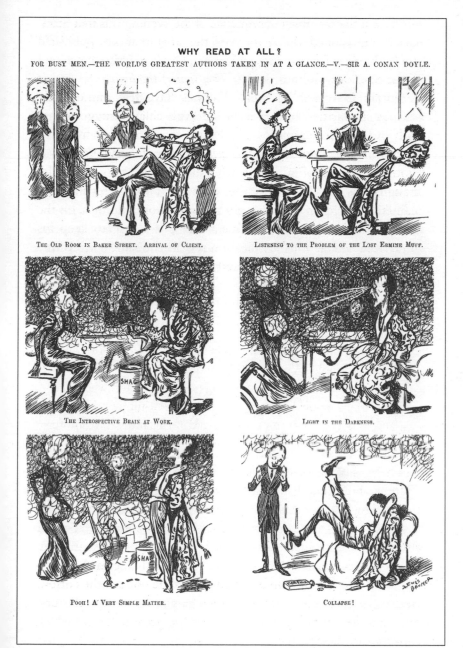

**WHY READ AT ALL?**

FOR BUSY MEN.—THE WORLD'S GREATEST AUTHORS TAKEN IN AT A GLANCE.—V.—SIR A. CONAN DOYLE.

THE OLD ROOM IN BAKER STREET. ARRIVAL OF CLIENT.

LISTENING TO THE PROBLEM OF THE LOST ERMINE MUFF.

THE INTROSPECTIVE BRAIN AT WORK.

LIGHT IN THE DARKNESS.

POOH! A VERY SIMPLE MATTER.

COLLAPSE!

There were dandies and aesthetes in the cricket of the nineties as well: the dashing cavaliers who cut and drove through the off-side, and who arrived at the ground in their immaculately pressed flannels and blazers. Ranjitsinhji, the great Indian batsman who ultimately played for England, was always beautifully attired and in many senses was the very personification of the British fascination with the exotic Orient. Cardus wrote of one of his innings, for example, that it was 'one more swaggering pageant reaching to a glittering horizon with Ranji holding the East in fee and bringing to Lord's and London a Kohinoor innings as a tribute!'

Conan Doyle himself was not among these dandies, though, for as a cricketer he embodied the Victorian straight bat more than the *jouissance* of the nineties. 'Steel true, blade straight' was the epitaph on his gravestone after he died, reflecting his outwardly moral nature, his straightforwardness and his industrious masculinity. In his autobiography he dedicated an entire chapter to 'some recollections of sport'. In life he gave the impression of beng a good-natured, jovial and chivalrous man with a keen sense of decency. Cricket was not his only sport, either, for he loved all kinds of outdoor pursuits and games. He had helped to found Portsmouth Association Football Club in 1884, and played for them as a goalkeeper and a full-back. He also cycled, played tennis and golf and was an enthusiastic skier on trips to Switzerland in the relatively early days of the sport. Rather less strenuously he became a successful billiards player and, after they had been invented, a motorcyclist too. But cricket was his great enthusiasm and he took it very seriously – for an Allahakbarrie at least. In the summer of 1889 he scored 111 not out for Portsmouth against the Royal Artillery and later he played ten games at first-class level, for MCC, and many other games at a very high standard.

Conan Doyle had enjoyed a good start to 1891 and during a productive period of six weeks between the beginning of April and mid-May he penned some of his most famous Sherlock Holmes stories: 'A Scandal in Bohemia', 'The Red-Headed

League', 'The Boscombe Valley Mystery' and 'The Adventure of the Five Orange Pips'. Conan Doyle's 1890 cricket season had been curtailed by a shoulder injury but he was certainly well enough to play in 1891 when he propelled the Allahakbarries to another victory. It's not known exactly what Conan Doyle's contribution was to his first game for the Allahakbarries against Shere, but Barrie wrote that 'Soon it became clear to Anon that the more distinguished as authors his men were the worse they played. Conan Doyle was the chief exception to this depressing rule'. Mackail adds that not only was Conan Doyle an exception to the rule, but also a 'striking if not almost embarrassing one'. If Conan Doyle was able to produce anything like his 111 not out from 1889, or the remarkable bowling figures which he came away with in future Allahakbarries games, there's no doubt that virtually on his own he would have helped the Allahakbarries to overcome the elderly Shere village side. Barrie paid testament to Conan Doyle's ability as a bowler when he wrote in the 1893 book he produced for the Allahakbarries: 'Doyle. A grand bowler. Knows a batsman's weakness by the colour of mud on his shoes.' In fact he was so good that at times he had to be dropped by Barrie in order to make the game fairer for the opposition.

Conan Doyle and Barrie became firm friends straight away and remained so for the rest of their lives. The last of Barrie's Auld Licht's novels, *The Little Minister*, was published at the end of 1891 to great acclaim and success. At the beginning of March 1892 the two of them visited George Meredith at Box Hill along with the writer, Arthur Quiller-Couch, who was another of Barrie's friends. Conan Doyle then went to Barrie's hometown of Kirriemuir at Easter that year, via Edinburgh, where Barrie checked on Joseph Thomson, who had recently returned from another expedition in poor health, and Conan Doyle almost certainly visited his father, who was in a lunatic asylum called Morningside in the city, though it seems he kept this a secret from his friend. In Kirriemuir the two of them walked and fished together, and in 1893 they collaborated on a fairly disastrous musical called *Jane Annie, or, The Good Conduct Prize*. George Bernard Shaw called it 'the most unblushing piece of tomfoolery that two respectable citizens could conceivably indulge in public'.

Barrie was not the only friend that Conan Doyle made in the Allahakbarries. He also became good friends with Jerome K. Jerome, who at the start of 1892 had just become the editor of the *Idler*. The magazine was founded by writer and publisher Robert Barr in the spirit both of Jerome's previous *Idle Thoughts of an Idle Fellow*, and also of an informally gathered bohemian gang of writers who called themselves the Idlers, and who regularly got together on Arundel Street, just off the Strand, for eating, drinking, smoking and conversation. Conan Doyle and Barrie were both regulars at the 'Idler at Homes', as they called them, and they were also joined by H. G. Wells, who at that time was combining his writing with teaching – in fact, he was one of the teachers of another, much younger, future Allahakbarrie: A. A. Milne. These occasions were celebrations of the joys of bohemian bachelor life, although by now a number of them were already married: Conan Doyle had married Louise in 1885, when he was twenty-six, and Jerome had also married, in 1888. But they had both celebrated the bachelor life in their books: Jerome in *Three Men in a Boat*, and Conan Doyle in his Sherlock Holmes stories, in which Holmes and Watson enjoy adventure, smoking and conversation. The Holmes stories are boyish in many ways, and fell into the category of 'comfort reading' for Conan Doyle's fellow-writers; 'the class of literature that I like when I have the toothache', according to Robert Louis Stevenson. Male companionship and bonding was a key part of their dinners, clubs (Conan Doyle and Barrie were members of a number of clubs between them, including the Reform, the Garrick and the Savage clubs) and other activities, including cricket, where as well as the game there were always 'hours for feasting, and smoking, and talk'.

Jerome was responsible for introducing Barrie to his future

wife, Mary Ansell, at the start of 1892. Barrie had long had a weakness for pretty young actresses. While he had been working in Nottingham, for instance, in 1883, he decided that he wanted to try and woo the actress Minnie Palmer who was in town performing with a touring company. He wrote a one-act play for her. Yet after he had been given an audience in her dressing room, he found that he was completely unable to speak. As he was drawn into the theatres of London and started writing his own plays, he found more opportunity to flirt with actresses and did so shamelessly. He was an altogether more confident character than he had been in Nottingham, though none of these flirtations developed into anything more serious (or more fun). All except one, that is.

Barrie was about to start rehearsing his new play, a comedy called *Walker, London*, about another scene of male bonding: holidays on the houseboat in the Thames. He wanted a different leading lady to the one being suggested by the theatre manager, and asked Jerome whether he knew anybody. 'He didn't want much,' recalled Jerome in his autobiography. 'She was to be young, beautiful, quite charming, a genius for preference, and able to flirt. The combination was not so common in those days. I could think of no one except Miss Ansell.' She was in a touring production of Jerome's at the time, called *Wheelbarrow Farm*, which also starred Bernard Partridge, under his stage name Bernard Gould, in the lead role, but Jerome said that he thought this was a much better opportunity for her to make her name. A meeting was arranged, with Jerome's friend Addison Bright the intermediary, and Barrie liked her, though he still had to convince the theatre manager that she was right for the part. There were arguments and ruffled feathers, but Barrie kept insisting that 'Miss Ansell plays the part' and on 25 February she appeared at Toole's Theatre on the opening night, just a week after the opening of Wilde's *Lady Windemere's Fan* at the St James's Theatre. The play was a huge success. It ran for two years and it made Barrie more money than he had earned before. If there had been any doubt in his mind about his destiny to be a playwright before, they had now vanished.

Just as it seemed that things could hardly be better, though, there was a tragedy in Barrie's life, which he discovered on his thirty-second birthday, 9 May 1892. His sister, Maggie, was engaged to marry James Winter, a local church minister who was well liked by Barrie and the rest of the family. The wedding was just three weeks away. But a telegram announced that Winter had been thrown from his horse and killed. It was a tragedy for Maggie, of course, and for Barrie too. He felt especially guilty because he had bought the horse for his friend, and so now he took it upon himself to help his sister out of her grief. He went immediately to Kirriemuir and the following day wrote to Conan Doyle:

*My dear Doyle,*
*The minister to whom my sister was to be married in three*
*weeks was flung from his horse and killed on Sunday night: he*
*had been conducting a service and was riding home. He was*
*my dearest friend. But it is the blow to her that we fear as she*
*is delicate.*

As a consequence there were no Allahakbarries games this year, though after an interval he took his sister to Shere where they spent most of the summer together in Anchor Cottage.

Meanwhile, in June 1892, Conan Doyle went on holiday to Norway with some of his relatives, including his sister, Constance, or Connie, as well as Jerome. When they came back he captained the Idlers cricket team against his local side in Norwood, south London, where he had moved with his family in June the previous year. The team also included Jerome and Robert Barr, Conan Doyle's brother, Innes, and Ernest William, or E. W. Hornung, known as Willie and a future member of the Allahakbarries. Hornung was a writer as well, and a contributor to the *Idler*, who later became famous with his caddish cricketer and gentleman thief A. J. Raffles. Hornung became Conan Doyle's brother-in-law by marrying Connie the following year.

The game against Norwood ended in a draw, and the Idlers played well. They scored more than a hundred, which led to Jerome indulging in some Barrie-like whimsicality: telling his team-mates not to applaud so enthusiastically for it would make their opponents think that they had never reached a century before. The Idlers team was a forerunner of other authors' teams and a *Punch* XI, which overlapped with the Allahakbarries. But the Allahakbarries were special, for that was always J. M. Barrie's domain, and there could never be an Allahakbarries game without him. For all the other sides, no other individual was so indispensable, however great a cricketer they may have been.

*The Adventures of Sherlock Holmes*, which had been serialised in the *Strand Magazine*, were published in a single volume in October 1892 and Conan Doyle was becoming increasingly famous. One of the responsibilities that this fame brought with it was the need to deal with a large amount of mail, some of which asked for the help of Sherlock Holmes on a variety of cases, requests which on occasion also provided inspiration for new stories. Over the next few months the next set of Sherlock Holmes stories were serialised in the *Strand Magazine*, and in December 1893, in *The Final Problem*, Holmes was missing, presumed dead, after a struggle with his arch-enemy Moriarty above the Reichenbach Falls in Switzerland. The fact that Watson could see no body as he looked over the precipice left open the possibility for Holmes's resurrection, though (probably a subconscious rather than a deliberate ploy) and some years later the most famous detective of all emerged again.

There was a further game against Shere in 1893, recorded in Barrie's first booklet about the team, which he presented to the Allahakbarries at a specially arranged, though informal, dinner at Solferinos Restaurant on Rupert Street, Soho on 30 November of that year. After a year with no cricket in 1892, yet spending most of that summer in Shere, his determination to play the game was greater than ever. He was taken seriously ill in February when he was in Scotland and Mary Ansell visited him. But he recovered, even from the additional blow in May of terrible reviews for the musical he had worked on with Conan Doyle. And as he made the preparations for the match this year, trying to coordinate a whole circus of players, wives and even a 'skulker', a 'subsidised crowd' and a photographer, he set about it with his usual vim, verve and maniacal energy: insisting, cajoling, joking and ordering. He was healthy again, and bustling through the filthy, crowded streets of central London in May with his head filled with glory on the cricket pitch, and dreams of green hedgerows full of songbirds and early-summer blossom in Shere.

The booklet gives the details of the outing with the usual disregard for facts and figures about the game itself, in preference to jokes about the members of his team. Mackail writes that 'he has given full play both to his fancy and to distinctly uncomplimentary remarks about his team.' It consists of ten typewritten pages, with a cover that marks it as being private: Barrie printed it for the members of the team only and it was strictly not for public consumption. The first page is an extensive list of all those involved in the match, in various different ways, and it is here that the jokes begin. Jerome K. Jerome is listed as being the 'Subsidised Crowd', which is assumed at least to be a reference to him being 'an idler', but perhaps as well because Jerome was no longer good enough to get into a team which was beginning to feature some reasonable cricketers, though Barrie did write, perhaps sarcastically, that 'Jerome once made two fours.' F. Anstey is listed as being the 'skulker'. His real name was Thomas Anstey Guthrie and he was another popular humorist of the time who also wrote for *Punch*. More prosaically, Barrie lists himself as captain and Marriott-Watson as the Secretary and Treasurer of the club, which almost suggests that the relative anarchy (compared to most cricket clubs) of the Allahakbarries was beginning to unravel and develop some order. Marriott-Watson was married by this time and his wife is also listed on the page as one of the patronesses, though her name is 'Graham R. Tomson'. This was actually her pen name, and the middle and surname of her second husband; Marriott-Watson was her third. She was a prolific poet and writer, the same age as Barrie, and she settled in Shere as Rosamund Marriott-Watson with her husband. Another female writer, Elizabeth Robins Pennell, is listed as the other patroness. She was an American, born in 1855, and married to the artist and author Joseph Pennell. They were both friends with the American painter James Whistler and together they later wrote a biography of Whistler, which was published in 1908. (There was another link between the Allahakbarries and Whistler too – Charles Whibley was his brother in law.) She also contributed to publications including the *Pall Mall Gazette* and the *Daily Chronicle*. There are other new names on this list and some highly unusual ones, too. In particular, the honorary presidents of the club are listed as being Beau Austin, Esq., Terence Mulvaney, Esq., Old Mel, Esq., and Sergeant Troy, Esq. All of these, except for Old Mel, are fictional characters. *Beau Austin* was a drama written by W. E. Henley and Robert Louis Stevenson; Terence Mulvaney was one of Rudyard Kipling's *Soldier's Three* and Sergeant Troy is a character from Hardy's *Far From the Madding Crowd*. Old Mel is simply George Meredith. Barrie no doubt felt that as literary men the team must at least make a nod to those writers who had influenced them, and these are undoubtedly his writing heroes, with the possible exception of Kipling (who was also not a lover of cricket). Other sources have suggested that Kipling played for the Allahakbarries but there is absolutely no evidence that he did. This document is probably the reason for the assumption. Neither did H. G. Wells or G. K. Chesterton play, as is sometimes assumed, though Barrie appealed on more than one occasion to Wells.

The umpire for the game was another explorer, George Kennan. Kennan was an American who had travelled extensively through Russia, and in particular Siberia, and who spent many years campaigning for revolution against the Tsarist regime in Russia. It is unlikely that he knew much about cricket, and therefore was singularly unqualified to umpire a match – another joke of Barrie's no doubt. He was a well-known writer and lecturer on his travels, and it's likely that Barrie had met him either through Gilmour's connection with the Royal Geographical Society or through Thomson. Gilmour, in fact, is conspicuous by his absence from this account of the 1893 game: it's probable that he was occupied by business in his role as secretary to the Earl of Rosebery, who at the time was foreign secretary and who in 1894, after Gladstone's retirement, became prime minister.

There is another list that follows this first one, simply entitled 'The Eleven'. This follows the same format as the list of the 'Celebrities at Home' team which had appeared in the *Edinburgh Evening Dispatch* in 1889, four years earlier, by listing each member of the team with a pithy description of their attributes, or more usually their deficiencies, as cricketers. Barrie writes of himself: 'An incomparable Captain. The life and soul of his side. A treat to see him tossing the penny. Hits well off his pads. Once took a wicket.' He writes about Watson that he is 'an invaluable man in the train going down. Very safe bat in the train. Loses confidence when told to go in.' And of Bernard Partridge: 'The Demon. Terrific delivery. Bowls all over the field. No one is safe. Breaks everything except the ball. Aims at the wicket and catches square leg in the stomach.' The epithet of 'demon' had been given to the notorious Australian fast bowler Fred Spofforth after he destroyed the MCC team in 1878 with figures of ten for twenty, which included the wicket of W. G. Grace, who he clean bowled for a duck. A few years later, at the Oval in 1882, Grace behaved rather shabbily in the match that gave birth to the Ashes when he ran out the Australian batsman Sammy Jones in between balls as he wandered down the pitch to do 'a bit of gardening'. The Australians were outraged and Spofforth stormed into the England dressing room between innings to tell Grace that his behaviour would cost England the match. Fired up with righteous anger Spofforth routed the England batsmen and was rewarded with victory and the decisive match figures of fourteen for ninety. Australia won by seven runs. After the match, the *Sporting Times* ran an obituary which stated that English cricket had died, and 'the body will be cremated and the ashes taken to Australia'. The English media then christened the next England tour to Australia (1882/83) as 'the quest to regain The Ashes'. Barrie makes clear that Partridge is not quite the same demon as Spofforth. But Spofforth was not far away: he had retired in England and still played club cricket for Hampstead, where at least one Allahak- barrie also played later in the 1890s.

There were some new players in the team as well. Barrie writes of George Ives that 'if he ever gets a ground to suit him, should take wickets.' Ives was an idiosyncratic combination of writer, criminologist, sex psychologist and keen amateur cricketer. He was also gay, though not overtly so, and had a brief affair with Lord Alfred Douglas, famous for his relationship with Oscar Wilde. For most of his life Ives kept notebooks with cuttings about a variety of subjects including murders, theories of crime and punishment, and cricket scores. He was also, according to Conan Doyle's biographer Andrew Lycett, the model for Hornung's cricketing cad, Raffles. 'Hornung may not have under- stood this sexual side of Ives's character,' writes Lycett, 'but was intrigued enough to use his friend as a model when he created his fictional gentleman thief Raffles, who enjoys a remarkable intimate relationship with his sidekick Bunny Manders.'

The illustrator and artist Henry Justice Ford was another of the new Allahakbarries and he came from a famous cricketing family. He was the same age as Barrie, and had been born in London to a solicitor father who was also an enthusiastic cricketer. He had six brothers, three of whom all played first-class cricket for Middlesex and one, his youngest brother Francis, for England as well. His eldest brother, William Justice Ford, was renowned for being one of the most prodigious strikers of a ball in England. When he played for Middlesex against Kent in 1885, he scored forty-four runs in the remarkably quick time of seventeen minutes and seventy-five out of ninety in three-quarters of an hour. His longest measured hit was 143 yards 2 feet. There are many other stories about his hitting too: for example *Wisden* told the tale in his obituary in 1904 that 'On another occasion, when playing at Torquay, he hit a ball out of the ground (above the ordinary size), across a road, and so far into another field that it put up a brace of partridges.'

It was this kind of legend that inspired Barrie to write of Ford that he is 'nicknamed "lost-ball Ford" because he and the ball are seldom in the same field.' He was undoubtedly a decent cricketer, though not of the standard of his brothers, and loved all kinds of games, particularly cricket, golf, billiards and chess. Ford was probably most famous for illustrating many of Andrew Lang's ten Fairy Books between 1889 and 1910, books which Barrie no doubt read, and which formed some of the background to Barrie's own interest in writing about fairies. Lang also wrote prolifically on folk-lore, mythology, anthropology and history, and his interest in many of these subjects overlaps the themes of some of Barrie's work, in particular the question of a 'return to nature' that is evident in Barrie's plays including *The Admirable Crichton* and *Peter Pan*.

Before the very brief write-up in the booklet of the 1893 match, Barrie offers nine 'Hints to the team by their captain'. Here are a selection of them:

1. Don't practise on opponents' ground before match begins. This can only give them confidence. [ . . . ]
5. No batsman is allowed to choose his own bowler. You needn't think it. [ . . . ]

8. If bowled first ball, pretend that you only came out for the fun of the thing, and then go away and hide behind the hedge.

9. Never forget that we beat Shere.

The Allahakbarries beat Shere again in 1893, and Barrie attributes his team's success entirely to himself, in his usual gleeful style: 'He set his field with exemplary coolness, and standing at cover point quickly dismissed Shere for the paltry total of 56. The wickets were nominally taken by Doyle, but entirely at the instigation of the captain.' In reply, the Allahakbarries played well with Ford scoring a rapid thirty and Conan Doyle and Charles Furse both getting into double figures too.

> He received valuable help from Watson (who played a masterly innings of 2), from Whibley (who defied the best bowling in Shere for nearly a minute), from the hard-hitting Partridge (who would be invaluable against his own bowling), and from Tomson, who looked like scoring at any moment.

Barrie was anticipating that the victory would be captured on film by the photographer, the *New York Times'* London correspondent Harold Frederick, 'but he forgot to pull the string or let down the lid or something, and we all came out as a sunset in ye olden times.' In fact there are no surviving team photos of the Allahakbarries in these early days.

The night that Barrie presented the Allahakbarries C. C., 1893 booklet to the team, on 30 November 1893 was a happy one, with Barrie full of high jinks and merriment. But the following day he received a telegram from Scotland telling him that his mother was dangerously ill and he hurried to see her. She recovered, but in March 1894 Barrie was also struck down with a severe illness while visiting Kirriemuir and he remained in bed for weeks. He had a feeble constitution, no doubt aggravated by his heavy smoking, and as he grew older he spent much more time, particularly during the winter months, struck down with chest infections and severe colds. There was no cricket again this year, as early in the summer Barrie was too weak, then on 25 June his latest play *The Professor's Love Story* opened. And finally, this summer, Barrie married the very pretty Mary Ansell on 9 July at his parents' home, Strath View, in Kirriemuir.

The following year they moved into their first house together at 133, Gloucester Road, South Kensington and in June Barrie got his cricketers back together again. This followed a dramatic cricketing event, which had taken place in May when W. G. Grace scored his hundredth first-class hundred at Bristol playing for Gloucestershire against Somerset. Grace, aged forty-seven, went on to score 288 out of his side's total of 465 and by the end of May had become the first person ever to have scored more than a 1,000 runs in a month. Earlier in the year, A. E. Stoddart had captained England to a convincing 4–1 series victory against Australia, regaining the Ashes. *Punch* celebrated the victory by penning the poem which contained the lines:

> Then wrote the queen of England
> Whose hand is blessed by God
> I must do something handsome
> For my dear victorious Stod.

Gilmour, Marriott-Watson, Bernard Partridge, Charles Furse and Henry Ford all played in the Allahakbarries game in June. Conan Doyle, though, was unavailable as he had travelled to Switzerland for the sake of his wife's poor health (she had tuberculosis), and later in the same year the Conan Doyles went to Egypt for the same purpose. Most of the team stayed overnight after a banquet at the White Horse and Barrie felt relieved and happy that even as a married man, he could still lead his friends on boyish expeditions into the countryside. It's unclear, though, whether they won or lost this game.

But there was bad news in August as Joseph Thomson became

the first member of the Allahakbarries to die. He had been in poor health ever since returning from an African expedition in 1891 and contracted pneumonia in 1892. He travelled to South Africa in 1893, and to Italy and southern France in early 1895 in an effort to regain his health but he died on 2 August 1895 in London, aged thirty-seven. Barrie wrote that 'I have known few men whom I have esteemed as much as Mr Thomson.' Worse was to come in September, just a month later, as Barrie's mother and his sister Jane Ann died within two days of one another. Barrie had written to his mother almost every day that he had been away from home, and her loss was a terrible shock. Soon after, he began writing about his mother, a project which took up more and more of his time, and which ultimately developed into the book called *Margaret Ogilvy*. In the early months of 1896 he worked hard on this and another book, *Sentimental Tommy*, alternating his work with trips to Kensington Gardens with Porthos, the Barries' young St Bernard, where they walked, played and even wrestled together.

And then, as Barrie was recovering from the loss of some of the people most dear to him, there was cricket at Shere once more in the summer of 1896. But as well as a game against the village side, Barrie now had enough Allahakbarries to form two teams that could play each other: Artists against Writers. This gave him the licence to carry out more assaults on convention on the cricket pitch and so he arranged that the two worst batsmen in each team should face the two worst bowlers. He was one of the batsmen, and the invention is a direct contradiction of the 'hint' he gave to his team in the 1893 book that 'no batsman is allowed to choose his own bowler. You needn't think it.' The Writers, aided and abetted by wides, no balls and other extras from the Artists' bowlers, prevailed on this occasion.

This encounter helped to inspire the next series of matches against a team of mainly artists in the village of Broadway in Worcestershire. If the Allahakbarries were playing in the golden

*Allahakbarries compelling Birrell and Gilmour*
*to go in first*

age of cricket then they were about to have their very own golden age within a golden age, what Barrie called 'the scene of contests and suppers of Homeric splendour, at which fair ladies looked sympathetic as their heroes told of their deeds of long ago, including Gilmour's five.'

# ❧ II ❧

# THE GOLDEN
# MIDDLE ORDER

# 4

## ARTISTS v. WRITERS:
## THE GAMES AT BROADWAY

The name Broadway is of Roman origin, and is believed
by the cognoscenti to be compounded of two words,
broad and way. However this may be, it was certainly to
Broadway that Caius retired when he fled from the city.
Here Caesar probably played many fine innings of a
Saturday afternoon. But all this was long ago, in the days
of top hats and underhand bowling.

> J. M. Barrie, *The Allahakbarrie Book of*
> *Broadway Cricket for 1899*

The Allahakbarries played three times at Broadway in successive years between 1897 and 1899. If their games in general
can be described as theatre, all artfully staged and choreographed
by Barrie, then Broadway, where this theatricality reached new
levels, was the most apposite of names as a place for them to
play. 'Rivalry ran at its noblest when the Allahakbarries had their
bouts with Broadway in Worcestershire,' wrote Barrie. And it
was here too that Barrie reached the peak of his exuberant powers
as captain of the team, and also where he brandished the second
of his two booklets about the Allahakbarries, this one a far more
elaborate affair than the previous effort.

Although Broadway was, and still is, a picturesque village in

Worcestershire, there were plenty of links with America which made it seem not so far removed from the theatre district of Broadway, New York, as might be suggested by the seven or eight days by boat that it then took to sail across the Atlantic. Barrie visited New York, and America, for the first time in the autumn of 1896, leaving Liverpool on Saturday, 26 September and arriving the following Saturday, 3 October. The trip was arranged by Addison Bright, the friend of Allahakbarries Jerome K. Jerome, and Bernard Partridge, who had just become Barrie's theatrical agent.

Barrie was greeted by reporters off the boat, which shows that by now his fame had travelled far beyond British shores. But his attitude to celebrity was always an ambivalent one and he guarded his privacy zealously. When newspaper men started to come to the Allahakbarries matches by the end of the 1890s, Barrie saw it as a terrible intrusion. When his friend William Robertson Nicoll printed a picture of Barrie's wife Mary soon after their marriage, it caused a spat between the two men. Yet Barrie was also one of the most intensely personal authors there has ever been, writing directly and explicitly about his own experiences and those of his family and friends. A point in case was his book about his mother, which was published in December of 1896. Barrie's own family were critical of the book, and the critic George Blake later censured Barrie for this in *Barrie and the Kailyard School*:

> One may well wonder why *Margaret Ogilvy* was ever written, except for private circulation, but Barrie threw the portrait of his mother into the whirlpool of commerce: in cold fact, cashing in on his popularity. Not many men would expose their own domestic affairs in this fashion, but Barrie was one of the few.

While he was in New York in October 1896, Barrie met Charles Frohman for the first time. Frohman was one of the most powerful men in American theatre and the year before he had founded the Theatrical Syndicate, which exerted a virtual monopoly on all contracts and bookings throughout the country. This suggests that Frohman was a smart and fairly ruthless businessman, but his empire was founded on a passionate love of theatre which had begun in childhood and which was his one true obsession in life. He was a short, rotund and un-athletic man, which helps to explain one of his nicknames: the Beaming Buddha of Broadway. No cricket for Frohman. Croquet, certainly, when he visited Barrie in England in the summer months, but no cricket. He was almost exactly the same age as Barrie and the two men, both curiosities in their own way, became great friends. They were determined, brisk, obsessive and hard-working characters. Barrie said of Frohman that he was a 'Niagara of a man' and that you 'could have lit a city' with his energy. Frohman, meanwhile, was enthusiastic about Barrie the man and his plays too, beginning with the adaptation of Barrie's book *The Little Minister*, which opened the following year, in September 1897.

There were Americans in the British version of Broadway as well; quite a few of them. And they liked cricket, or certainly seemed to after Barrie had cajoled them into playing. Americans loving cricket might not be quite as unusual as it generally is now, as cricket was then popular in certain parts of the east coast, in particular in Philadelphia. In 1897, for example, the Gentlemen of Philadelphia toured England playing first-class matches and in 1896 P. F., or Plum, Warner had taken an England side over to the United States. A number of the Americans in Broadway had connections with Philadelphia. The American actress, Mary de Navarro, whose mother was from Philadelphia, was one of the key characters at the centre of the artistic colony in Broadway, and she became known as the Allahakbarries' 'Dear Enemy', as she assumed the captaincy of the Broadway team, though she herself did not play. Barrie also referred to her as 'Worcestershire's loveliest resident'.

Broadway is sometimes referred to as the 'jewel of the

Cotswolds' and like Shere presents a chocolate-box image of an English village, though in contrast to Shere it is full of honeyed stone buildings, a colouring which is characteristic of the Cotswold oolitic (meaning 'egg stone') limestone. This detail is significant because eggs, particularly duck eggs, played an important part in matches between the Allahakbarries and Broadway. The village has one main street – the broad way – which slopes down the lower part of Fish Hill from east to west. This was also the main road between Worcester and London for centuries and it was a busy stagecoach stop with as many as twenty coaching inns at one time in its history.

The railway came to nearby Evesham in 1865 and there was a collapse in the staging industry and consequent loss of income to the village, which became a quiet backwater with just a handful of inns. Broadway was 'rediscovered' in the 1870s as artists, particularly from London, began to come to the village. William Morris stayed in the folly called Broadway Tower which stands high above Broadway itself and from where on a fine day it is possible to see views to thirteen different counties in England. Morris stayed there with his family and the pre-Raphaelite painter Edward Burne-Jones in the mid-1870s and these visits helped Broadway to gain a reputation in London as a peaceful and beautiful retreat for artists to come and paint. The famous American portrait painter John Singer Sargent painted the famous painting *Carnation, Lily, Lily, Rose* in the mid-1880s in two gardens in the village, one of which, the garden of Russell House, was used as a ground for the first of the Allahakbarries matches in 1897.

The American painter, Frank Millet, lived in Russell House, which is at the bottom of the long Broadway high street. Barrie was introduced to Millet and the Broadway gang through another American artist and a keen cricketer as well, Edwin Abbey, who was also a friend of Arthur Quiller-Couch. Back in 1892 when Quiller-Couch, or Q, as he was widely known, had been in

London, he stayed with Abbey and his friend the English land-scape painter Alfred Parsons who lived at Bedford Gardens on Campden Hill in Kensington.

Barrie wrote to Q from Broadway on 20 April 1897, where he and Mary were taking a short holiday and staying at Frank Millet's house, though Barrie had taken work with him – the dramatisation of *The Little Minister* which he was working on for Frohman.

> We've come here for a week. A land of orchards, very beau-tiful and as English as anything could be. We bicycled (oh, my ankles!) from Stratford – kept shouting every minute 'What a scene for Alfred Parsons!' when suddenly remembered that it *is* Alfred's own country and he did last year the very road and orchard which we had specially fixed for him to do.

He also mentions the de Navarros and their house, Court Farm, which is at the top of the high street, up the hill, and the other end of the village from Russell House where the Barries were staying. Barrie describes Court Farm as a 'glorious old farmhouse, all over oak and ingle nooks with 10 acres of ground'. And he concludes his letter by way of apologising to Q about his handwriting, which had become almost illegible: 'The reason that my writing is worse than ever is that the table is werry low and the chair werry high so that I dive at the paper.'

Mary de Navarro moved to Court Farm in Broadway with her husband, Antonio, or Tony, de Navarro, in 1894. She was best known by her maiden name of Mary Anderson. She was born in Sacramento, California in 1859, and by 1890, at the age of thirty-one, she had already enjoyed a successful career as an actress in America and Britain, though at the end of her career she had a breakdown brought on by exhaustion and some negative critical reviews. Oscar Wilde wrote his first play for her, *The Duchess of Padua*, though she rejected it. Antonio was an American barrister from New York with origins in Spanish nobility, and was a keen sportsman, and a particularly good player of tennis and baseball, though not cricket. He was also trying to get some writing published and Barrie helped him over the next few years by giving him feedback on his manuscripts and tips on writing and developing characters. 'I knew there would be something fine and rare about your story and yes sir there is,' he wrote to Antonio in June 1897. They were an extremely attractive couple, helped no doubt in Barrie's eyes by the fact that she was an actress, a breed that he had always been attracted to. He flirted with the striking Mary and played a rather straighter bat with her lawyer husband, who did not seem to worry about the attention of this curious little chap.

'We were a very merry little colony in Broadway,' wrote Mary de Navarro in her memoirs: 'all friends – fencing, gardening, riding together. It became a joke among us that the many friends – artists, writers, musicians – who came to see us, all wanted houses in the village.' It sounds like a vision of Barrie's own idea of an island paradise – an arcadia of friends and good living removed from the maw of the city. As well as the de Navarros and the artists Alfred Parsons and Frank Millet there were other artists such as Herman Herkomer, brother of the more famous artist Hubert von Herkomer, who painted Queen Victoria's death-bed portrait, and famous musicians including Kennerley Rumford and Harry Plunket Greene. But Barrie's visits were among the highlights of life in Broadway according to de Navarro, who wrote that 'far above everything there was the "little man" who had to be in everything; always occupied, always happy.'

They had a son called Jose, though this name was later changed to one of his nicknames – Toty. Mary de Navarro had an album for her son, in which many of her famous friends wrote or drew tributes. The list of people who contributed to the album shows what an exalted circle the de Navarros moved in, with major names from art, music and literature including Edward Elgar,

Henry James and John Sargent. Barrie's own contribution is a stunning piece of what de Navarro called 'delicious chaff':

'The truth about Mary de Navarro'
An interview with Jose
I found Jose in his own room at Court Farm. A bottle was conspicuously near his mouth and he hastily concealed it beneath his bib. I courteously looked the other way. 'What can I do for you?' he said, craftily crossing his arms over the bump in the bib.

I explained that I had come to hear the truth about his mother; and at this he looked grave.

'Would you mind finding out on tip-toe,' he said, 'whether she is on the stairs?' I did this joyfully as I saw that discreditable revelations were in the air; and as soon as I could assure him that we were quite alone, Jose began to laugh.

'Excuse me,' he said, 'but the fact is I can never think of that lady without giving way to unrestrained mirth.'

'But why?' I asked.

'Well,' he said, 'she is so quaint.' He leant forward and whispered, 'I have sometimes thought,' he said musingly, 'that she was created for my own particular entertainment. If you don't believe me, you just go down and ask her who is the child in this house.'

I obeyed him, and returned with her reply. It had been 'Jose is his name, of course!'

'Exactly what I expected,' he said, chuckling so much that the bump in the bib heaved like a ship at sea. 'Oh! What a woman!'

'What do you mean?' I asked, thunderstruck.

'She is the child,' he explained. 'She is much younger than I am. My dear Sir, I never see my mother without thinking she has come out of her egg-shell that very morning. I pretend I am the child, but it is only to humour her, bless you.'

'But Jose you seem to forget that she was once a great
ac . . .'

'I can't believe it,' he said sternly. 'That child of nature!
Pooh!'

'But in the plays of Shakespeare it was universally
acknowl . . .'

'Yes, I dare say,' said Jose, with something very like a sneer.
'But that was because he wrote them for her. You may take my
word for it, Sir, she is the child. Many a laugh have my father
and I had over it when she was out teaching the cows to chew
grass. If you want a proof, take this album she has started. The
woman has been courted by all the world, and instead of being
quite spoilt by it, she goes and starts an autograph book, just
like a little girl.' Just then we heard a footstep on the stairs.
Jose winked at me, and resumed his bottle.

This tongue-in-cheek, gently mocking and teasing, and even
somewhat combative tone of voice was used by Barrie again and
again in his letters to Mary de Navarro, which are often full of
Barrie's special brand of gleefulness and absurdity. He laughed
at the fact she always called the game 'crickets' instead of cricket
and lampooned her competitive spirit, saying that *he* did not care
which side won, 'but far otherwise was it with that implacable
one, who never (such is the glory of the woman) could follow
the game, despite deep study'.

The idea of a cricket match was first mooted on that trip to
Broadway in April 1897 which was also the 'first memorable
meeting of the two captains': Barrie and Mary de Navarro. This
meeting took place at the atmospheric old coaching inn on the
high street, the Lygon Arms, where many famous guests had
stayed over the centuries, including Oliver Cromwell and King
Charles II (in separate rooms). On Barrie's thirty-seventh birthday,
on 9 May 1897, he wrote a letter to Mary de Navarro with plans
for the match that summer. It is an extraordinary letter, full of

the kind of boyish excitement which anticipates the start of summer and the long days of outdoor games to come. It was the first of a series of exuberant missives that he fired off that summer. 'By common consent you were proclaimed an Allahakbarrie of the deepest dye', he wrote at the start of the letter, pretending that his team had gathered together as a committee in order to elect her so. It was Queen Victoria's diamond jubilee, as well as the ten-year anniversary of Allahakbarries CC, and for Barrie that meant a great excuse for a very special game of cricket. 'The general feeling is that the Diamond Jubilee should be celebrated in no ordinary way,' he wrote.

A certain royal personage
Expects
Something
Big
from our representative elevens. Knighthoods are in the air for everyone who
Breaks
His
Egg
The affair may even be graced by the presence on the field of
A
Spirited
Old
Lady
The man in the shirt is going about asking in a scared whisper –
'What is this about a Broadway Week End?' The team shudder and are exultant by turns. The captain denies all interviewers. He has been seen entering the homes of artists, literary gents, musicians and other suspicious characters. When he left they were mopping their brows. Single wicket is being played in the Spectator office. When Mr David Bispham ought to begin

to sing he flings balls at the audience and yells, 'How's that, umpire?' When Mr Partridge is asked on the steps of the Haymarket Theatre what his name is he replies 'Short leg.' . . . . Dr Conan Doyle is pale with emotion.

The 'spirited old lady' is presumably a reference to Queen Victoria, though during the celebration of the jubilee she was far from spirited, and continued to wear the black mourning dress trimmed with white lace, which she had worn since the death of Albert many years earlier. David Bispham was a famous American opera singer.

The reference to 'knighthoods are in the air for everyone who breaks his egg' refers to the origin of that strange piece of cricketing terminology – the duck. A cricket score of nought was originally referred to in public school slang around the middle of the nineteenth century as a duck's egg, because a zero symbol resembles the shape of an egg. When a player had made a score, therefore, he was said to have broken his duck's egg. This became common usage in print in the 1860s and was soon contracted to duck, without any reference to the egg being made at all. But Barrie turned the duck eggs into an extended joke, which made an appearance in his 1899 book about the team when he described a strange machine called the 'Quackuary'. He explains:

> The Quackuary is a sort of rustic steam-press in which the eggs laid by the Allahakbarries and their rivals are hatched by machinery. On the morning of a match all the female members of Russell House are up betimes hieing them to the cricket ground with aprons, into which they may be seen gathering the eggs. Many of the ducks which come waddling towards us are Allahakbarries, and they are quacking excitedly at the prospect of more little brothers and sisters.

An egg also makes its way into Peter Pan, when Captain Hook asks Peter (who is also described as a captain – of the lost boys) 'Pan, who and what art thou?', and Peter replies 'I'm youth, I'm joy. I'm a little bird that has broken out of the egg.'

The game was arranged for Saturday, 19 June, just three days before Queen Victoria's diamond jubilee procession through London. Barrie organised his players in London and made arrangements in Broadway. He asked Mary de Navarro to book rooms for his team at the Lygon Arms. And in a letter just five days before the game he included a list of his team which included Conan Doyle and Hornung, his old friend Gilmour, the *Punch* cartoonists E. T. Reed and Bernard Partridge, the artists Charles Furse and Henry Ford, the editor of the *Daily Chronicle* H. W. Massingham and Barrie's theatre agent Addison Bright. The make-up of the team had changed from the very early days, and there were a number of far more competent players than there had been at the beginning. Thomson was dead, and neither du Chaillu or Jerome had played since the very first games. From this team of 1897 only Barrie, Partridge and Gilmour had been playing ten years earlier. The openers had given way to the middle order.

Barrie added at the bottom of his team list that 'You needn't be alarmed' and that 'I can't play a bit', though all in a spirit of blithe confidence which should have been well founded considering the fact that he had two decent players in the form of Conan Doyle and Ford. As an after-thought he also wrote: 'I suppose you have wickets. If not, let me know. We shall bring the other necessaries.'

The Allahakbarries, accompanied by their wives, arrived at Evesham railway station at 12.27 p.m. on Saturday and there were horse-drawn brakes and traps waiting to take them the seven miles to Broadway. As they approached the village green, at the bottom of Broadway's high street, they were all waving and cheering while the Broadway team 'were in the road to welcome them, all like children out of school.' The game was a close one and Mary de Navarro remembered that 'the high, nervous tension, even consternation we all experienced during the game was not at all merry'. Barrie wrote to her after returning to London on the Monday to thank her for the weekend.

> It was a glorious outing and we can never thank you sufficiently for all you did for us. May the Broadway week become an institution. Did you see the article on our match in today's *Chronicle*? Methinks I recognise the hand of Massingham, and I am thirsting for next year that I may propose his health in barbed words.

The editor of the *Daily Chronicle*, Massingham, had indeed committed something of a cardinal sin in Barrie's eyes by breaking ranks and writing an in-depth match report in his newspaper, though it is noticeable that he gets the name of the Allahakbarries completely wrong, calling them 'The Allahibaris'.

This mistake is a detail that was not lost on Barrie. 'Massingham guesses our name incorrectly,' he wrote to de Navarro, 'I look on that as a great triumph.'

But Massingham's report also provides one of the first accounts of any detail of an Allahakbarries game – 'perhaps the most important and interesting match of the season' – which was not written in Barrie's own hand. And this is most likely where the perceived insult lay. Barrie wanted not only to control the match, but also the way it was written about afterwards, so that he could refine the facts and finesse the fiction to achieve the precise dramatic effect he was aiming for.

Massingham stages the contest as being Literature against Art: 'Literature in London and Art in Broadway', though he admits that not all the Allahakbarries team are writers and not all the Broadway team artists. There were artists in the Allahakbarries side and at least one writer, the author of children's stories, Charles Turley Smith, who was the nominal 'on-field' captain for Broadway. After this first meeting 'Turley', as he was known to his friends, became one of Barrie's closest companions.

'The captain of Literature was Mr J. M. Barrie. The Grace of his eleven was Mr Conan Doyle; the Disgrace was Mr Barrie's strange tactics, of which more anon,' wrote Massingham in a way that probably did not please Barrie, despite being tongue-in-cheek, and attempting to emulate his captain's own style.

The Allahakbarries batted first and Massingham describes Barrie's very short innings: 'The captain scored one rapidly, and seemed set for a lengthy innings, when on the next delivery he was bowled'. The Allahakbarries were looking in trouble at three for 'a large number of wickets' but then Conan Doyle and Massingham came to the centre and began to accumulate some runs: 'Mr Doyle dispatched the ball among the surrounding heights for 4s, while the editor obstructed his wicket with a successful maladroitness unparalleled in the history of modern cricket.' The Allahakbarries made seventy-four altogether and as Conan Doyle bowled as well as he had batted, it seemed inevitable that the Allahakbarries would overcome the Broadway side. Until, that is, the famous Irish baritone singer and great friend of Edward Elgar's, Harry Plunket Greene, came in and 'played a forcing game'. This meant that the Broadway side crept closer to the required total and by the fall of the ninth wicket, the two teams were tied on seventy-four runs each. The artists Herman Herkomer and Frank Millet were the batsmen who required just a run between them in order to win the match. Massingham takes up the story:

> The moment, I can assure you, was most exciting. To stop stolen runs, the field crept in on the batsmen like a chorus of operatic conspirators. The brilliant but Machiavellian idea then occurred to the captain to order Mr Doyle to cross over to the other end and bowl two overs in succession. This was loudly applauded by those 'Allahibaris' who did not know the rule, and secretly acquiesced in by those who did. But the opposing captain came out and mildly but firmly insisted that cricket was the game they were playing, and that the captain of the Allahibaris must have been thinking of something else.
>
> So the other bowler went on. There was a stillness as of death, followed by a full pitch. It was driven by Mr Herkomer for two. The game was won and a shout went up from the pavilion that made the Cotswolds shiver. Next ball Mr Herkomer was bowled. Mr Millet carried out his bat for a finely played o.

There was a feast that evening at the de Navarro's house and many toasts, to which Barrie replied with 'much felicity and at great length'. There was even dancing and Mackail tells us that 'Yes, Barrie, danced too, on this eve of the Diamond Jubilee, and again everyone was happy and childish, and again it was all his doing.' They agreed at the dinner to make the game an annual fixture. But the morning after Barrie had second thoughts about the outcome of the match: 'at breakfast . . . Mr Barrie stated that by mental arithmetic he had arrived at the conclusion that the score of the Allahibaris was 78 and not 74, and that consequently they were the victorious team. The motion, however, was not seconded, and fell to the ground.'

Barrie was thirty-seven years old and at his exuberant best: full of life and energy for this game, and the other game, which was persuading his team to go along with his schemes in the first place. He had succeeded in staging a piece of high theatre, and on returning to London doubtless many of the eminent and well-established individuals reflected on how the funny, quirky and boyishly mischievous Barrie had made them, for a weekend at least, forget about their more onerous responsibilities in life and make fools of themselves on a cricket pitch. This was his plan: to turn them into children and for him to be their chief, their captain; directing them hither and thither with the impetuosity and wilfulness of a schoolboy. There is a sense of this in Mary de Navarro's remembrance of Barrie at Court Farm:

Often in passing by the old ingle-nook in the hall, I can still see the slight figure of Barrie sitting in it, smoking a long churchwarden pipe, his limpid eyes looking as innocent as those of a baby, while, as I learnt to my sorrow, he was planning murder to my team: serenely puffing away, and death to the Broadway team in his heart!

*Result of the test match, 1897.*
*Barrie being bowled by*
*Mary de Navarro*

But this time he had not succeeded. The Allahakbarries had been defeated by de Navarro and her artists and musicians. Barrie had scored just one run himself. And although he was still jubilant because he had succeeded in arranging the whole thing, his body was telling him that he was certainly not a boy anymore. He had 'pain at the knees', bruises and aching muscles. But in October that year he endured far more pain when he fell off the stage while rehearsing *The Little Minister* at the Haymarket theatre. He was knocked unconscious but was only concussed and made a quick recovery, writing to H. G. Wells with his by now customary vitality and bullishness at the end of the month to tell him that he too should play for the Allahakbarries.

> I have you now;- you have a secret desire to spank them to leg and lift beauties to the off, and you probably can't, and so you are qualified for my cricket team. Elected whether you grumble or not.

Wells' father, Joseph, had played as a professional for Kent in first-class matches a few times when H. G. was a child, but Wells did not share his father's enthusiasm for the sport and he certainly never turned out for the Allahakbarries, despite Barrie's best efforts. Wells wrote about a day that he had spent with his father when he was eighteen, when his father 'discoursed very learnedly on the growing of willows to make cricket bats and how long it took for a man to learn to make a first-class cricket bat. That was a great day for father and me.' P. G. Wodehouse was later rather facetious after Wells had mentioned his father in a cricketing connection. Wells had invited the young Wodehouse and a number of other writers to dinner and, as Wodehouse remembered

> we had barely finished the initial pip-pippings when he said, a propos of nothing: 'My father was a professional cricketer.' If there's a good answer to that, you tell me. I thought of saying

'Mine had a white moustache', but finally settled for 'Oh, ah', and we went on to speak of other things.

Conan Doyle had moved into his new house, called Undershaw, at Hindhead in Surrey in October after a relaxing summer of cricket, family holidays to English seaside towns, and some thought about writing a stage version of Sherlock Holmes. Undershaw, built on a plot of four acres, had extensive views to the south and had been built to order with eleven bedrooms, servants' quarters, a stable, an electrical generator and a tennis court, costing a total of £8,000. Despite the Allahakbarries' loss, Conan Doyle had undoubtedly been the hero of the team with both bat and ball, though his inclusion in the side remained a controversial point between Barrie and de Navarro, who wrote that she was nervous about having to play against 'a centurion'. 1897 was a significant year for Conan Doyle, not only because of his grand new mansion, but because this was the year he met his future wife, Jean Leckie, for the first time. His present wife, Louise, had been suffering from tuberculosis for five years. 'I had everything in those few years to make a man contented,' he wrote, 'save the constant illness of my partner.' But when he met Jean, a mezzo-soprano singer, on 15 March, he fell in love immediately and she fell in love with him, though Conan Doyle's biographer Andrew Lycett insists that 'so long as he was chaste, this type of dalliance was acceptable.'

Barrie and de Navarro bickered in a good-natured way, not just in letters to one another, but in their respective memoirs as well, published many years later. In *The Greenwood Hat*, Barrie wrote that de Navarro 'had a powerful way of wandering around the field with the Allahakbarries' top scorer, who when he came back would tell anon sheepishly that he had promised to play for her in the second innings.' And he also poked fun at her for her knowledge of the game, recalling a time when despite the fact that the Allahakbarries had passed the Broadway score, she turned to Barrie, rather hopefully, and said 'Yes, but you have still several men to go in'. She replied in her own published memoirs, *A Few More Memories*, that she liked *The Greenwood Hat* immensely, 'in spite of the jaundiced, libellous attack it contains on me as a cricket captain!' and she counter-attacked: 'the brilliant Barrie was not a shining light in the cricket field. I never saw him make a single run. His speciality seemed to be in poultry' [assumed to be a reference to scoring ducks].

On New Year's Eve 1897 Mr and Mrs Barrie went to one of the most fashionable parties in town, an annual event given by a distinguished society lawyer of the time Sir George Lewis, and his wife Lady Lewis. Barrie was seated next to 'the most beautiful creature he had ever seen': Sylvia Llewelyn Davies. She was the daughter of *Punch* cartoonist and novelist George du Maurier, married to Arthur Llewelyn Davies and the mother of their boys, of whom there were three at this time: George, Jack and Peter, though shortly there were two more as well: Michael and Nico. They were a model family: good-looking, intelligent, funny and charming, and Barrie was smitten by them. After this first meeting, all their lives were strangely, joyously and tragically connected.

In May the following year, 1898, Barrie resumed the annual preparations for the next cricket match, though this time he planned to make it a long weekend in order to make room for 'sports of a wild nature' as well as the cricket. Mary de Navarro scrawled in pencil on the back of one of Barrie's letters what these sports would be: hurdle, sack races, egg and spoon race, animal race, obstacle race, three-legged race, donkey race and wheelbarrow. Barrie also reprised the idea which he had first had a few years ago and suggested that the batsmen choose which bowlers they face up until forty runs have been scored, 'to give those who are not players a chance of making some runs.' It's not clear whether he got his way. The core of the team remained the same as the previous year but both Furse and Hornung could not make it so Barrie proposed bringing some new players with him. These were the novelist A. E. W. Mason, the *Punch* writer Owen Seaman, the publisher Sidney, or S. S., Pawling and George Meredith's son Will, who was also a publisher.

Mason was one of the younger members of the group, aged thirty-three in 1898 and an author and later a Liberal politician. His biographer Roger Lancelyn Green wrote

> When one thinks of A. E. W. Mason, one thinks first of the swift, breathless, joyous rush of adventures: Mason as an actor; Mason as a struggling journalist leaping suddenly into fame with his second novel; Mason the traveller exploring the Sudan, Morocco, Spain . . .
>
> To the exceptional nature of [his character], all his friends bear witness: to his eager interest in everything, to his powers as a conversationalist, and his even greater powers as a raconteur; to the exhilarating joy of being in his company and listening to his wonderful laughter – laughter that, said E. V. Lucas, was famous in both hemispheres.

He had a distinctive appearance: handsome, confident and dark-haired with a large nose and lively, engaging eyes. His first novel, *A Romance of Wastdale*, was published in 1895, but he is best remembered for his adventure novel *The Four Feathers*, written in 1902, of which there have been seven different film versions made, the last in

*Caricature of A. E. W. Mason*

2002. The 1939 version of the film starred C. Aubrey Smith, a cricketer who grew up just a short walk from Broadway at Chipping Camden, and who later became a Hollywood actor. While he was on the set of the film, Smith invited a previous England captain, Archie MacLaren, to star as an extra on the film as a Crimean War veteran. According to David Rayvern Allen, 'Aubrey had secured the "extra work" for Archie so that in between takes they would get a good chance to have a "decent natter."' He was nick-named 'round the corner Smith' because of his peculiar approach to the wicket when bowling. 'It is rather startling when he suddenly appears at the bowling crease', W. G. Grace said of him. In all he took 346 first-class wickets as well as five wickets in his only test match, and played in annual Authors versus Actors matches at Lord's, which ran from 1905 to 1909.

Barrie recalled in a speech that, whereas his own bowling was slow, 'Mason, on the other hand, is fast, but somewhat erratic.' Elsewhere he said of Mason's bowling 'that one never knew in advance whether he was more likely to send the bails flying or to hit square leg in the stomach.'

Owen Seaman played a decisive role in the 'test match' between the Allahakbarries and Broadway in 1898. He had been writing for *Punch* since 1894, when his first contribution, 'The Rhyme of the Kipperling' was published. Meanwhile, the beefy S. S. Pawling, just two years younger than Barrie and partner with William Heinemann of publishing firm W. Heinemann Ltd, had no doubt been recruited for his lethal fast left-arm skidders and his robust batting style. Barrie disingenuously wrote to Mary de Navarro that 'Pawling is or was fairly good I believe': he surely knew that Pawling had played three first-class games and taken nine wickets for Middlesex.

The date of the match was set for Saturday, 11 June 1898 and Barrie tried once more to lure H. G. Wells along. He wrote to him just a few days before the match:

Are you coming to my cricket match? It takes place on Saturday next the 11th at Broadway, Worcestershire, against a team of artists etc. got up by Mrs de Navarro (Mary Anderson that was). We had a great time last year, and none of us can play. We are going down the previous day, for which she has arranged sports of a wild nature, a supper also at which there are great doings. Cricket on Saturday, return on Sunday. Our train leaves Paddington Friday morning at 9.50. Book second class to Evesham and bring evening dress.

But Wells could not be persuaded. So the party of more than twenty, including seven wives and Doyle's sister, got the 8.30 train from Paddington to Evesham on Friday and arrived at lunchtime before playing the games in the afternoon in the garden of the de Navarro's residence of Court Farm. The results of these 'sports' on the Friday afternoon were not recorded with one exception: Barrie and Mason between them won the three-legged race.

After a high-spirited supper on the Friday night, probably at the Lygon Arms, the day of the test match dawned. The Allahakbarries were out to get their revenge on the Broadway side and achieved it through the heroics of three players: Conan Doyle, who top-scored with forty-six, Barrie, who remarkably took seven Broadway wickets with a new leg-break delivery (presumably orthodox left-arm spin which turns away from a right-handed batsman, rather than a Chinaman, which turns in the opposite direction) which he claimed surprised him even more than it did the batsmen. Owen Seaman hit the winning runs for the Allahakbarries. That's one version of the match, at least, though Philip Comyns Carr suggested that Conan Doyle didn't play, because he had devoted himself to a higher standard of cricket, and that Barrie had invited him and two of his university chums to play. According to Carr:

I turned up with my two cricketers, and we won the match, though neither side, if I remember right, scored more than thirty-five for two innings, and the winning hit was made by neither of my Oxford friends, but by Owen Seaman, the editor of *Punch*. He afterwards celebrated the event in verse.

Carr's account, written more than fifty years later, is inconsistent and it seems likely that he has blurred the memories of a couple of years together. It's not even clear whether he played in 1898, though he certainly did in 1897 and 1899. And according to Barrie's letters to Mary de Navarro, Doyle definitely played in 1898, though not the following year. But Carr is right about Seaman hitting the winning runs in 1898, and, yes, so proud was he of this heroic feat, that he wrote a poem to commemorate it.

'THE WINNING HIT':
AN ODE TO MYSELF ON MAKING 2 NOT OUT
IN THE TEST MATCH OF 1898
*by Owen Seaman*

Bloody the battle, and the sun was hot
When on our ranks there fell an awful rot
One bearded warrior, playing like a blue,
Had made a prehistoric swipe for two,
When three, his fellows, noted for their pluck,
Through inadvertence got a paltry duck.
Upon the warpath, which was far from flat,
The foeman's champion had secured a hat,
And one might recall the dropping of a pin
When you, heroic sailor soul, walked in.
Virgin, and chosen for your facial oddity,
In you your captain found a rare commodity.
Omitting not what other men omitted,
You went to make the winning hit and hit it.

Thanks to Seaman, the heroic Alla-hakbarries had squared the series at one match all. It meant that the following summer one or the other of the teams would move ahead.

———

The Barries went to Scotland for the remainder of the summer, with Barrie spending much of his time fishing in burns. That winter he met another future member of his team, Maurice Hewlett, who was a lawyer and civil servant, and a writer too, whose historical novel *The Forest Lovers* was published in 1898. He also wrote a play the same year called *Pan and the Young*

*O. Seaman and the bat he did it with*

*Shepherd*. He was a year younger than Barrie, had been married for eleven years and had two young children – a boy called Cecco and a girl called Pia – by the time the two men met. Barrie later named one of the pirates in *Peter Pan* Cecco after Hewlett's son. In the map of Kensington Gardens in the frontispiece to Barrie's story *The Little White Bird*, there is also a tree marked as 'C. Hewlett's tree'. On the same map, the meaning of the phrase on the left hand side is now clear to us: 'cricket is called crickets here' is another of Barrie's jokes with a personal meaning which would only be understood by very few of his readers – he is poking fun at the American Mary de Navarro, who according to him could not get the name of his favourite game right.

The Second Boer War began in October the following year, 1899. It signalled the beginning of the end of Britain's splendid isolation, and the start of a new foreign policy, the *entente cordiale*. Britain was facing up to the fact that its economic power and global influence was fast diminishing. Was it an *entente cordiale* that existed between Barrie and Mary de Navarro as well? It was far friendlier than that, in fact, but the competitiveness between the two of them became even greater in 1899; and Barrie was starting to treat cricket a little more seriously. 'Feeling this year', Barrie writes, 'ran very high'.

In 1899 the team began once more to keep the scorebook which had been neglected ever since their first game, now twelve years previously. It is the only known scorebook of the Allahakbarries and is now kept in the archives at Lord's. Until now the Allahakbarries had only played one game a year but Barrie decided in 1899 to start playing more games: 'in the exceptional circumstances the Allahakbarrie captain thought himself justified in arranging some trial matches for the first time in the history of the club.' His first cricket letter of the year to Mary de Navarro was early on – in March. The de Navarro's sailed to New York later that month and Barrie wanted to make sure that the match was in the diary before they left. He writes:

> I hope you will have a fine voyage both ways and a good time with your people. May heaven direct your sails, and please tell your mother that I shall never never never forget that she told me I was handsome.
>
> Our love to the lady who never says that.

'The lady who never says that' is of course Mary de Navarro. Barrie suggests 9 and 10 June as the dates for the game that year but they did not actually play the deciding test match until the beginning of July.

In the exchange of letters between the two in March that year, Barrie sent one of his more remarkable letters, which Mary de Navarro later called 'a curious mixture of "vitriol and the milk of human kindness"'.

The ladye Marye de Navarro throweth yᵉ gloue to yᵉ puissant Sir James of Kirriemuir, and challengeth hym to combat in yᵉ tented field.

Barrie looks, in height at least, to be at a disadvantage in the contest with Mary de Navarro, the opposition captain for the Broadway games between 1897 and 1899.

'She was to be young, beautiful, quite charming, a genius for preference, and able to flirt.' Mary Ansell on stage in 1892, the year she first met Barrie.

Barrie in 1904, just a few weeks before the first performance of *Peter Pan*.

A. E. Stoddart (batting) wears an I Zingari cap as his Middlesex teammate, Gregor MacGregor, keeps wicket. This portrait hangs in the Long Room at Lord's.

W. G. Grace appears for England for the final time at Trent Bridge in 1899. In the same row (left to right), flanking Grace's mighty shoulders, are three of the other big names of the era: C. B. Fry, K. S. Ranjitsinhji and F. S. Jackson.

'Before me he stands like a vision/Bearded and burly and brown'. Grace at Crystal Palace, the ground where he was dismissed by Arthur Conan Doyle.

Augustine Birrell demonstrates his unique stance, A. E. W. Mason smokes at silly-point and T. L. Gilmour manages to look like he might keep wicket.

Barrie looks on as other members of his team inspect a novelty item on the cricket field: a three-wheeled motorbike.

E. W. Hornung prepares to pad-up.

Conan Doyle shares a story in the field.

Young members of Shere Cricket Club in 1897.

Married v Single at Shere in 1899. Barrie is third from the left in the back row. George Meredith is third from the left in the second row from the front.

*Left*: The 'dear enemy of the Allahakbarries', Mary de Navarro, as Rosalind in *As You Like It*, Barrie's favourite Shakespeare play.
*Right*: Sylvia Llewelyn Davies takes guard.

George Llewelyn Davies bats, his brother Jack keeps wicket.

Barrie with Michael Llewelyn Davies on the lawn at Black Lake Cottage.

A plate from the *The Boy Castaways of Black Lake Island*, a record of the adventures of the Llewelyn Davies boys at Black Lake Cottage in 1901.

The Allahakbarries in 1905. E. V. Lucas hands a ball to Michael Llewelyn Davies as Barrie looks on. Also in the back row: Maurice Hewlett (left) and Harry Graham (second from right). Front row (left to right): Henry Ford, A. E. W. Mason, Charles Tennyson, Charles Turley Smith.

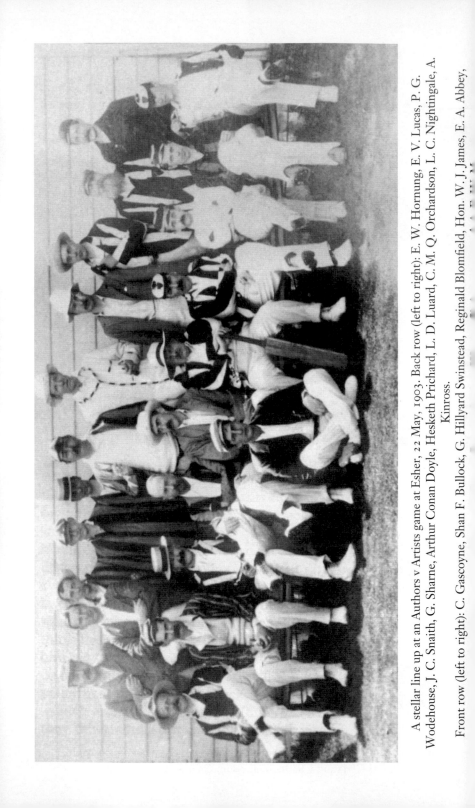

A stellar line up at an Authors v Artists game at Esher, 22 May, 1903. Back row (left to right): E. W. Hornung, E. V. Lucas, P. G. Wodehouse, J. C. Snaith, G. Sharne, Arthur Conan Doyle, Hesketh Prichard, L. D. Luard, C. M. Q. Orchardson, L. C. Nightingale, A. Kinross.

Front row (left to right): C. Gascoyne, Shan F. Bullock, G. Hillyard Swinstead, Reginald Blomfield, Hon. W. J. James, E. A. Abbey,

*Dear Lady*
*I am naturally greatly elated by your letter, and the kind things*
*you insinuate rather than express. What particularly delights*
*me is the note of uneasiness which you are at such pains to hide,*
*but which bobs out repeatedly, thro'out your bold defiance. The*
*other day I showed my big dog to a child, and he kept saying, to*
*give himself confidence, 'He won't bite me; he won't bite me;*
*I'm not afraid of his biting me,' and it is obvious to the Alla-*
*hakbarries that even in this manner do you approach me. They*
*see also a wistfulness on your face as if, after having lorded it*
*over mankind, you had at last met your match. Not, they say,*
*that it will be your match. Hence the wistfulness of your face as*
*summer draws near. As one captain speaking to another, I*
*would beg you not to let your team see that you are hopeless of*
*their winning. It will only demoralise them still further.*

*I have no intention of changing my team this year. If I can*
*get them I shall bring down last year's winners without alter-*
*ation. Also I offered last year not to put on Doyle and Pawling*
*to bowl unless you put in your cracks, and when the fatal day*
*arrives I am willing to make a similar offer again.*

*Lastly, you say 'Be then like unto me.' If you would kindly*
*tell me how it can be done I shall process to do it right away.*
*Don't think by this that I mean I want to lure your players*
*onto my side. I mean I want to be like you in your nobler*
*moments. Teach me your fascinating ways. Teach me to grow*
*your face. Teach me how you manage to be born anew every*
*morning. In short, I will make you a sporting offer. Teach me*
*all these things, and I will teach your team how to play cricket.*

The Allahakbarries began their campaign in May. On 19 May,
ten days after Barrie's thirty-ninth birthday, and a day after a
rather grand dinner at the Savoy Hotel in honour of Barrie's old
Edinburgh professor, Professor Masson, the Allahakbarries
played an Artists XI at Denmark Hill in south London. The

team was led by a friend, and another American cricketing enthusiast, Edwin Abbey, who had been one of Barrie's main links to the Broadway set and who may have played in at least one of the games there. Abbey was a slightly older man than Barrie, aged forty-seven in 1899, and was a prominent artist who was chosen to paint the coronation of King Edward in 1902. In him, Barrie had possibly met his match in terms of enthusiasm, for Abbey brought with him a distinctly American energy to the cricket pitch. Barrie wrote that 'Abbey would have tried to stop a thunderbolt to save the third run.' He and Antonio de Navarro were feared for their throws from the outfield, a hard and direct bullet that they had both learnt playing baseball. Barrie comments on this when he writes that: 'The only fault [Abbey] found in cricket was that it was not sufficiently dangerous. He tried to remedy this. As soon as you struck the ball you remembered Abbey and flung yourself on your face.' Conan Doyle in particular was a great admirer of what he saw as being the inspiring vitality of America, and a number of his stories, including the first Sherlock Holmes story, *A Study in Scarlet*, feature American characters.

But Conan Doyle, who turned forty in 1899, was not playing in the match at Denmark Hill as he was busy appearing in more serious games of cricket that season. However, Conan Doyle's young friend, just twenty-three years old, was playing in his first ever Allahakbarries game against the Artists on 19 May. His full name was Hesketh Vernon Hesketh-Prichard, though he was more commonly known simply as Hesketh Prichard. During his lifetime Prichard became everything that Barrie aspired to be. He was six feet four inches tall and a fearsome fast bowler who played first-class cricket. He was also an explorer, adventurer, big-game hunter and reputedly one of the best rifle shots in the world, as well as a journalist and author.

The game was a twelve-a-side match with both teams having the same twelfth man – the sculptor F. W. Pomeroy, who is most famous for the four figures facing upstream on Vauxhall Bridge in London. The Allahakbarries team was almost identical to that which had played at Broadway the previous summer except for the addition of Prichard and the loss of Doyle. The Artists batted first and their number four batsman, George Hillyard (G. H.) Swinstead hit the Allahakbarries' bowlers all over the ground and made a century, which included ten fours. The other artists only managed twenty-six runs between them. With studied understatement Barrie wrote that 'Mr Swinstead made a fair score'. Prichard starred for the Allahakbarries by taking five wickets and then in the Allahakbarries innings he scored twenty-six, Ford thirty-two and Pawling thirty-four. Barrie made three runs with one hit, but it was Swinstead's match for he took an astonishing eight wickets in all which meant that the Artists won by a narrow seven runs, all thanks to the efforts of one man.

The Allahakbarries played again on 1 June, against a similar team of artists, though it is not included in the scorebook, but it appears that they won by 171 runs. Then they played Bradbury, in Kent, on 17 June and a week later the London members' club, the Savile Club, though there are no records for either game.

The de Navarros returned to England from their trip to America in June and Barrie resumed his efforts to organise the match for the first weekend in July. He greets Mary de Navarro with a letter that begins: 'Welcome back, and I applaud your long hesitating promise to play fair this time'. Barrie reveals that Birrell, 'who can't play at all' and Hornung, who 'is of no consequence as a cricketer' will both be playing, but only 'if you don't sneak in any good men.' The threat that hangs over this promise from Barrie is one that he stated in an earlier letter in which he wrote that 'I could easily get another good player in his place but would it not be better to get a duffer like ourselves?'

But this year Barrie is particularly excited by the prospect of a mysterious event: 'On the Friday night there is a unique and impressive ceremony to take place among the allahakbarries from which I can't be absent as no one knows what it is except myself and I was hoping you could attend it.'

In a replay of the previous year, they arrived at lunchtime on Friday to indulge in sports in the afternoon. And then in the evening, at a dinner at the Lygon Arms, Barrie unveiled two surprises to his team. Philip Carr remembers that 'after the dinner, he made a speech, at the end of which he threw across the table to each of us what he called "your blue", a silk cap of the most hideous assortment of colours that he had been able to purchase at the shop in Regent Street where all the club colours in the world were sold.' Barrie also had a blazer made for himself in these colours. He then handed each member of the team his second Allahakbarries' booklet. The first had been very small with just a few pages, 'but the second was swollen to thirty, just as *Wisden* grows and grows.' It was called the *Allahakbarrie Book of Broadway Cricket for 1899* and it was full of Barrie's usual jokes as well as illustrations from other members of his team and the Broadway eleven too. Its title was inspired by Ranjitsinhji's *The Jubilee Book of Cricket*, which was published in 1897, though it was certainly a less serious work than that of the great batsman. The *Punch* cartoonist E. T. Reed had drawn a crate full of ducks sitting on the platform of Evesham railway station, with the label 'Allahakbarrie Cricket Club'. The drawing was called 'An indispensable part of their luggage'. Another drawing, reproduced from a photograph, features what looks like a tug-of-war, but which Barrie calls 'Allahakbarries compelling Birrell and Gilmour to go in first.' Only fifty copies were printed of the original book but it was reprinted in 1950 with an introduction by Philip Carr and a foreword by Sir Donald Bradman, who became a friend of Barrie's in the 1930s.

Barrie sets the scene for the third test match at the start of the book, with the title 'Broadway as a Cricket Centre', with more than a hint of absurdity, by depicting Broadway as an idyllic rural setting for cricket.

In the leafy month of June, when old Sol progresses to his height of passion and sluggish draughts move gently through the vibrating light of a drowsy noontide, ruffling the dainty plumage of sweetly trilling songsters performing their ablutions in shaded pools, it is then that the panting climber of the precipitous paths of Parnassus longingly looks with lingering gaze over the seething masses of the madding crowd toiling intently in dusty thoroughfares to green fields dotted with white figures on reasonable terms.

He claims that Broadway 'dates back to the time of the Romans' and that 'here Caesar probably played many fine innings of a Saturday afternoon. But all this was long ago, in the days of top hats and underhand bowling.' He leads the reader on an imaginary journey along the high street, from the Evesham end at the bottom of the hill, where the 'Quackuary' is, up past the village green, pointing out the houses where various members of the team have stayed and, on the left hand side, the 'banqueting hall of the Allahakbarries.' This is the Lygon Arms, 'an ancient structure, heavy with historic associations' where a 'Stuart king slept immediately before being caught and bowled for nothing'. He finally arrives at Court Farm, the home of the de Navarro's where he notes that Mary de Navarro 'is looking a little pale today.'

And now for the third test match.

Barrrie gives some background and team news in his little booklet, in particular the deliberations of the selection committee: 'Mr Barrie called a committee meeting to consider the composition of the team for the 1899 Test Match, present, himself and Reed. After a careful exchange of views the following were elected as a nucleus of the eleven: J. M. Barrie, Esq., Reed (E. T.).'

They discuss Conan Doyle, 'but it was stated on authority that he had decided to devote himself henceforth to second-class cricket.' They also deliberate between some first-class cricketers and some rather more familiar faces. 'We now want a hard hitter. Shall it be

Gilmour or A. E. Stoddart? It was decided to play Gilmour if the pitch was treacherous, and Mr Stoddart if it was sticky.' The pitch was evidently treacherous, for Stoddart was left out and named as a reserve instead. Not being picked was certainly unusual for an Ashes-winning captain of England, and iconic batsman, but not being picked by a five-foot-tall Scotsman must have been a unique experience for Stoddart. 'The committee' also favoured Meredith over the Middlesex and England wicket-keeper G. MacGregor, though he also is listed alongside Prichard as being a reserve. It is likely through a number of connections that Barrie and others in the team knew Stoddart and MacGregor: Pawling had played with Stoddart at Middlesex and Hampstead and Conan Doyle would have known them both too. But it is probable that they never actually turned out for the Allahakbarries, though they may have both been at the match. Then again, it might have just been a fantasy (and a joke) of Barrie's that he would have such cricketing heroes to call upon. Nonetheless, Prichard, who had a distinguished amateur first-class career, certainly played as a twelfth man for both sides.

The booklet was written prior to the game so Barrie gives a 'Forecast of the Allahakbarrie Score in the 1899 Test Match' with room at the end for the players to fill in exactly what really did happen 'Lest the forecast should be wrong.' Barrie uses this forecast to give full expression to a number of long-running jokes about the team – and quite a few new ones too – in epigrammatic sentences. It begins:

> This annual engagement, which is now recognised as a first-class fixture, came off tomorrow at Broadway in ideal cricketing weather. By 11.15 the pavilion was thronged with beautiful women and brainy men.

The joke that runs almost entirely through the forecast is Partridge's accumulation of runs using his pads alone: 'Partridge opened the ball by bagging a brace of lovely cuts, each for 3 and both off his pads.'

Use of the pads was a very topical issue at the turn of the century. There had been increasingly more drawn games in the decade since the foundation of county cricket in 1890, rising from twenty-odd per cent to almost double that, as batsmen became more and more dominant over the bowlers. In 1900 there was a proposal to change the LBW law in order to make it easier for bowlers to get batsmen out. Derek Birley describes how 'The hon. Alfred Lyttleton, no less, had proposed the motion in a lengthy MCC debate, because "the present cricket [was] somewhat dull." Other old stagers deplored the deliberate use of pads, which once had been thought unethical and unsporting.'

Partridge seems undeterred by this consternation, though, as shown in one of the illustrations by artist and fellow member of the team, Henry Ford. The sketch is called 'Partridge's golden dream' and shows Partridge asleep, and with his pads on, dreaming of tens of disembodied pads come to life and hitting runs all over the pitch.

Partridge sleeps now

The final pages of the booklet include Owen Seaman's poem and a reprise of Barrie's 'Hint to the Team by their Captain' which had first appeared in the 1893 booklet.

There were members of the press there to record what really happened, much to Barrie's annoyance, and the score was also recorded in the Allahakbarries scorebook. It was not ideal cricketing weather. The *Evesham Journal and Four Shire Advertiser*, in fact, reported that the 'weather was almost as disastrous as it could be, heavy storms passing over the ground at frequent intervals during the day'. The paper also curiously calls the Broadway side the 'Allabazans' in opposition to the Allahakbarries, of which there is no mention in any other source, and was most probably invented by the journalist who wrote the piece. 'Many did not expect that there would be any cricket at all, but the members of the Allahakbarries and the Allabazans are nothing if not keen. They had come to play cricket, and cricket they were determined to play. They had not their fearful and awful averages to consider, or perhaps some of them would have been a bit shy at batting on such a sodden wicket.'

Broadway batted first and they had a good opening stand, with Charles Turley Smith making twenty-one, but once the openers had gone the rest of the wickets fell quickly, with Mason and Barrie taking three wickets each. The Broadway total was eighty-nine, which included eleven extras. Seaman and Ford opened the batting for the Allahakbarries and also put on a good first stand. Seaman was out lbw for fifteen and Partridge who came in next failed to live up to Barrie's forecast by being bowled for a duck by Smith. But then Pawling came to the wicket and immediately lashed the ball to all parts of the field, making a half century that included nine boundaries. Ford also helped himself to a half century as the Broadway fielders watched in despair. Barrie, meanwhile, prowled around the boundary edge with an umbrella under his arm, a cup of tea in his hand and a pipe in his mouth. When Pawling was out for fifty-two, he awarded him 'a beautiful clay pipe, with fine amber mouthpiece, in a case' for being the man with the highest score. The innings continued long after the Allahakbarries had won the match, so Barrie was able to get in and make eight runs himself, before his team were bowled out for 153. They had triumphed again: the Allahakbarries were the champions of this three match series.

The Barries set off the following week for the spa town of Schwalbach where Mary Barrie was taking the waters for her poor health. Barrie wrote to Mary de Navarro from Germany and struggled to contain his joy at victory:

> *I am really writing this letter in order to say that:*
>
> *How I wish the match were the next Saturday instead of the last. Oh, that everything would always be next Saturday. And generally at Broadway.*
>
> *This is not a sporting place. I long to stop the passerby and say to them 'Sir (or madam) I challenge you to anything you like.'*
>
> *Drinking the waters is the only thing they go in for. It is not my game but in desperation I am ready to play them even at that.*
>
> *The place is almost entirely full of ladies, each with her little drinking mug. There is scarcely a team of men in the countryside.*
>
> *Such as they are, are a weakly looking lot.*
>
> *I think Broadway could play them.*
>
> *(That slipped out. I meant to be so nice in this letter. Forgive me, Mamie. I ought never to refer to cricket in a letter to you.*
>
> *(I believe that is another slip. This is very unlike me).*
>
> *We are to be here for the whole of July. I am wearing my colours, but the other people little know that an allahakbarrie is in their midst.*

Barrie later remembered in *The Greenwood Hat* that

> In their love for [Mary de Navarro] the Allahakbarries tried
> to let her side win, but we were so accomplished it could not
> be done. I take back all my aspersions on the team. I remember
> now that we always won. The Allahakbarries were invincible.

# 5

## THE MIGHTY CONAN DOYLE,
## AND OTHER CRICKETERS

'The team had no tail, that is to say, they would have
done just as well had they begun at the other end. Yet
when strengthened in the weaker points of their
armour, namely in batting and bowling, by outsiders
surreptitiously introduced, they occasionally astounded
the tented field.'

J. M. Barrie, *The Greenwood Hat*

———

1899 was a significant year in the life of W. G. Grace who at the
age of fifty-one was still playing first-class cricket, though with
his famous beard now heavily flecked and streaked with grey. But
he played his last ever test match, against Australia, at Trent
Bridge that year after realising that he was overweight and slow
in his late middle-age. He took the decision himself to retire as
he was now a liability in the field at this level. England went on
to lose the series as the Australian renaissance, which had begun
in the 1897/8 series continued. Grace played his last match for
Gloucestershire, the county he had played for since 1870, in 1899
as well, though it was far from being his last match in first-class
cricket. A new club called London County had been formed in
Crystal Palace, south London, and they had invited Grace to join
them as their secretary and manager as well as playing for them.

He accepted, thinking that he did not have to have divided loyalty between the two sides. But the authorities at Gloucestershire disagreed and gave Grace the ultimatum to choose one or the other – and on 28 May 1899 Grace, affronted by the treatment given to him by Gloucestershire, chose London. Other famous players, such as Ranjitsinhji and C. B. Fry, who both played for Sussex, also played on occasion for London County, but with the approval of their county. Conan Doyle, playing for MCC against London County at Crystal Palace the following year, in 1900, took his one and only first-class wicket, and it was that of the most famous cricketer of all: W. G. Grace.

Conan Doyle had not been able to play for the Allahakbarries in 1899 as he was playing, according to him, 'on the fringe of first-class cricket'. He actually played forty games in all that summer, including a number of two-day games, a schedule that left little time for writing. He was an all-rounder, a fact recognised in his *Wisden* obituary, which reveals that 'Although never

"THE FIFTIETH YEAR OF GRACE."
NOT OUT.

a famous cricketer, he could hit hard and bowl slows with a puzzling flight.' Conan Doyle's diary reveals that his slow bowling was well prepared and considered: 'Must cultivate the faster leg ball with swerve. Move along the crease. Bowl two balls with leg swerve over the wicket and then one with off break from the extreme edge of the crease.' He took 106 wickets in all in the 1899 season and though his batting average was just twenty-one, he was also capable of some destructive hitting: sixty-seven runs in an hour in a second-class match against East Gloucestershire, for example. In a second-class match for MCC against Cambridgeshire on 30 and 31 August 1899 he achieved a triumphant return of seven for sixty-one off thirty-nine overs. He was playing alongside B. J. T. Bosanquet, the spin bowler who has been credited with inventing the googly, played for England seven times and who in 1904 was the *Wisden* cricketer of the year. But on this occasion he was outshone by Conan Doyle, and only managed to take one wicket. In his autobiography, *Memories and Adventures*, Conan Doyle recalled that probably the strangest thing that happened to him on the cricket pitch was when he was literally set on fire while batting at Lord's.

I was playing for the Club against Kent, and faced for the first time Bradley, who was that year one of the fastest bowlers in England. His first delivery I hardly saw, and it landed with a terrific thud upon my thigh. A little occasional pain is one of the chances of cricket, and one takes it as cheerfully as one can, but on this occasion it suddenly became sharp to an unbearable degree. I clapped my hand to the spot, and found to my amazement that I was on fire. The ball had landed straight on a small tin vesta box in my trousers pocket, had splintered the box, and set the matches ablaze.

Conan Doyle also had his own coterie of friends and relatives with whom he played cricket, and he hosted an annual cricket week at his house near Hindhead, Surrey, in August. He called his team the 'Undershaw XI' after the name of his house. Barrie was usually in Scotland during August, so he did not attend these cricketing weeks, which featured games against Haslemere, Grayshott and other local clubs, but it appears from photographic evidence alone that Barrie did play more cricket in the summer of 1899 as he is pictured in a team photo at a Shere Cricket Club 'Married v Single' game with George Meredith and A. E. W. Mason.

Conan Doyle's brother-in-law, E. W. Hornung, or Willie to his family and friends, was one of the Allahakbarries who did turn out for the Undershaw XI weeks and he was a great enthusiast of the game, though like Barrie he was blessed with neither great physical attributes nor skill. But he qualifies for this chapter not by virtue of his own prowess as a cricketer, but because of his most notorious fictional character, Raffles.

Hornung was born in 1866 in Middlesbrough, the youngest son of businessman John Peter Hornung, and was a thin and feeble child, short-sighted and afflicted by severe asthma. He was educated at Uppingham but he left school early, in 1883, because of his poor health and went to Australia to recuperate. He spent three years there and thoroughly enjoyed it, regaining his health, though having little opportunity to play much cricket. Hornung was employed as a tutor but also travelled widely and when he returned to England in 1886, determined to be a professional writer, and with his family in difficult financial circumstances, the articles and stories he contributed to magazines were mainly about different aspects of Australian life. His first novel, *A Bride in the Bush*, published in 1890, was also set in Australia, and there followed seven more novels as well as a collection of short stories. He was a witty man and a sparkling conversationalist, so much so that Conan Doyle wrote after his death, in a rather double-edged way, that 'he was a Dr Johnson without the learning but with a finer wit. No one could say a neater thing, and his writings, good as they are, never adequately represented the powers of the man, nor the quickness of his brain.'

This sparkling wit, though, must have been one of the qualities that persuaded Conan Doyle's sister, Connie, to marry
Hornung in 1893, as she was an attractive woman and had many
suitors to choose from. They lived in Kensington, very near to
Barrie, for most of their lives. Hornung's association with Arthur
Conan Doyle ultimately turned out to be a very profitable one,
as it was Sherlock Holmes who provided the inspiration and
Conan Doyle the first name for Hornung's most famous character, A. J. Raffles. The first Raffles book, a collection of short
stories called *The Amateur Cracksman*, was published in April 1899
and dedicated 'To A. C. D. This Form of Flattery'. Raffles is an
exceptional cricketer and a dandy. He has an 'indolent, athletic
figure'. He's handsome, debonair, witty, masterful and brave too,
but, in a cunning inversion of the Sherlock Holmes character, he
is also a criminal. This was something that Conan Doyle disap-
proved of, one of a number of incidents that put a strain on the
relationship between the two men:

> I think there are few finer examples of short-story writing in
> our language than these, though I confess I think they are
> rather dangerous in their suggestion. I told him so before he
> put pen to paper, and the result has, I fear, borne me out. You
> must not make the criminal a hero.

The very first Raffles story was actually published in *Cassell's
Magazine* in 1898, where it was described as 'Being the Confes-
sions of a late Prisoner of the Crown, and sometime accomplice
of the more notorious A. J. Raffles, Cricketer and Criminal, whose
fate is uncertain.' The tales are narrated, in a similar way to those
of Sherlock Holmes, not by the hero himself, but by a faithful
companion and in this case 'sometimes accomplice' Bunny
Manders. The two men had known one another at school where
Raffles had been the captain of the cricket team and at the start
of the first story, in the early 1890s, now young men, they have
just become reacquainted. Manders is in desperate need of money

and asks his old schoolmate if he has any suggestions for what he could do to get some. Raffles says that he has a solution and fools his friend into helping him to steal from a jewellery shop on New Bond Street. He afterwards welcomes him to the not-so-honourable fraternity of gentlemen burglars. 'Why should I work when I could steal?' he asks Manders. 'Why settle down to some uncongenial billet, when excitement, romance, danger, and a decent living were all going begging together?' Which sounds rather like Peter Pan not wanting to grow up and go to an office every day.

'Raffles may or may not have been an exceptional criminal,' relates Manders, 'but as a cricketer I dare say he was unique. Himself a dangerous bat, a brilliant field, and perhaps the finest slow bowler of his decade, he took incredibly little interest in the game at large . . . He professed to have lost all enthusiasm for the game and to keep it up only from the lowest motives. "Cricket," said Raffles, ". . . is good enough sport until you discover a better . . . What's the satisfaction of taking a man's wicket when you want his spoons? Still, if you can bowl a bit your low cunning won't get rusty, and always looking for the weak spot's just the kind of mental exercise one wants."'

Raffles played for the famous I Zingari team and the Gentlemen of England, and there is an element of snobbery that distinguishes the 'amateur cracksman' from professional thieves, whom Raffles calls 'professors', just as in the Sherlock Holmes stories there is the same snobbery between the amateur Holmes and the professional police force. Holmes has foresight; he is sharp, perceptive and intelligent. The Scotland Yard detectives like Lestrade, by way of contrast, are clumsy, oafish bunglers. In cricket the distinction was made between the flair, thrust and imagination of young gentlemen amateurs and the plodding, workaday play of working-class professionals. One of the stories in *The Amateur Cracksman* is even called 'Gentlemen and Players', which was an annual match between amateurs and professionals played at Lord's that had begun in 1806.

Raffles is an aesthete who embodies the most famous description of how young *fin-de-siècle* aesthetes ought to behave: from Walter Pater's notorious *Studies in the History of the Renaissance*. Pater advised young men 'to burn always with this hard, gem-like flame, to maintain this ecstasy', and to seek 'the highest quality to your moments as they pass, and simply for those moments' sake'. George Orwell, an old-Etonian, though nonetheless a possibly surprising fan of Raffles and of cricket in general, noted that Raffles 'will take extra risks in the name of "sportsmanship", and sometimes even for aesthetic reasons.' That is one of the things that distinguishes him from the professional thieves. Hornung's biographer Peter Rowland even suggests that the character was based on Oscar Wilde. The fact that Hornung's only son, who was born in 1895, was named Arthur Oscar, though came to be known as Oscar, just one week before the start of Wilde's famous libel case against the Marquess of Queensberry in April, certainly suggests that Hornung had some sympathy for the Irish playwright. And there are a number of reasons, though no convincing single one, to agree with Rowland. Wilde was certainly no sportsman, though, and it seems more likely that fellow Allahakbarrie George Ives was the real inspiration for Raffles, though it is curious to note that Ives also knew Wilde personally.

Raffles was certainly not the only cricketing dandy around. Cricket was ideally suited to dressing up, a favoured pastime of the turn-of-the-century upper and middle classes. The men wore smartly pressed flannels and many amateurs emulated Ranjitsinhji by donning a silk shirt. Brightly coloured silk ties were worn around the waist instead of belts and there were garishly striped caps and blazers of a variety of different colours. Even Grace enlivened his rather formidable appearance with a brightly coloured scarf tied around his enormous waist.

Although Raffles was a likeable and handsome rogue, Hornung did not endorse the controversial and criminal activities of his hero. He saw it as an amusing parody of the Holmes stories, and an opportunity to have some fun with established social mores and his favourite game. He clearly saw the commercial opportunities in the venture as well, and the Raffles books were extremely successful, with further collections of short stories published in 1901 (*The Black Mask*) and 1905 (*A Thief in the Night*). This may even have been one of the reasons that Conan Doyle decided to resurrect Sherlock Holmes in *The Hound of the Baskervilles*, which he wrote in 1901 and which was first published as a serial in the *Strand Magazine*. Hornung himself was far from being a Raffles-like aesthete, and the Raffles stories were, outwardly at least, meant to be cautionary tales: by the end of *The Amateur Cracksman* Manders is in prison and Raffles missing, presumed drowned. Hornung's actual ideal of youth was not aestheticism, as personified by Raffles, but a far more English sense of asceticism – duty, discipline, male companionship, exercise and cold baths. He was a firm believer in both cricket and the public-school system and often quoted Sir Henry Newbolt's famous 1897 three-verse poem 'Vitai Lampada', literally '[They pass] the torch of life', which is all about cricket as a preparation for battle, and which was later used as propaganda in the First World War.

> There's a breathless hush in the Close to-night
> Ten to make and the match to win
> A bumping pitch and a blinding light,
> An hour to play, and the last man in.
> And it's not for the sake of a ribboned coat.
> Or the selfish hope of a season's fame,
> But his captain's hand on his shoulder smote
> 'Play up! Play up! And play the game!'

The sand of the desert is sodden red –
Red with the wreck of a square that broke
The Gatling's jammed and the colonel dead,
And the regiment blind with dust and smoke.
The river of death has brimmed its banks,
And England's far, and Honour a name,
But the voice of a schoolboy rallies the ranks –
'Play up! Play up! And play the game!'

This is the word that year by year,
While in her place the school is set,
Every one of her sons must hear,
And none that hears it dare forget.
This they all with a joyful mind
Bear through life like a torch in flame,
And falling fling to the host behind –
'Play up! Play up! And play the game!'

This is a long way from Barrie's imaginings of cricket as an idyllic rural pursuit, free from the pressures of modern life. It is cricket as cultural indoctrination, sport promoted as politics; the extension of the cricket field on to the battlefield. Jeremy Paxman wrote in his book *The English*, that 'It is hard not to be carried along in its rhythm, even if there is something so breathtakingly stupid about the poem that it is hard to imagine how on earth it could ever have been taken seriously. Yet in the balmy days before August 1914, the idea that life was essentially a version of the Game seemed almost plausible.' He is right: the motif at the heart of this poem was entirely absorbed by the cricketing establishment and indeed the political establishment too and in the years that followed 'playing the game' was at the very heart of what it meant to be English, at least for the 'leisured classes'. It meant following an entire moral and behavioural code which was based on team games, and most importantly cricket. And it also meant that the Newboltian ethos was easy to impart to schoolboys, those same boys who later died in their thousands in the fields of northern France.

Raffles ultimately followed in the same direction as Newbolt's schoolboys; for all his misdemeanours he was also a patriot and he celebrates the Diamond Jubilee ('For sixty years, Bunny, we've been ruled over by absolutely the finest sovereign the world has ever seen') by sending the queen a gold cup which he has stolen from the British Museum. And this is how he ultimately makes good: by dying in the Boer war in South Africa fighting, with characteristic panache, for queen and country at the end of *The Black Mask*.

The motive of wish fulfilment is a powerful one, for Hornung was not an athlete, and so he turned his hero into one of the most exceptional cricketers of his generation. 'There are eminent men of action,' he wrote in 1902, 'who can acquit themselves with equal credit upon the little field of letters, as some of the very best books of late years go to prove. The man of letters, on the other hand, capable of cutting a respectable figure in action, is, one fears, a much rarer type.' Conan Doyle was of course one of these rare men who manage to succeed in both action and letters, and it is he who commented on Hornung's own prowess on the field of play by writing that he 'would I am sure have excelled in the game himself if he had not been hampered by short sight and villainous asthma. To see him stand up behind the sticks with his big pebble glasses to a fast bowler was an object lesson in pluck if not in wicket-keeping.'

But Conan Doyle had another friend who played for the Allahakbarries who really did play for the Gentlemen of England against the Players at Lord's and who also excelled as both a man of action and a man of letters. Hesketh Prichard, who had played for the Allahakbarries against Broadway, was still a young man at the turn of the century. He was born in 1876 in India where his Scottish father was an army officer. His father died of typhoid in India before Prichard was born and he and his mother moved back to England soon after. Like Barrie and Conan Doyle, Prichard also had a significant Edinburgh connection as he went to Fettes School in the city, which is where his talent for cricket was first noticed: the school magazine described him as 'the best bowler we have had for a long time. Fast right hand, with a good break back on a bowler's wicket. At present is hardly steady enough, and he wants experience. Unfortunately he is leaving, but he ought to do something in the future.' He certainly fulfilled that prophecy.

After school, in the mid-nineties, Prichard qualified as a lawyer, and combined writing with travel to Europe and Africa. He wrote stories and articles rather unusually together with his mother under the pseudonyms H. Heron and E. Heron. In February 1897, after they had had articles published in the *Cornhill Magazine*, Prichard met Conan Doyle at a dinner in Mayfair organised for authors and contributors to the publication. The two became friends straight away and talked long into the night. Conan Doyle later had a significant role in Prichard's cricket career, recommending him to W. G. Grace, who picked him to play for London County in 1899. Prichard's biographer and friend Eric Parker wrote that 'W. G. had a great opinion of him, and liked to have him on his side whenever possible', and on one occasion the two men shared a century stand together in a charity match against Bristol. Conan Doyle also recommended Prichard to another friend of his, the captain of Hampshire County Cricket Club, Major E. G. Wynard. He played most of his first-class cricket for Hampshire, playing his first game in 1900, and he took 339 wickets in all during a first-class career which was regularly interrupted by his other activities, particularly exploration, hunting and writing. He was clearly a destructive bowler, as in just eighty-six games he took five wickets twenty-five times and ten wickets five times, and all at an average of just twenty-two. He was selected three years in a row, between 1903 and 1905, to play for the Gentlemen against the Players at Lord's and in one of these games, in 1904, he performed heroics with ball and bat for the gentlemen to win by the narrowest of margins. He also played for the most famous touring sides including I Zingari and the Free Foresters and later toured the West Indies and Philadelphia for the MCC.

It's possible that it was Barrie who introduced Prichard to the newspaper proprietor and owner of *Pearson's Weekly* and the *Daily Express*, Arthur Pearson, a man who brought further adventure into Prichard's life. In 1899, as Pearson was preparing to launch the *Daily Express* the following year, he wanted some exciting stories of travel and adventure to unknown places to put in his new half-penny paper. Prichard suggested that an account of a journey to Haiti would fit the bill and got the commission. His reports so impressed Pearson that when Prichard returned he was sent off again in 1900 to Patagonia to investigate reports of a mysterious beast which some experts thought could be a living example of the thought-to-be-long-extinct giant ground sloth, or mylodon. Though Prichard did not find the sloth, he did succeed in thrilling the readers of the *Daily Express* with his epic tales of adventure, which he later published in his book *Through the Heart of Patagonia*. One of the more exciting passages from the book is when Prichard steers an old steam-ship, the *Ariel*, down the un-mapped Leona river, having little idea whether it was navigable or not. At first he and his small crew went cautiously, facing the boat against the current so that they did not go too fast, but they were suddenly turned prow-first and had to run full tilt down the river.

> There was now no straining and grunting from the engines as there had been while we were battling against the current. You barely felt the throb and vibration, and it was only when you looked at the banks that you realised how swiftly the boat was rushing onwards. Perhaps we achieved seventeen knots. The shores slid by.

We were now in a world of our own, whose boundaries were the curving banks and the reaches of the river as they opened out in front of us. One's senses were too much occupied, one's nerves too much on the stretch to be aware of anything beyond. We, the launch and the river were playing a gigantic gamble, in which the stakes on our part were perilously heavy.

Prichard explored over ten thousand miles of southern Argentina, named a lake after his mentor Arthur Pearson, a river, the Rio Caterina, after his mother, and discovered a previously unknown sub-species of the puma.

1900 was also a significant year for the laws of cricket. The over was extended from five balls to six. A declaration, which had previously only been allowed on the third day of a match, was now able to be made after lunch on the second day, and enforcing the follow-on was made optional when a side led by 150 runs or more after the first innings. It is curious to note as well that the score of a six for a hit over the boundary rope did not become standardised across the country until 1910 – for now big hits were often only awarded four runs. For the Allahakbarries, the changes in the laws made little difference, though Barrie, now in his fortieth year, might have preferred a five-ball over to a six-ball one. Not that he appeared tired. He was as zealous and energetic as ever this year in organising games against the Artists, a game against themselves and against the village of Shackleford, which was close by to the Barries' new country residence.

Mary Barrie had for some time been looking for a country house and in April 1899 she found it nestling in a remote and quiet spot, deep in pine forests near Farnham, and reached by horse and cart down a sandy track. It was called Black Lake Cottage after the brackish pond nearby and the estate comprised of four acres of garden and four acres of woodland. Mary had a talent for design, decoration and gardens and she set about transforming the cottage into a dazzling country retreat. It was the venue for annual cricket festivals, for the next six summers from 1900, at first occupying weekends and then whole weeks, hidden far away from the prying eyes of the press hounds in the heart of the woods. Its south lawn, at the back of the house, was large enough for games of golf-croquet and also cricket of the more informal kind, such as gentlemen (left-handed) versus ladies.

———

On the damp streets of London on Friday, 18 May 1900 newspaper boys were out in force with unusual news of what their notices called the 'latest cricket', which gave the score of 'Baden Powell not out 216, Kruger 0.' Colonel Robert Stephenson Smyth Baden-Powell, who was three years older than Barrie and later the founder of the Boy Scouts as well as one of the more enthusiastic devotees of *Peter Pan*, had commanded troops in the town of Mafeking on the border of the Transvaal, which had been surrounded by Boer forces ever since the start of the Boer War in October 1899. But on 17 May British forces relieved the siege after what is now generally agreed to have been 217 days, adding one to Baden-Powell's score. The man who according to the British newspapers had scored a duck, Paul Kruger, was the state president of the South African Republic. The 'Relief of Mafeking' meant that on the evening of 18 May there were huge celebrations in central London and Baden-Powell became a national hero. During the siege he had created a regiment of boys below fighting age – the Mafeking Cadet Corps – who he used to run errands, often quite dangerous ones, as manpower was so limited in the town. They provided Baden-Powell with inspiration for the Scouts, the organisation that he founded in 1907, and an enterprise in which he was helped considerably by his enduring fame and popularity from the Mafeking siege.

According to Baden-Powell's biographer Tim Jeal,

Wilde and other 'decadent' *fin-de-siècle* poets and artists had seemed to threaten an entire culture with their self-indulgence and effeminacy. Their antithesis was the ideal soldier living simply, ignorant of art and intellectual matters, disciplining his mind and body and placing his love of country above all else. Such a man was proof against degeneration inseparable from soft urban living. He personified the self-control which society would need if anarchism, socialism and sexual licence were not – as Max Nordau put it – to lead 'to its certain ruin because too worn out and flaccid to perform great tasks'. And when such fears in Britain were at their height during the disastrous Boer War, no soldier epitomised that saving manly spirit more perfectly than R. S. S. Baden-Powell.

Baden-Powell himself urged the younger generation that they shouldn't

> be disgraced like the young Romans, who lost the Empire of their forefathers by being wishy-washy slackers without any go or patriotism in them. Play up. Each man in his own place and play the game. Your forefathers worked hard, fought hard and died hard to make the Empire for you. Don't let them look down from heaven and see you loafing about with your hands in your pockets, doing nothing to keep it up.

So where did the Allahakbarries fit in this scheme of things – were they the effeminate bohemians that were threatening British culture with their degeneracy? Or were they part of the Newbolt–Baden-Powell imperialist asceticism; the subordination of the individual to the team, the spirit of the game and the nation? Were they foppish dandies or sturdy heroes? Clearly there was something playfully subversive about the side – their fundamental lack of thoroughness, joking about cricket (which ought to be taken seriously) and claiming to not care about winning, for example – which suggests that they might be considered to be on the margins of the type of political orthodoxy expressed by Baden-Powell, Newbolt and the like. But they were also not as bohemian as a bunch of writers playing cricket might have expected to have been. Conan Doyle, though sometimes unconventional, was a man of military bearing with strong belief in the nation and the empire. Barrie was in many ways utterly un-bohemian – he preferred to go to fairgrounds and play games than to listen to music or look at art, for example. He had always viewed cricket as a rather more bucolic and bumptious pursuit than Newbolt evidently did, in which jesting had a full part: more rural conservatism than aggressive imperialism. So, if anything, the Allahak-barries straddled the divide suggested by Jeal: they were bohemian heroes, subversive conservatives, unconscious imperialists and a mass of other strange and often oxymoronic collocations.

The first Allahakbarries match of the new century was a reprise from the previous year of the game against the Artists at Denmark Hill. It took place a fortnight after Barrie's fortieth birthday, on 24 May, and it's likely there was some agreement to give Barrie an unexpected present that day, for he opened the batting and made an unprecedented and never-to-be-repeated nineteen runs. The author Albert Kinross, who later played in Artists v. Authors games at Esher, commented in his book of cricketing memoirs, *An Unconventional Cricketer*, that 'We all liked [the American artist] Abbey and did our best *not* to get him out, and the Artists, I think, had much the same feeling towards Barrie.' He was certainly proud of his achievement. He boasted of it a couple of weeks later when he wrote to Antonio de Navarro to say that 'We are all very sorry that the match can't take place this year'. But it was good news that he wanted to communicate.

I made a perfect 19 (nineteen) against the artists, and if when we come back to Broadway, Mamie finds that I am constantly lifting my hat to her I may say that the reason is that I have my glorious score pasted on the inside of it.

Mamie is his affectionate nickname for Mary de Navarro. He adds a postscript to his letter too – 'Did I mention that I had made 19?'

The Artists, who were much the same side as the previous year, had batted first and the star of the previous fixture, G. H. Swinstead, performed intrepid deeds again by making a score of sixty-five, of which an astonishing forty-eight runs came from boundaries.

Charles Turley Smith, formerly of Broadway, also played in this game for the Allahakbarries, but the real cricketer of note who made his debut this year against the Artists was J. C. Snaith. Born in 1876, the same age as Prichard, the left-handed John Collis Snaith played his one and only first-class game for Nottinghamshire in 1900. He made a reasonably promising twenty-one in his only innings in that game, but never got the opportunity to follow it up. He certainly excelled in club cricket and for the Allahakbarries proved to be a dangerous and greatly feared bowler who could skittle sides out – something which he accomplished the following month in the next match against the Artists. Charles Tennyson, who later played for the Allahakbarries described him as 'a medium or slow-medium left hand bowler, and on certain types of wicket he had the power of bringing the ball in very quickly off the pitch time after time, just bail high, with a "naturally unnatural" break from the off, which was fatal to second class batsmen.'

The essay in which this description appears is called 'The Too-Serious Snaith', for Tennyson writes that he was an intense and introverted man who found it difficult to socialise and generally led a very private life. He was pale, gaunt and wore scholarly glasses, had straight black hair and slightly stooping shoulders. He enjoyed playing chess with a select group of companions and loved more than anything else to play cricket. And of course he was a writer, though not a writer with the fame of many of the other members of the Allahakbarries team. Tennyson, however, writes that Snaith's story *Willow the King*, which was published in 1899, 'has often been referred to as the best cricket story ever written'.

Snaith was so ardent about his cricket that one member of the Allahakbarries recalled that on the south lawn of Black Lake Cottage, 'when the traditional match of Gentlemen (left-handed) against Ladies was being played with customary hilarity, Snaith smote Mrs Barrie on the ankle with a fast Yorker and was with difficulty restrained from claiming lbw.'

He was sometimes called 'the gloomy scribe', such was his generally overcast disposition, and it seems that the rest of the team aimed some gentle jokes in his direction. He had first been introduced to Barrie in 1898 and, quite typically, Barrie saw him as an interesting character study. And when Prichard published the book about his travels to South America, *Adventures through the Heart of Patagonia*, in 1902, which described his hunt for the giant sloth, Barrie 'immediately invented a shy and formidable and even more mysterious animal, The Giant Snaith, about which he delighted to weave grotesquely appropriate fantasies in his slow rich Scottish drawl.'

He does not, however, seem to have found his way into Barrie's written fiction, but his exploits on the cricket pitch must have delighted the little Scot. In this first match of the season he took an unspectacular but useful four wickets and scored sixteen, but they still lost the match by twenty-two runs. Far better performances were just around the corner, though, and he proved to be one of the team's strongest players. Another cricketer who played in this game for the Allahakbarries as well as a handful of others, was Harry Wilson, a Yorkshire-born bowler who played six first-class matches for Worcestershire and took six for eighty-six on his County Championship debut against Surrey in 1903.

On 11 June the Allahakbarries played against themselves in a so-called 'Duffer's Match' with Barrie captaining one team and A. E. W. Mason the other. None of the more impressive cricketers were playing that day and so, with a couple of exceptions, the Allahakbarries reverted to their original state of being not very good at cricket. The actor Gerald du Maurier, brother of Sylvia Llewelyn Davies (and father of the novelist Daphne du Maurier), made his debut for the team and top-scored with twenty-one out of a total of sixty-seven. He played a number of fictional characters created by members of the Allahakbarries during his acting career, including Captain Hook and Mr Darling in Barrie's *Peter Pan*, and Raffles in the stage version of Hornung's stories.

Mason's team thrashed Barrie's bowlers around in their innings and George Ives demonstrated that he made a worthy life model for Raffles by making sixty-one, though not, it is assumed, by also stealing from his fellow players. Ives did have a connection with criminality as he spent a lot of time studying criminology and later became a well-known reformer of the penal system. In the years running up to the First World War he published a number of books on the subject of crime and punishment including *Penal Methods in the Middle Ages* (1910), *The Treatment of Crime* (1912) and *A History of Penal Methods: Criminals, Witches, Lunatics* (1914).

Just a few days after this game, on 14 June 1900 a team called 'Arthur Conan Doyle's XI' played against the Artists, but with a number of Allahakbarries among them including Barrie himself. The score for the game was recorded in the Allahakbarries scorebook. But there were also a number of unfamiliar characters, and most strangely of all no Arthur Conan Doyle despite the team being named after him. In fact the match was probably a tribute to him as he had been in South Africa since 21 March. He had attempted to get drafted to fight in the conflict, and urged in a letter to *The Times* in December 1899 that other men, proficient as many country gentlemen were in shooting and hunting, should join up too. He also tried to promote to the War Office what he considered to be an extremely useful military invention, which he claimed would turn a regular gun into a howitzer by simply putting his device onto the end of an ordinary rifle. He did some preliminary tests on it at Frensham Pond, where the Allahakbarries played for the first time in 1901. The War Office, however, turned down the offer. And Conan Doyle was eventually recruited as a doctor rather than a soldier, which, after all, was what he was qualified to be. He served in a field hospital, which turned out to be situated on a cricket pitch in Bloemfontein. In April 1900 he was busy helping to deal with a typhoid epidemic after the Boers had cut off the water supply and later that month watched the waterworks being retaken and the supply restored. He remained in South Africa until 4 July. On the voyage back from Cape Town he met a young *Daily Express* journalist from Devon called Bertram Fletcher Robinson, who the following year inspired him to write *The Hound of the Baskervilles* by telling him the legend of a demonic hound on Dartmoor.

Conan Doyle would have been proud of Snaith's performance in his tribute side: he took eight wickets and made fifty in the match, out-performing even Prichard, who took two wickets. But despite their quality players, the side were defeated by the triumphant Artists who in less generous mood than earlier in the season, bowled Barrie out for a duck. Unlike his previous success against the Artists, this innings was certainly not mentioned in despatches.

But Barrie was looking forward to the next cricket event of the season: a weekend at his new country house. The idea was to recreate the festival atmosphere of the Broadway weekends, and to play some cricket, of course. He and his wife arrived at the cottage in early July just as the workmen were completing the renovations to the property. Barrie was making notes for *The Little White Bird* and thinking about the production of his latest play *The Wedding Guest*, which was to open at the Garrick Theatre in September, as well as making arrangements for the match.

On Friday, 20 July he and Mary were joined at the cottage by many of the usual Allahakbarries who had journeyed by train and carriage from London, as well as a few new ones. The team on this occasion included George Meredith's son Will, A. E. W. Mason, Henry Ford, Owen Seaman and Augustine Birrell. Birrell also brought his stepson along, Charles Tennyson, the grandson of Alfred Tennyson. He played his first game for the Allahakbarries the following day, when the side made the eight mile journey across heathland and through woods to the small and peaceful village of Shackleford to play Edgar Horne's XI. Edgar Horne lived at the manor house in the village called Hall Place, which is now the home of Aldro preparatory school. Horne, later the chairman of Prudential and a Surrey MP, had his own cricket pitch and had assembled a team to play the Allahakbarries.

Barrie's side had two other new recruits playing in this game. They were George Cotterill and Walter Frith. Walter Frith was the son of the famous Victorian painter, William Powell Frith, and was a novelist and dramatist, though he had no outstanding success with his writing. The *New York Times*, for example, damned his play *The Man of Forty* with rather faint praise when it opened at Daly's Theatre in November 1900. 'Its reckless use of coincidence, its unsophisticated construction, its lack of the desirable theatrical quality called "sympathy" are not to be disputed. Yet its merit is considerable, and it "acts" surprisingly well.'

Cotterill, meanwhile, born in 1868, had been a successful amateur footballer in the 1890s and played for Corinthians and England, though he retired from serious football in 1898. He also had a brief spell in the late 1880s, between the age of eighteen and twenty-two, playing first-class cricket as an amateur for Cambridge University and Sussex. He was a slow bowler but had indifferent results with both bat and ball, taking just three first-class wickets and averaging only ten with the bat. But Barrie must have felt that he could star for the Allahakbarries.

Horne's team batted first and Barrie had a good day throwing down his lobs to them, as he took four wickets with Shackleford

*The night before the match, an Allahakbarrie\* preparing a spot to suit his bowling*
*\*J. M. Barrie*

all out for seventy-three and only two batsmen making it into double figures. Not a grand total you might think, but the Allahakbarries could only make forty-six in reply, with Cotterill the only one to get into double figures, making up exactly half the team's score with twenty-three. In the second innings, with a lead of twenty-seven, Shackleford made a further sixty-six runs with Mason 'running through' the opposing side by taking six wickets.

The Allahakbarries might once have panicked when faced with a total of ninety-four to win, but they now made light work of accumulating the runs with all three of the new boys starring: Cotterill made twenty-three, Frith twenty-six and Tennyson was not out twenty-two. They only lost three wickets in their run chase with Ford and Seaman also contributing to the tally. It was another victorious game for the Allahakbarries, though the weekend's fun was far from being over. Back at Black Lake Cottage there were sports of an even lighter kind: golf-croquet, feasts and probably a further game of cricket with the men playing left-handed against the ladies.

The Llewelyn Davies family were not at the cottage this year, though ever since Barrie's first meeting with Sylvia Llewelyn Davies in 1897 they had formed an ever-growing part of Barrie's life. The oldest of the Llewelyn Davies boys, George, named after his grandfather, George du Maurier, was now seven, but the latest addition to the family had only just arrived: Michael had been born on 16 June that year, which was why the rest of the family could not be there. But the following summer was a different matter as the Llewelyn Davies boys found in the woods surrounding the cottage not just trees and pine cones, needles and roots, but Indians and pirates and adventures of the most thrilling kind; adventures that were mostly written, directed and even photographed by Barrie.

Mackail wrote that 'The host was forty now, but he didn't look it. His face, that is to say, had hollows and lines and shadows, and sometimes it seemed that centuries of experience had been etched into its strange modelling. Then he smiled, and it was a face that was neither young nor old. His hair was as thick and dark as ever; his figure was still slight.'

Barrie stayed on at the cottage during August 1900 but Conan Doyle was busy writing about what he had learnt on his visit to South Africa earlier that year (later published as *The Great Boer War*), preparing to stand as an MP in Edinburgh (he lost the election) and even found time to play his first-ever game of first-class cricket between 23 and 25 August. It was in this game, against London County at Crystal Palace, where Conan Doyle took his only first-class wicket playing for MCC, that of W. G. Grace. Conan Doyle later celebrated it in his poem, 'A Reminiscence of Cricket'.

> Once in my heyday of cricket,
> One day I shall ever recall!
> I captured that glorious wicket,
> The greatest, the grandest of all.
>
> Before me he stands like a vision,
> Bearded and burly and brown,
> A smile of good humoured derision
> As he waits for the first to come down.
>
> A statue from Thebes or from Knossos,
> A Hercules shrouded in white,
> Assyrian bull-like colossus,
> He stands in his might.

With the beard of a Goth or a Vandal,
His bat hanging ready and free,
His great hairy hands on the handle,
And his menacing eyes upon me.

Grace had admittedly already scored a century by the time
Conan Doyle claimed his wicket and he was not out to a great
ball either, but to a short-pitched 'gift', which Grace attempted
to hit out of the ground: 'His huge figure swooped as he hooked
it/His great body swung to the blow.' But he did not connect bat
and ball as he would have liked and the hit went soaring high
into the air, 'Up, up like a towering game bird/Up, up to a speck
in the blue,' before dropping safely into the wicket-keeper's
gloves: 'There was 'plunk' as the gloves shut upon it/And he
cuddled it up to his shirt.'

Conan Doyle did not use much of his own skill to record his
success, but there was no doubt of the result:

Out – beyond question or wrangle!
Homeward he lurched to his lunch!
His bat was tucked up at an angle,
His great shoulders curved to a hunch.

Walking he rumbled and grumbled,
Scolding himself and not me;
One glove was off, and he fumbled,
Twisting the other hand free.

Conan Doyle was one of five Allahakbarries, honorary or
otherwise, to have had strong playing links with Lord's cricket
ground: Pawling played three matches for Middlesex, who are
based at Lord's, and Prichard captained an MCC tour to
Philadelphia. The other two Allahakbarries that Barrie mentions
in the 1899 book he produced about cricket in 1899 are Gregor
MacGregor and A. E. Stoddart. They were team-mates at
Middlesex and also played for England together. They are also

the subject of a well-known portrait which now hangs in the long room in the pavilion at Lord's, with Stoddart preparing to face the bowling wearing an I Zingari cap, and MacGregor poised behind the wicket. MacGregor's first-class career lasted for almost twenty years, between 1888 and 1907, for Cambridge University and then Middlesex. He was another man with an Edinburgh connection, (he was born there) and he came to be regarded as one of the finest wicket-keepers of his generation, though he played his last of only eight test matches in 1893.

Conan Doyle had an unfortunate run-in with his brother-in-law, Willie Hornung, at Lord's in August 1900. Conan Doyle's wife, Louise, had been ill with tuberculosis since 1893 and Conan Doyle had been spending time with Jean Leckie, later his second wife. Hornung, who spent a lot of time at Lord's watching cricket, saw Conan Doyle with Leckie and the following day the two men argued when Hornung expressed his disapproval of what he suggested was inappropriate behaviour. 'Of course when I saw this carping tone I refused to speak further upon so sacred a matter', reported Conan Doyle to his mother, 'and I left the house not angrily but in a serious frame of mind which is more formidable.' This was just one among a number of occasions when relations between Conan Doyle and his sister's husband became strained and later that year Conan Doyle wrote to his mother to say that 'I don't feel better by contemplating the fact that William is half Mongol half Slav, or whatever the mixture is' – a reference to the fact that Hornung's father was Hungarian.

Barrie reveals that on the first trip to Broadway in 1897 S. S. Pawling and Conan Doyle shared a house together, but whereas much of Conan Doyle's life was well documented, very little of Pawling's seems to have been. He was born in Berkshire in 1862 and in 1893 became a partner of the publisher William Heinemann. He played three first-class games for Middlesex in 1894, against Kent, Sussex and Surrey, appearing alongside both Stoddart and

MacGregor in all of them. Although he failed with the bat he did take nine wickets in these three games, which suggests that he was a talented bowler. The author Albert Kinross, who played against him in Authors v. Publishers matches in the 1900s wrote that he was actually an 'uncommon bowler who could send down a fast in-swinger with an authentic fizz – a brute of a ball to start on and bad enough at any time. I speak with feeling, for it was one of these that laid me low.'

Pawling also regularly played club cricket for Hampstead for many years. As it is just up the road from Lord's, the Middlesex and Hampstead clubs had close connections with each other and Stoddart and MacGregor played for both sides, alongside other retired first-class players such as Australia's demon bowler Fred Spofforth.

Stoddart was an extremely athletic man and a fine cricketer who played sixteen tests and captained England, most notably in the 1894/5 tour of Australia when England won the series 3–2 and Stoddart averaged fifty-one. He was born in 1863 in County Durham and moved to Marylebone in London with his family when he was fourteen. His father was a wine dealer.

Stoddart made his debut for Middlesex in 1885, aged twenty-two, the same year that Barrie had arrived in London, and there's no doubt that Barrie saw him many times on his regular pilgrimages to Lord's. Stoddart often opened the batting, sometimes with MacGregor, and was a flamboyant, attacking batsman. He was well known for excelling on pitches that other batsmen found difficult to play on. And he was more than just a great cricketer too – he also played rugby for England ten times and helped to organise the very first British Lions rugby tour of Australia in 1888.

However, Stoddart's success in Australia in 1894/5 was not repeated in the 1897/8 tour. The Ashes were lost with Australia pummelling England 4–1. Stoddart's mother died just before the first test and he was too distraught to play in either of the first two matches. Ranjitsinhji, batting at number seven with a throat infection, scored 175 in the first Test and took England over 500 for the first time in a game. They won the first match of the tour by nine wickets but lost the next four heavily.

Stoddart's last full season for Middlesex was in 1898 and in 1899 he played just one game and in 1900, his final season, he played just two: what could have been a very muted conclusion to an outstanding career. But it was in his final game at Lord's, against Somerset in June, that Stoddart made his greatest ever first-class score of 221, bowing out in glory. It was recorded in his obituary in *Wisden* that he was 'A splendid batsman to watch . . . Mr Stoddart had all strokes at his command, but was especially strong in driving and hitting on the leg side. Again and again he proved his greatness by his ability to make runs under conditions which found other batsmen at fault, his play, both on fiery and on soft wickets, being quite exceptional.'

However, it was Ranjitsinhji who was the star of the English cricket season in 1900. He was at the very height of his powers and made over three thousand first-class runs in the season at an average of seventy-six – far ahead of any other batsman. But his efforts were not enough to help his county, Sussex, win the County Championship that year, which was instead won by Yorkshire, largely due to an impressive young professional bowler called Wilfred Rhodes.

Barrie's new play *The Wedding Guest* opened at the

*K. S. Ranjitsinhji*

Garrick in September 1900, near the end of the cricket season. Barrie wrote to Sylvia Llewelyn Davies that he expected 'the men of the world to stamp on the thing'. And he was right: the critics loathed it and Barrie retreated into his shell for a while, mourning what he told his old friend Gilmour was his 'bleeding and broken play'.

As a diversion from this criticism, Barrie indulged himself in the run up to Christmas by writing a pantomime for private performance. The previous year, Barrie had taken the two eldest Llewelyn Davies boys to see the pantomime *The Babes in the Wood* at the Coronet Theatre in Notting Hill. This year the pantomime was performed at Barrie's house at 133 Gloucester Road, mainly by members of his cricket team. Indeed, the programme that Barrie had so characteristically had printed for the occasion to give to the child spectators, revealed that:

> The Allahakbarrie Cricket Club has the honour to present for the first and only time on any stage an entirely amazing moral tale entitled *The Greedy Dwarf* by Peter Perkin.

This grand event took place on 7 January 1901 and starred Barrie himself as Cowardy Custard, A. E. W. Mason as Sleepy-head, Gerald du Maurier as Allahakbarrie, Addison Bright as Bruin, a Bear, and Will Meredith as a policeman. All these were Allahakbarries. Of those that weren't, Sylvia Llewelyn Davies played Prince Robin, Mary Barrie played the heroine and the Barries' dog Porthos played Chang, a dog. In her later book, *Dogs and Men*, Mary wrote that:

> I was the heroine, escorted every morning to her school in the woods by her big dog. The point here was, that he got a biscuit before leaving her, and when, as it happened on this occasion, he didn't get it, he refused to budge. He would neither shake hands nor go back home, until the mistake had been rectified. All this he did to the life, especially in the biscuit part of it.

In the second act he defended the hero from the devilry of the villain – his master.

This was done by holding him in the wings, until a given signal, when he was let loose. Then he rushed onto the stage, sprang upon the villain, and wrestled with him until he was overthrown. It was a consummate performance; and the curtain came down to thunderous applause. Again and again he was called before the curtain, and ended by walking across the footlights amongst the children, who then discovered that he was a real dog, and not a man, like the bear, made to resemble one.

It was a wonderful afternoon, only marred – and there is always something to mar all perfect things – by a child infecting all the rest with measles. Harrowing for their poor mammas, but I think the children thought it was worth it.

In the final act of the play Miss Mary Contrairy had the unenviable task of having to spell out 'Allahakbarrie' for the edification of the audience. Barrie's future biographer Denis Mackail, who was then aged nine, was among the audience of children watching the extravaganza:

> The children in front, only few of whom had ever seen a play before, would never forget that afternoon. None of them, perhaps, would remember the plot, simple as it was and almost implicit in the programme; but to see grown-up people dressed up, and fighting each other, or being brave, or romantic, or funny; to know at least some of their faces, and yet to find them transformed like this – here was richness, and amazement, and silent joy.

Queen Victoria died two weeks later and an era ended. The status of Britain as the world's wealthiest and most powerful nation, a status that Victoria had so readily epitomised, was becoming increasingly weak. But Britain's bullish belief in itself had not been obviously dented. The new monarch was rather different to Victoria. In March that year Conan Doyle sat next to him and later described Edward as 'an able, clearheaded, positive man, rather inclined to be noisy, very alert and energetic. He won't be a dummy king.' Whereas Victoria had been austere, Edward was jolly. The mourning queen gave way to the sporting prince. Patrick Morrah, in *The Golden Age of Cricket*, wrote that:

> Taking their cue from the flamboyant, pleasure-loving king, the leaders of British Society burst forth into a spectacular good living. They were individualists; where their fathers had tended to conform to type, working tenaciously to improve their fortunes and build a better world, the Edwardians went each his own way, conscious that they had inherited that world and that it was theirs to do what they liked with.

Morrah is not alone in exhibiting the common tendency to caricature the Edwardian years as full of long and sunny summer days, garden parties, champagne and good cricket: the kind of jolly whimsicality (a word, incidentally, which Barrie hated) that the Allahakbarries themselves seem to represent. But it was also a time when there was beginning to be increasing political dissent about the vast inequalities of wealth in British society. It was becoming clear to more and more people that the decadence of the upper classes could only be afforded because of the industry of the workers, something that Robert Tressell eloquently portrayed in his 1910 book *The Ragged Trousered Philanthropists*. The Labour Party was founded in 1900 and there was growing interest in socialism and universal suffrage. Home Rule of Ireland and free trade were contentious political topics. And despite the notable victory at Mafeking in 1900, Britain remained at war in South Africa. It was a controversial conflict and many spoke out against it, men such as David Lloyd George for instance. Nonetheless, rampant militarism was fast becoming a significant part of the Edwardian years and, while Barrie was entertaining children with his pantomime at the start of the year, Conan Doyle was beginning to teach local men how to shoot. He set up the Under-shaw Rifle Club which had three ranges of fifty, seventy-five and a hundred yards. Within a couple of years, he said, there would 'not be a carter, cabman, peasant or shop-boy in the place who will not be a marksman.'

# 6

## THE *PUNCH* XI

*The sun in the heavens was beaming;*
*The breeze bore an odour of hay,*
*My flannels were spotless and gleaming,*
*My heart was unclouded and gay;*
*The ladies, all gaily apparelled,*
*Sat round looking on at the match,*
*In the tree-tops the dicky-birds carolled,*
*All was peace till I bungled that catch.*

P. G. Wodehouse, 'Missed'

———

In June 1901 the Allahakbarries played the Punch Bowl Cricket Club at Frensham Pond, just a short distance from Barrie's holiday retreat in Surrey, Black Lake Cottage. There was a whole bathtub of alcoholic punch on the boundary edge and thirsty fielders were meant to help themselves to it. Many of them drank so much that it impaired their cricketing talents or at least exaggerated their lack of skill. That evening at dinner Barrie asked the assembled teams: 'Did you notice that when one member of the punchbowl team was hit on the shin, the whole team swelled?' Somewhat ironically, though, none of the Allahakbarries that day were associated with *Punch* magazine.

*Punch* men had formed the spine of the team for many years by the start of the 1901 cricket season. There had been the cartoonists Bernard Partridge, George Morrow and E. T. Reed, and the writer Owen Seaman, who had famously hit the winning runs against Broadway in 1898. In the 1900s a number of other satirists earned the distinction of both playing for Barrie's team and writing for *Punch*. They included Barrie's great new friend E. V. Lucas, a very young P. G. Wodehouse and A. A. Milne, who was crowned by Barrie as the 'last member' of the team in 1910. Charles Turley Smith, who first played for the Broadway side before switching to the opposition, was also a contributor to the magazine. More tangentially, Arthur Conan Doyle's uncle Dicky had been an illustrator for the journal. There was another significant connection with *Punch* as well. George du Maurier, who was the social cartoonist from 1864 until his death in 1896, was the father of both the actor Gerald du Maurier, who played once for the Allahakbarries and appeared in a number of Barrie's plays, and Sylvia Llewelyn Davies, whose children provided much of the inspiration for *Peter Pan*. Du Maurier had recommended Bernard Partridge to the then editor Francis Burnand when he joined the magazine as a cartoonist in 1891. And he was a novelist as well. His 1894 novel *Trilby* was an enormous best-seller and brought two new words into common usage in the English language: trilby (as in the hat) and svengali.

Partridge remembered that the members of the *Punch* Table

> dined on the corner of the old office at the corner of Fleet Street and Bouverie Street, meeting before dinner in the Editor's room above. The meal itself – five courses, with champagne – was a rollicking affair of high spirits, badinage and leg-pulling, but after coffee and liquers had been served and the toast of the 'new boy' proposed by Burnand and drunk, without speeches – we settled down to the business of thrashing out the two cartoons for the coming week.

The *Punch* Table was essentially a weekly editorial meeting of the senior contributors and to be invited on to the table was seen as a great honour. Seaman, du Maurier, Partridge, Lucas and Milne all

" We found Mr. Barrie by the Round Pond
in Kensington Gardens."

"Oh, I'm no good except as a change bowler.

" He briskly signalled to the nurses in charge
to propel us in the direction of the Bayswater
Road."

sat at it at one point or another, Wodehouse did not. *Punch* magazine celebrated its sixtieth birthday in 1901. In its early days it had combined satire with genuine radicalism but as the century progressed it had increasingly become part of the establishment press and extracts from it were regularly printed in *The Times*.

It was a busy start to 1901 for Barrie as he was working on three different major projects all at the same time. There were two plays – *Quality Street* and *The Admirable Crichton* – and his book *The Little White Bird*, which was not really a novel but could not be described as anything else either. It is a strange and sprawling story, narrated by a character called Captain W., and mainly set in Kensington Gardens. Barrie uses it to express his own feelings of wanting to be a father (the Barries had now had a childless marriage for seven years) and he also introduces the character of Peter Pan for the very first time. The chapters featuring Peter were later published separately as *Peter Pan in Kensington Gardens*.

The Gardens were also the setting for the first Allahakbarries game of the year. They were a wilder place then than they are now – livestock even grazed there – and for Barrie, who was fascinated by a retreat from modern civilisation and the idea of islands, the pull of a green oasis in the centre of London was strong. The place became an obsession to him: an island that could be reached without setting sail; a rural idyll that he could escape to without having to jump on a train to Broadway, Shere, Boxhill or Scotland. He took his large St Bernard dog, Porthos, for walks through the park, where he saw nurse maids pushing prams down the Broad Walk which runs from Bayswater Road to the north of the gardens to Kensington Road to the south, containing the children of the well-heeled families who lived nearby. 'All perambulators lead to Kensington Gardens', he wrote. And this is where the inspiration for the characters of the lost boys in *Peter Pan* came from: they were the children who had fallen out of their prams. The gardens combined in one place Barrie's preoccupations with fantasy, childhood and nature and so it seems obvious that he would also want to play something else which combined all these things: cricket.

On 20 May 1901, the fixture soon after Barrie's birthday on 9 May was played against a team of artists captained by the indefatigable American Abbey, just as in the previous two years. The previous two years it had taken place at Denmark Hill but this year it was in the more salubrious surroundings of west London, just to the south of the round pond. The Allahakbarries were fielding a strong side that included Conan Doyle and Snaith, and Barrie undoubtedly felt confident that his team would gain revenge for the previous year's loss. Among the others playing were some of the regulars including Hornung, Meredith and Mason as well as the *Daily Telegraph*'s cricket and rugby correspondent, who at that time was Captain Philip Trevor (later promoted to Major and then Colonel). He was educated at Marlborough and Sandhurst, and had served in the Burma Field Force and in the Boer War. He published a number of books about cricket including *The Lighter Side of Cricket* (1901) and *The Problems of Cricket* (1905) and was a good friend

*Allahakbarries examining the state of the wicket:*
*Barrie in straw hat with Bernard Partridge on his left.*
*Conan Doyle is in the centre*

of Conan Doyle's. Indeed, when Conan Doyle had thrown a fancy-dress party to celebrate moving into his new house at Hindhead in 1897, Philip had actually turned up disguised as his host. It was, without exaggeration, Conan Doyle's match. The Artists went in to bat first but were blown away by Conan Doyle's bowling as he took eight wickets and restricted the highest scoring artist to

*Bowlers at practice:*
*Barrie and Partridge*

twenty-seven runs. Then in reply he alone scored ninety-four runs, which included fourteen boundaries, and Snaith scored forty-seven for the Allahakbarries to win easily. Barrie also joined in the fun by scoring a boundary in his seven not out. There was even a snippet in the magazine *Cricket*, which stated that 'Dr. A. Conan Doyle's performance with bat and ball was remarkable.'

Five days later the press had got hold of the story that Conan Doyle was planning to resurrect Sherlock Holmes, as reported in *Tit-Bits* on 25 May. The original idea for *The Hound of the Baskervilles*, which came from Conan Doyle's friend, the journalist Bertram Fletcher Robinson who he had met on the voyage back from South Africa in 1900, was not originally meant to be a Sherlock Holmes story. But Conan Doyle and the editor of the *Strand Magazine*, Herbert Greenhough Smith, who was planning to serialise the novel, saw that there was considerable publicity value in bringing back the great detective. Conan Doyle was writing the story in May and at the start of June was at Princetown in Dartmoor, adding some local colour to the sketched-out plot. 'Holmes is at his very best, and it is a highly dramatic idea – which I owe to Robinson. We did 14 miles over the Moor today and we are now pleasantly weary. It is a great place, very sad and wild, dotted with the dwellings of prehistoric man, strange monoliths and huts and graves.'

Conan Doyle claimed in turn to have provided the inspiration for Barrie's play *The Admirable Crichton*, which Barrie was writing in the early part of 1901, when the two men had been on a walk. He suggested that an interesting story might be this: a man and his master are shipwrecked on a desert island; the man is much better adapted to survival in this environment and so becomes the master. Barrie does not appear to have acknowledged the debt, if it exists, but he also transformed this basic idea into a multi-layered political satire and social comedy.

Crichton is the butler to the aristocratic but socially liberal Loam family at Loam Hall. He is with the family and their friends when they all get shipwrecked on a tropical island and whereas they are all extremely impractical, Crichton is endowed with the necessary skills to survive and even flourish in this new environment. He reluctantly assumes the leadership of the group and is ultimately accepted as the leader by all the others. In the third act, two years have passed since they were stranded on the island

and Crichton has established agriculture and buildings. He begins
to take on the privileges of a monarch while Lord Loam provides
musical entertainment and does odd-jobs. The others call him
'Guv', one of the three daughters, Lady Mary Loam, falls in love
with him and they decide to get married. But just as the ceremony begins they see a ship on the horizon and Crichton decides
to send a signal. They are rescued and on their return to England
the previous social order resumes. No mention is made of Lady
Mary's engagement to Crichton who decides to resign in order
to spare everyone's embarrassment.

At the start of June 1901 the Barries bought their first
mechanically powered vehicle, though it did not run on an internal
combustion engine, but with the power of steam. It came with
a chauffeur too, named Alfred, but neither the steam-powered
car nor the chauffeur lasted long. They were soon replaced by
petrol cars and other chauffeurs with the expertise required to
drive them. Barrie liked the steam car, which he treated as an
amusing toy, but he always preferred to walk, or take a train or

a cab rather than drive in the petrol cars. He ultimately came to dislike all cars. According to Mackail 'It was they . . . that had changed and spoilt the world in which he had grown up, they slaughtered thousands, and they stood for all the rottenness and restlessness that he loathed.'

Barrie was out playing cricket again on 22 June though this time it was for the Authors against Esher, at Esher. The score is, however, recorded in the Allahakbarries scorebook and many of the regular Allahakbarries were playing in the game including Barrie's old friend Marriott-Watson, who was now living in Shere. There was also Conan Doyle, who had returned from researching *The Hound of the Baskervilles*, as well as Snaith, Ives, Mason and Hornung. Indeed, Albert Kinross remembered that it was Hornung who organised all the Authors games, though his brother-in-law, Conan Doyle, asserted his superiority as a cricketer and was the captain of the side.

> I had seen a paragraph in the paper saying Hornung was getting up a side of Authors to play against a side of Artists, so I wrote and asked whether he had room for me. I did not know him, but cricket is cricket. He replied at once in the most friendly spirit and I was able to get him down to Brondesbury for some net practice, which he needed. Like so many men who are hardly average players, he was an out-and-out enthusiast.

The authors who had not played for the Allahakbarries included Conan Doyle's friend Major Frederick Gordon Guggisberg and a vicar and missionary called Frederic Meyrick-Jones who had also played eighteen first-class games for Cambridge University and Kent between 1887 and 1896. Guggisberg was a Canadian-born author, though not a novelist, playwright or poet. He had served for the Royal Engineers and in 1903 published a book titled *Modern Warfare*. He wrote about a variety of military topics and later co-wrote with his actress wife Decima Moore an account of their life in the Gold Coast and Ghana called *We Two in West Africa*.

By strange coincidence, Moore had also appeared in the ill-fated comedy musical *Jane Annie* which Barrie and Conan Doyle had written together back in the early 1890s. The following year, in 1902, Guggisberg arranged a two-day match between the Royal Engineers and Allahakbarries which was one of the greatest mismatches in early twentieth-century cricket. He was a good cricketer and playing for MCC in 1901 (though not in first-class games) averaged more than fifty-eight. Conan Doyle, in the same year, could only manage an average of 21.84 for MCC.

Esher batted first and made seventy-one against the high-class bowling attack of Snaith and Conan Doyle who between them took all ten wickets: Snaith taking eight and Conan Doyle two. The last five wickets fell for just five runs with four batsmen on the Esher side all waddling back to the pavilion with ducks. The Authors put in Meyrick Jones and Guggisberg at the start of their reply and Meyrick Jones scored an astonishing 135 runs. Kinross wrote that 'the finest player I ever saw at Esher was a parson of the name of Meyrick-Jones. Like the great Studd, he had given to missionary work what might have gone into first-class cricket. He hadn't held a bat that season, yet he took a century with an ease and variety which weren't far short of genius.'

The rest of the team were not quite so successful: Conan Doyle got a rare duck, Snaith made seventeen, Hornung five, Barrie two and A. E. W. Mason was not out for three. They had made 230 runs in all. Sensing the need for a bit of batting practice, Esher went in again and declared on sixty for three after they had probably run out of time. But it did mean that Barrie was able to steal in and take a couple of wickets.

Five days later, on 27 June, with the cricket season now in full swing, the Allahakbarries went down to Black Lake Cottage where Barrie had been based for some weeks, finishing his play *Quality Street*. His team travelled the short distance from the cottage to Frensham Ponds to play their alcoholic game against the Punch Bowl Cricket Club. The club was almost certainly named after the Devil's Punchbowl, rather than a bowl for alcoholic cock-tails. The Punchbowl is a local landmark, a large, dramatically scooped and sandy valley, five miles south of Frensham and very close to where Conan Doyle lived. But the name provided them with a good excuse to enjoy a drink. Conan Doyle was not playing, probably because he was resting after having played for the Gentlemen of the MCC against the Navy the previous day. He scored thirty-one and bowled eight overs without taking a wicket as the Gentlemen won by 136 runs. He had just finished writing *The Hound of the Baskervilles* and managed to fit in plenty of cricket over the summer, including another confrontation with Grace. The old Allahakbarrie Jerome K. Jerome, whose writing and editing career had taken a downward turn since a high point in the early to mid-1890s, had continued the theme of dogs in Conan Doyle's life in 1901 by giving his friend not a spectral hound, 'its muzzle and hackles and dewlap . . . outlined in flickering flame', but a simple bulldog which Conan Doyle decided to call 'Derby the Devil'. A photo of the dog was Conan Doyle's Christmas card to friends that year.

Although Conan Doyle and Jerome were not there, many of the other familiar Allahakbarries and members of Barrie's inner circle were at Frensham to enjoy the punch and the cricket, including Mason, Maurice Hewlett, Ives, Will Meredith, Snaith and Charles Tennyson. It was also the first and probably the only outing for the team for the well-known classicist and friend of George Bernard Shaw, Gilbert Murray.

The Allahakbarries batted first and Ives made a stylish seventy-two. In total the Allahakbarries made 158. The *Punch* Bowl team, who had no doubt been indulging in the punch, were deceived by Barrie's slow bowling and Snaith's chinamen – a cricketing term for slow left handed balls which turn into a right-handed batsmen from the off-side. Barrie took a valiant five wickets and Snaith four. The Punch Bowl side declared on ninety for nine with the last batsman perhaps realising that he would struggle even to make it to the wicket in his pads, let alone hit a ball, due to his inebriated state. So he stayed where he was and no doubt drank some more punch. The Allahakbarries were victorious once more.

Pawling, meanwhile, who did not play in any of the Allahakbarries games in 1901, was having a successful time playing club cricket for Hampstead alongside A. E. Stoddart. On 26 June, against Guy's Hospital, Pawling took six wickets for six runs and Stoddart made fifty-six, and a few days later on 29 June, playing against Arkley the duo again scored a double success with Pawling taking four for nine and Stoddart making eighty-three. Pawling took a total of forty-eight wickets in the season for Hampstead and Stoddart topped the batting averages for the club that year with 50.9.

Just over a week after the Allahakbarries' boozy bucolic adventure, on 5 July, two of the original team, T. L. Gilmour and Augustine Birrell, joined the team for a reprise of the previous year's fixture against the Shackleford team captained by Edgar Horne. Owen Seaman also joined the team. Apart from these additions, and the loss of Gilbert, Ives and an unknown player, the Allahakbarries were otherwise identical to the team that had played at Frensham. It was the last Allahakbarries game of the season and as usual it formed part of more festivities at Black Lake Cottage, including the ubiquitous games of golf-croquet that Barrie loved so much. It was held on a Friday and for the rest of the weekend there were, for the second year running, feasts and more informal sports in the garden of the cottage.

Owen Seaman had not played for the Allahakbarries since the final and triumphant game against Broadway in 1899. He had been a contributor to *Punch* since 1894 and had been invited to join the famous table in 1897. He became the assistant editor in 1902 and then editor in 1906. One of the first things he did when he became editor was to appoint A. A. Milne as his assistant editor, despite the fact that the two men did not get along at all.

The situation was not helped by the fact that the two men's politics were at such odds with one another (Milne was an earnest liberal, Seaman a staunch conservative). But they also simply had very different personalities from one another too. Milne called him 'a strange, unlucky man. All the Good Fairies came to his christening, but the Uninvited Fairy had the last word, so that the talents found themselves in the wrong napkin and the virtues flourished where graces should have been. Humour was drowned in Scholarship, Tact went down before Truth, and the Fighting Qualities gave him not only the will to win but the determination to explain why he hadn't won.' Milne's portrait of Seaman as a rather oafish and miserable character, the general perception of him as a schoolmasterish and, over time, increasingly pompous and priggish editor, inspired the rumour that Seaman was in fact the inspiration for the gloomy character of Eeyore in Milne's Winnie-the-Pooh stories. But Milne's biographer Ann Thwaite, as well as others, have dismissed the notion, and it is true that Milne went on to write that Seaman 'had, truly, a heart of gold', though perhaps Eeyore did too.

Seaman was born in 1861 and was a successful student at both his school and at Cambridge. His father was a prosperous small businessman and shopkeeper, though R. G. G. Price in his *History of Punch*, writes that Seaman had a 'deep insecurity' about his family background. After university, in the 1880s, he taught at a school, and in the 1890s became a professor of literature. He also became a barrister, though never actually practised law, for by that time, in 1897, he had been invited onto the staff at *Punch*. His talent, at least in his earlier years with *Punch*, was for comic light verse, of the type with which he celebrated hitting the winning runs against Broadway in 1898. Barrie wrote that Seaman 'knew (or so he said) how to cut', but it is clear that Seaman was an Allahakbarrie of the original strain of that breed – a man who longed to be good at cricket but never truly would be. The reference to 'cutting' also seems to be a pun on the art of the satirist, in which case Barrie is possibly casting doubt on Seaman's abilities to 'cut' with both bat and pen.

The Allahakbarries batted first against Shackleford, and Snaith, Turley Smith and Walter Frith batting at three, four and five in the order all made good scores of forty, twenty and twenty-seven respectively. The other batsmen could only make thirteen between them, with Barrie scoring just two, giving them a total of 100, though it is strangely recorded in the scorebook as being just eighty-three. Either score would have been good enough to win the game, though, as the young Charles Tennyson took eight wickets and at sixty-eight for nine, with one batsman by the name of Curzon yet to go in, it seems that Horne admitted defeat and declared. It meant that Barrie had won every game he had played in during the 1901 season and his assertion that the Allahakbarries were 'invincible' was proving to be more and more accurate.

After the party had broken up at the start of July, Barrie sat quietly in his first-floor south-facing study, looking out on to the now empty lawn to the tall pine trees beyond, and finished his play *Quality Street*. By the end of the month he had posted the manuscript to Charles Frohman in New York and was looking forward to some more play. It arrived not in the form of cricket but with the Llewelyn Davies family, who had rented a cottage at nearby Tilford, which has one of the most famous and picturesque cricket pitches in England. The village green is cut into a generous triangle by three roads, which in 1901 were still sandy tracks. The River Wey passes the green on the eastern side and directly adjacent to it is the Barley Mow pub.

George, Jack and Peter took part in Barrie's elaborately choreographed games during August, which were largely based on one of Barrie's favourite books from his own childhood: *Coral Island* by R. M. Ballantyne. In Ballantyne's book three boys – Jack, Ralph and Peterkin – become ship-wrecked on an island in the South Seas and so Barrie set out to create a South Seas island, in their collective imaginations at least, in the thick woods and shallow sandy ponds which surrounded his home just outside Farnham. Barrie and his dog Porthos between them played a variety of roles in these games. Barrie was the pirate Captain Swarthy, who Andrew Birkin describes as 'a dark and sinister figure who displayed cowardice in the face of his young antagonists, frequently forcing the four-year-old Peter to walk the plank into the murky waters of Black Lake.' Porthos faithfully played the pirate's dog and, wearing a papier-mâché mask, a fierce tiger as well. Barrie not only played out these adventures with the boys but also recorded them by photographing them as they 'set out to be wrecked', strung up pirates and had 'a last pipe before turning in'. And of course he took notes all the while as well, for these games, and lines uttered by the boys during their play, found their way into *The Admirable Crichton*, *The Little White Bird* and *Peter Pan*.

But Barrie also bound the pictures he had taken with narrative captions into a book with a much smaller audience than any of these works, in a similar way to that which he had done with the cricket books. The book, which featured thirty-five photographs in all, was called *The Boy Castaways of Black Lake Island* and subtitled 'Being a record of the terrible adventures of the brothers Davies in the summer of 1901 faithfully set forth by Peter Llewelyn Davies'. In 1894 Barrie had written that 'the next best thing to being boys is to write about them', which suggests that he was himself not so much the boy who wouldn't grow up, but a man attempting to vicariously experience childhood through his writing and through other people: his fellow cricketers, children and actors. He used all of them to construct fantasies that tore him away, however temporarily, from the certain knowledge, that isolated island, of his own adulthood and mortality. As the cricket writer Derek Birley notes in *A Social History of English Cricket*: 'Cricket itself, at this and every other time, was an ideal dream world for those seeking escape from reality', though the same could be said of inventing fantasies, theatre, or playing with children just as readily. These were all islands that Barrie could inhabit away from the rules and deathly certainties of the real world. Two copies of the book were printed by Constable's: one which Barrie kept for himself and the other which he gave to the boys' father, Arthur, who very soon after lost his copy, or so he said, on a railway carriage.

The Barries remained at Black Lake Cottage for a few more weeks after the boys and their family had returned to London. *The Hound of the Baskervilles* had meanwhile begun to be serialised in the *Strand* magazine and on 9 September 1901 the stage version of Sherlock Holmes opened at the Lyceum Theatre in London. A month later, in October, Barrie was also able to enjoy a theatrical celebration when *Quality Street* had its first performance in America. The play, though rather slight in plot, was the first of a series of efforts from Barrie that established him among critics and contemporaries as a master of stagecraft and drama, as well as a unique artist. The murmurings that had previously plagued him – that he should stick to writing novels rather than plays – began to cease and he was increasingly seen primarily as a playwright rather than a novelist.

Barrie had come a long way since he arrived in London sixteen years previously. He was now rich, famous and admired. He had a beautiful wife, many friends and belonged to some of the most exclusive gentlemen's clubs in London. He had a country house and his own cricket team. But he had also not entirely conformed in order to achieve this success. He had played the role of the outsider and the underdog with aplomb and courage. He retained his quirkiness and it seemed almost that the quirkier he became the more popularity he achieved, the ultimate truth of which he discovered with the strange and fantastic *Peter Pan*. And at forty-one he was still brimming with ideas, energy and playfulness and that slightly bossy, egotistical and even chiding streak which he had used many years ago to persuade his friends to play cricket with him. But there were also bouts of depression, difficulties with his marriage, terrible, debilitating headaches and an ugly cough, which was not helped by his love of pipes and cigars: he was still always smoking.

He had not written a sequel to the pantomime that he had performed with members of the Allahakbarries during the festive season the previous year but he did take the Llewelyn Davies boys to see *Bluebell in Fairyland*, 'A Musical Dream Play', at the Vaudeville. Barrie afterwards became obsessed with it, acting out various parts of the play and making a number of notes for his own fairy play, such as this:

> *Fairy Play* What children like best is imitation of *real* boys and girls (not so much *comic* incidents).

In the spring of 1902 Barrie made a new friend who very soon was on the staff of *Punch* and playing for his cricket team too. His name was E. V. Lucas. Barrie wrote to Arthur Quiller-Couch in 1905 to say that 'E.V. Lucas is the only man I've met of late years that I specifically took to. You would like him.'

The Barries met Lucas and his wife Elizabeth at the Hewlett's house in Northwick Terrace, just a couple of mighty hits away from Lord's, for dinner one evening and became friends immediately. Lucas had a very different personal outlook to the literary personality that he expressed in the pages of *Punch*. His writing was friendly and light and according to his daughter Audrey, who later wrote a portrait of her father, he 'once described himself as a bedroom author, meaning by this, that any of his works might with safety be put by the bedside of a very young girl or a very old lady.' He no doubt said this with some disdain for 'in private he was a cynical clubman, liking to entertain peers to sumptuous meals with champagne and brandy, very bitter about men and politics and the decadence of modern art.' He was also rumoured to have an extensive library of pornography. But he loved cricket and had done all his life. Indeed, a collection of his essays called *Cricket All His Life* was collected and published after his death by Rupert Hart-Davis, which the famous cricket author and broadcaster John Arlott called 'the best written of all books on cricket'. As a cricketer himself, he was described as 'a pretty bat and a good field', while Barrie wrote in *The Greenwood Hat* that 'Lucas had (unfortunately) a style'.

Lucas was born in 1868 in Eltham in Kent but his family soon after moved to Brighton in Sussex and Lucas was devoted to Sussex County Cricket Club his whole life: a side which in Lucas's early twenties had contained two of the most exciting cricketers in England: C. B. Fry and K. S. Ranjitsinhji. In Audrey Lucas's book about her father, written in the 1930s, she writes that in his childhood 'the whole family, girls and boys, went to the Sussex County ground whenever they could and talked as eagerly of famous cricketers as children now talk of film stars.' He did not have a university education and his first job was working in a bookshop in Brighton before writing for a local newspaper in Sussex and then the London newspaper the *Globe*. It was only in 1904, at the age of thirty-six, that he was invited to join the *Punch* table. He became a prolific writer, not just for the magazine, but also as an essayist and author of many books with diverse subject matter including travel, cricket and art as well as editions of poetry and a number of biographies including that of the American artist and cricketer familiar to the Allahakbarries, Edwin Abbey.

However, for all his hard work, he never reached the same heights of artistic achievement and fame as Barrie and many of the other authors who he was not only friends with, but who looked up to him, and according to Mackail 'it was this knowledge and disappointment, perhaps, that ended by confusing and tangling his life.' His *métier* for *Punch* was not so much satire as light essays and sketches on a variety of subjects, though he was occasionally criticised for being overly sentimental, particularly when it came to his favourite breed of dogs: the small and long-haired Pekinese. Curiously enough he shared this love of the

Pekinese with fellow Allahakbarries P. G. Wodehouse, who had many of the dogs throughout his life, and Denis Mackail.

Barrie's dog Porthos, who had played such a major role in the games with the Llewelyn Davies boys the previous summer, had died in 1901. He had been with the Barries since soon after their marriage in 1894. 'Buried with him were seven years of my youth,' wrote Mary Barrie later. 'He had known the girl just started out on the great adventure, hands outstretched, demanding what life had to give her . . . He had all the first warmth of my love for dogs. And he had shared with me those first seven years of my married life. None of the others could take his place.'

The Barries moved in May 1902 from 133 Gloucester Road, which had been their London home since 1895, to the opposite side, the north, of Kensington Gardens. And later that year they bought a replacement for Porthos, another large dog, a Newfoundland this time, called Luath (named by Barrie after one of Robert Burns' favourite dogs who was immortalised in the poem 'The Twa Dogs'). Their new house, Leinster Corner, was now far closer to the Llewelyn Davies family and also to the cricket pitches in Kensington Gardens where the Allahakbarries played their by now traditional early summer fixture against the artists on 15 May.

They fielded a strong team, though it did not include Conan Doyle who was on holiday in Italy at the time. But Barrie was able to field four players with first-class experience in the form of Snaith, Prichard, Meyrick Jones and Cotterill, as well as George Ives, who had distinguished himself with a fine innings the previous summer and who this season played his one and only first-class game alongside Conan Doyle for MCC at Lord's. Barrie said that he never cared about winning, but he could easily have put out a side of really poor cricketers if he had so chosen. There were of course a few duffers among them still, including Barrie, Hornung, Lucas (playing in his first game), Frith and Will

Meredith, of whom Barrie wrote that he 'would have excelled in the long field but for his way of shouting "Boundary" when a fast ball approached him.'

It was the first-class cricketers who were dominant for the Allahakbarries in this game, though. The Artists batted first and were bowled out for ninety-six with Snaith taking four wickets and Prichard six. Prichard had not played much the previous summer, as he had been busy preparing the manuscript for his book about his travels to Patagonia, so he was using this game to brush off the winter rust. He had a remarkably successful season playing for Hampshire in 1902. He starred in all twelve county games and came second in the county bowling averages with thirty-eight wickets at an average of 20.78. Against Sussex he took six wickets for thirty-nine runs including that of C. B. Fry and against Derbyshire, on a batsman's wicket, he took seven for forty-seven.

The cricket writer Neville Cardus described Prichard's bowling style after the First World War:

> His action was not in the least a tearaway action; he seemed always to be bowling well within his strength, with his mind definitely directing every stage in his action. He was not a fast bowler that became a passenger on the advent of rain; he could adapt himself to a bowler's wicket, which he did by slackening pace and bringing into play a break-back spun from the fingers. As with most good fast bowlers, his pace came from a full rotary swing of the arm following a loose-limbed run to the wicket. There was little in his action of the abrupt energy at the hips and back which is the mark of the 'slinging' type of fast bowler.

So was it unfair to unleash a bowler of his quality on the Artists, who were in danger of replacing the Allahakbarries at being a colourful but inept cricketing side: a team 'who, presumably, were better painters than cricketers'? No one seems to have taken exception and Prichard remained a regular for the Allahakbarries as well as a number of other part-time amateur sides, just as many other first-class players also played club and country house cricket at the same time as playing for their counties.

The Allahakbarries unleashed their new ace batsman, the missionary Reverend Meyrick Jones, against the Artists' bowling attack and he hit 118 not out in a total of 220 for four. It was a comprehensive victory, though one that the captain had barely participated in having not batted at all, and not taken a wicket either.

Barrie could have done with a few more of his adept players a few weeks later as the Allahakbarries played Guggisberg's Royal Engineers in what was scrawled in the scorebook as being a 'Grand Two Days Match' at the Royal Engineers Ground in Chatham, Kent on 6–7 June. Prichard and Ives were both missing and Conan Doyle could not play. Barrie had appealed to Conan Doyle to play in the game in a letter he wrote to him on 28 May but Conan Doyle had only arrived back in the country from his holiday in Italy on 31 May and it seems that he could not make it. Perhaps their recent spate of victories had made them over-confident and they almost succumbed to an innings defeat, though they did not do too badly in their first innings, making 146. But then the Royal Engineers came in to bat and an impressive first wicket stand, which Guggisberg contributed to with a half-century, blazed a trail for a large innings of 200. Snaith managed to take a respectable six wickets to keep the score down to one which his side might reasonably have been expected to challenge. After the Allahakbarries were then bowled out for sixty-one in their second innings, though, the Royal Engineers knocked off the winning runs without losing any wickets and won the game by ten wickets. The second day must have ended extremely early. In two innings the Allahakbarries had recorded seven ducks and Barrie had been not out for nought in both.

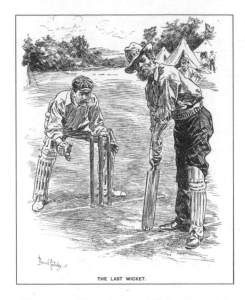

THE LAST WICKET.

Kitchener (Captain and Wicket-keeper).
*"He has kept us in the field a deuce of a time; but
we'll get him now we've closed in for catches!"*

The date of Conan Doyle's arrival back home was the same
day that the peace treaty was signed which formally brought the
Second Boer War to an end. Although the war was over, there
were more signs this year that Britain was increasingly preoccupied by the possibility of future conflicts. The National
Service League was founded this year, for example. Conan Doyle,
who had strong opinions about the country's readiness for battle,
which he had expressed in his book *The Great Boer War*, accepted
a knighthood from the new king in June and on 26 June Barrie
wrote to him to congratulate him: he was the first of a number
of Allahakbarries to receive such an honour.

> *'Dear Sir Arthur and still dearer Lady Doyle,*
> *My very hearty congratulations to you on this honour and may*
> *you both have many happy years to enjoy it. We toast you*
> *tonight in a bumper.'*

But they did not get round to making the toast as later that same day Barrie received the news that his father had died and he and Mary set off to Scotland for the funeral. There was no more cricket for Barrie or his team in 1902 and instead of his cricketing week at Black Lake Cottage this year, he had Scottish relatives to stay with him near Farnham, who brought with them an atmosphere of dour, lingering melancholy. Barrie himself was philosophical about his father's death and it is clear that it did not have the same impact on him as the death of his mother.

Barrie's cricket season may have been over but Conan Doyle's was near the beginning. He played a number of games this year and the highlight was a three-day match at Lord's between 14 and 16 July that he played in for MCC against Grace's London County. This was fellow Allahakbarrie George Ives' one and only first-class match, and he failed to make an impression with scores of seven in the first innings and two in the second. Conan Doyle, though, compiled his highest ever first-class score of forty-three, though he was out, stumped, to the man whose wicket he had so famously taken in the same fixture two years' previously: Grace had taken his revenge. Conan Doyle wrote that 'There was nothing more childlike and bland than that slow, tossed-up bowling of Doctor Grace, and nothing more subtle and dangerous. He was always on the wicket or about it, never sent down a really loose ball, worked continuously a few inches from the leg, and had a perfect command of length.' Nonetheless Conan Doyle struck him for two successive fours, and the wily Grace then held the next delivery back a little, 'which gave the delusion that it was coming right up to the bat, but as a matter of fact it pitched well short of my reach, broke sharply across and Lilley, the wicket-keeper, had my bails off in a twinkling. One feels rather cheap when one walks from the middle of the pitch to the pavilion, longing to kick oneself for one's own foolishness all the way.' Conan Doyle should not have been too upset: Grace did take thirteen wickets in the match.

The legendary professional all-rounder A. E. Trott was also playing for MCC in the same match. In 1899 he had hit a ball clean over the pavilion at Lord's; something which only he has ever achieved. His two greatest years were 1899 and 1900: he scored more than 1000 runs and took more than 200 wickets in both.

Conan Doyle also wrote a humorous cricketing piece for *Punch* this year, called the 'Anglo-American "Willow-and-Leather" Syndicate', which betrays anxiety about Britain's diminishing, and America's growing, influence in the world.

The Anglo-American 'Willow-and-Leather' Syndicate (President: Mr Pierpont Morgan; capital, ten million dollars) beg to intimate that their season will open at Lord's on the first of April. They have obtained an exclusive lease of this well-known ground, and their list of star artists fairly licks creation.

[. . .] At 3 precisely – Dr W. G. Grace will lead the way into the field, and will give his world-renowned performance, including the Deep-Square-Leg Trick, the Scratching-the-Ground-with-a-Bail Trick, etc, etc. At the conclusion of his turn he will be umpired out 'lbw' to a leg-break, and will then speak a stirring monologue. (Copyright strictly reserved).

4 – 5 – The Oxford and Cambridge elevens will play tip-and-run. The scene of the ground will be a careful reproduction of the famous 'Varsity match. Beauty and brightness will be seated on real drags; peers (warranted hall-marked), Cabinet Ministers and Judges will watch the proceedings from the pavilion. Real triple-distilled essence of British Aristocracy will pervade this turn. Huge attraction for visitors from the States.

In the real world of cricket, 1902 was one of the most exciting seasons of Ashes cricket of all time. It had not been an auspicious start to the series as this was a damper-than-average summer with the first two tests of the five test series being rain-affected draws. Australia won the third test at Bramall Lane in Sheffield and with two games to play the dramatic fourth test took place at Old Trafford. England batted second and in their final innings they required just 124 to win. It looked like they were going to make it with the fourth wicket falling for ninety-two runs: just thirty-two more required to win. But then there was a collapse and England crumpled to 116 for nine: eight runs required and one wicket left. Fred Tate, the last batsmen in, and playing in his first test, had already dropped a crucial catch in Australia's second innings. But before he could face a ball the rain came down and he had to wait in the pavilion for three quarters of an hour. He then managed to hit a four and with a further four runs left to win the game for England he was bowled two balls later. When Barrie later wrote in *The Greenwood Hat* that 'Henry Ford was, even more than Tate, an unlucky bowler', this is the incident he was referring to. Tate never played in another test match.

The final test at the Oval on 11–13 August was a dead rubber, with Australia already 2–0 up in the series, but it turned out to be a similarly thrilling game nonetheless. This time, England faced a final innings target of 263, though at forty-eight for five it seemed unlikely that they would get the runs. But Jessop, one of the great batting heroes of the 1900s, scored a fast and thrilling hundred (it took him just seventy-five minutes to reach three figures) which meant that the last pair of Rhodes (again) and George Hirst had to score fifteeen to win the game. This time they did win it by the single wicket, and although England had lost the series they had certainly gained the respect of the opposition.

A young P. G. Wodehouse, aged twenty-one, was watching at least some of the final day's play of this game from the Oval stands, though he was obliged to be back at his office before long at the Hongkong and Shanghai Bank on Lombard Street, where he was at that time still a clerk. It meant that he missed Jessop's barnstorming innings in the afternoon but a month later he walked out of the bank for the last time to become a writer. His cricketing exploits are a reasonable indication of how quickly he gained a reputation for his writing: the following year he was already playing for an Authors' XI and two years later he was well known enough to be invited to Black Lake Cottage to play for the Allahakbarries.

In the autumn of 1902 Barrie was having a busy and successful few months. In September *Quality Street* opened at the Vaudeville in London after its success in New York; in November *The Admirable Crichton* opened at the Duke of York's Theatre (with Gerald du Maurier among the cast) and Henry Irving playing Crichton, and very soon after *The Little White Bird* was published by Hodder and Stoughton to general critical acclaim. *The Admirable Crichton* and *The Little White Bird* are two extremely different works – one a comedic social satire, the other a strange, jumbled and sentimental story full of fairies and children. The critic A. B. Walkley wrote in his review of *The Admirable Crichton* in *The Times* that

> It deals with Rousseau's perpetual subject, 'the return to nature'. But it deals with that subject in a whimsical, pathetic, ironic, serious way which would have driven Rousseau crazy. Nevertheless it is as delightful a play as the English stage has produced in our generation.

*The Times* review of *The Little White Bird*, meanwhile, called it 'one of the most charming books ever written' and, 'in sober earnest . . . one of the best things that Mr Barrie has written.' The book is dominated by the character of David, who is the outlet for the frustrated paternalism of the narrator, Captain W. It is clear that David is based on George Llewelyn Davies and Captain W is a barely concealed Barrie. In this extract from the book, they play cricket together in Kensington Gardens:

> David wanted to play on a pitch near the Round Pond with which he is familiar, but this would have placed me at a disadvantage, so I insisted on unaccustomed ground, and we finally

pitched stumps in the Figs. We could not exactly pitch stumps, for they are forbidden in the Gardens, but there are trees here and there which have chalk-marks on them throughout the summer, and when you take up your position with a bat near one of these you have really pitched stumps. The tree we selected is a ragged yew which consists of a broken trunk and one branch, and I viewed the ground with secret satisfaction, for it falls slightly at about four yards' distance from the tree, and this exactly suits my style of bowling.

I won the toss and after examining the wicket decided to take first knock. As a rule when we play the wit at first flows free, but on this occasion I strode to the crease in an almost eerie silence. David had taken off his blouse and rolled up his shirt-sleeves, and his teeth were set, so I knew he would begin by sending me down some fast ones.

His delivery is undcrarm and not inelegant, but he sometimes tries a round-arm ball, which I have seen double up the fielder at square leg. He has not a good length, but he varies his action bewilderingly, and has one especially teasing ball which falls from the branches just as you have stepped out of your ground to look for it. It was not, however, with his teaser that he bowled me that day. I had notched a three and two singles, when he sent me down a medium to fast which got me in two minds and I played back to it too late. Now, I am seldom out on a really grassy wicket for such a meagre score, and as David and I changed places without a word, there was a cheery look on his face that I found very galling. He ran in to my second ball and cut it neatly to the on for a single, and off my fifth and sixth he had two pretty drives for three, both behind the wicket. This, however, as I hoped, proved the undoing of him, for he now hit out confidently at everything, and with his score at nine I beat him with my shooter.

In November, Barrie received an appreciative letter from Birrell, who had recently had an accident. 'In Common with the Whole Civilised World,' he wrote, 'you have doubtless shuddered at the spraining of my knee (don't pretend you haven't heard of it, it has been in all the papers: halfpenny, penny and threepenny, morning, afternoon and evening), but while the whole world shuddered, I lay chuckling & simmering in sweet content over your little white bird.'

———————

The first few months of 1903 had been, according to the *Daily Express*, 'one of the most miserable springs on record', but by 22 May a heatwave had set in, with the thermometers in London reaching almost eighty degrees Fahrenheit. It augured well for the start of Barrie's cricket season that day in Esher when the Authors, but not the Allahakbarries, played the Artists. The *Daily Chronicle* reported that 'the welcome change in the weather enables cricketers to enter into the spirit of the game with a whole-hearted enthusiasm which is difficult to arouse when the skies are dismal and the air cold and damp.'

The game is not recorded in the Allahakbarries scorebook but Mackail mentions that 'the press tracked them down' which Barrie for once forgave 'when they credited him with a "brisk 10."' It was probably the first time that Barrie had met P. G. Wodehouse, who was just twenty-one years old at the time. The *Daily Chronicle* provided an account which mentioned Wodehouse, who played well, but entirely omitted any mention of the little Scot:

On Saturday a team of authors captained by Sir A. Conan Doyle, visited Esher, and played the Esher C. C. whose side included S. A. P. Kitcat, the Gloucestershire amateur. The result of the match was a win for the Esher Club, whose innings total produced 158 against 132 of the writers. T. Westray, the well-known hockey player, with 39, was the chief scorer for the winners, other contributions including 34 by R. Howell and 27 by J. A. Peachey, Kitcat being not out with 9. P. G. Wodehouse was the principal contributor for the Authors, making 41 runs out of a total of 132, Sir A. Conan Doyle being next on the list with 29 to his credit. In the bowling department H. Prichard did best for the scribes, taking half of the wickets, while T. C. Snaith captured 4 and G. H. Swinstead one. On the Esher side, Kitcat and C. B. Peachey divided the honours.

There is a photograph which has survived of both teams with the players wearing ankle-high cricket boots and a selection of striped blazers and caps. There are also some fine moustaches on display. Hornung, on the back row, is smoking a cigarette and Wodehouse, in his first such game, a pipe, with E. V. Lucas standing between the two of them. Ives and Barrie, sat next to one another at the front, are both wearing their pads. Doyle stands in a commanding pose befitting that of a knight of the realm at the centre of the back row, but even he is dwarfed by Hesketh Prichard standing next to him and wearing a white sun hat. The American captain of the Artists, Edwin Abbey, is sat on the front row clutching a bat with A. E. W. Mason sat cross-legged on the floor by his feet.

Just a few days after the match, on 27 May, P. G. Wodehouse, who evidently had insider information, had a lyric published in *Punch* about the resurrection of Sherlock Holmes. Conan Doyle had been writing the first few stories in spring 1903 of what in 1905 was published as *The Return of Sherlock Holmes*. As ever, they had their first appearance in the *Strand* magazine, starting in the autumn of that year, which explains the title of Wodehouse's skit: 'Back to His Native Strand'. The first verse runs:

Oh, Sherlock Holmes lay hidden more than half a dozen years.
He left his loving London in a whirl of doubts and fears.
For we thought a wicked party
Of the name of Moriarty
Had dispatched him (in a manner fit to freeze one).
They grappled on a cliff-top, on a ledge six inches wide:
We deemed his chances flimsy when he vanished o'er the side.
But the very latest news is
That he merely got some bruises.
If there is a man who's hard to kill, why he's one.
Oh Sherlock, Sherlock, he's in town again,
That prince of perspicacity, that monument of brain
It seems he wasn't hurt at all
By tumbling down the waterfall.
That sort of thing is *fun* to Sherlock.

This light poem already has the distinctive mark of Wodehouse's particular brand of humour, though it is the second verse that demonstrates that he was a cut above many of the other comedy writers at the time. In it he targets the rather implausible manner in which the detective will be brought back to life, and perhaps hints at some of the other discrepancies in detail and plot which characterise some of the Sherlock Holmes stories:

> Sir Conan has discovered him, and offers to explain.
> The explanation may be thin,
> But bless you! We don't care a pin,
> If he'll but give us back our Sherlock.

According to Conan Doyle's biographer Andrew Lycett, Wodehouse was 'a devoted fan of all Arthur's work'. Later in life he professed that 'Conan Doyle was my hero. Others might revere Hardy and Meredith. I was a Doyle man, and I still am.' Sherlock Holmes was also a key point of reference for him as he is said to have mentioned his name more than five hundred times in his stories.

Pelham Grenville Wodehouse, known simply as Plum to his family and friends, was born in Guildford in 1881. He had been a cricketer at his school, Dulwich College in south London. He was tall, but not a beanpole, weighing in at more than twelve stone in his later schooldays. He sometimes opened the bowling for Dulwich with N. A. Knox — who later played twice for England — and, on one famous occasion, against Tonbridge, bagging seven wickets, including that of K. L. Hutchings, who later played more than 200 times for Kent before the war, to Knox's one. The school magazine, *The Alleynian*, might have been expected to be impressed, but its standards were evidently high:

> Wodehouse bowled well against Tonbridge but did nothing else. Does not use his head at all. A poor bat and very slack field.

Murray Hedgecock, the editor of an anthology of Wodehouse's cricket writings called *Wodehouse at the Wicket*, suggests that Wodehouse may even have written this rather stern report himself. He continued to write cricket reports for *The Alleynian* for much of his life, writing his last in 1939, long after he had become a rich, famous and prolific author who spent most of his time either in Hollywood or France.

In his final year at school, in 1900, Wodehouse took nine wickets for fourteen in one innings and in the match as a whole a remarkable fifteen wickets. *The Alleynian* summed up his cricketing career with the school that year: 'A fast righthand bowler with a good swing, although he does not use his head enough. As a bat, he has very much improved, and he gets extraordinarily well to the pitch of the ball. Has wonderfully improved in the field, though rather hampered by his eyesight.'

It was better than his general school report, which noted that 'He has the most distorted ideas about wit and humour; he draws over his books and examination papers in the most distressing way and writes foolish rhymes in other people's books.'

Wodehouse went straight to work for the bank after finishing school in September 1900, under pressure from his parents, though he did not enjoy the experience and within two years he had left. He started his journalistic career by writing for the *Globe* and was published by *Punch* and other publications including the *Daily Express* as well. One of his first pieces for *Punch* was called 'Under M. V. C. Rules' and it was about a new (and imaginary) game called vigoro, said to have characteristics of both tennis and cricket, to be played with a soft rubber ball, and playable all year round by both sexes. MVC stands for Marylebone Vigoro Club. R. G. G. Price, in his *History of Punch* wrote that 'P. G. Wodehouse wrote for a comparatively short time in the early years of the century; his comic exuberance burst out all over the place. He did not invent new kinds of article, but wrenched accepted forms to his purpose. The strong individuality, the fertility of comic detail and the life in his articles made them different from other people's.'

Wodehouse probably met Conan Doyle for the first time at Chatham in 1902 as he watched the older man take five for forty-five for an Authors side against the Royal Engineers. When Wodehouse later played for the Authors one of his team-mates, Albert Kinross, noted that he was 'still rather the schoolboy'. In fact, Wodehouse was beginning in 1902 and 1903 to make a good living from being 'rather the schoolboy' as he had begun to write a number of stories in the popular genre of boys' adventure stories, particularly those involving sport. He had these types of stories published in *Sandow's Magazine* (which was run by an ex-strongman), *Captain* and C. B. Fry's *Magazine of Sports and Out of Door Life* – all aimed at sporty boys with a taste for adventure. The most famous of Wodehouse's characters from this genre of writing was Mike Jackson, a star batsman for his school. Two stories – 'Mike and Psmith' and 'Mike at Wrykyn' – were published in one volume called *Mike* in 1909. And George Orwell later said that '*Mike* is certainly his very best book.'

Wodehouse became such a prolific writer and author (he wrote ninety-six books in all during his lifetime) that he very soon had little time for much else, including cricket. But in 1903 he was persuaded by Owen Seaman to turn out for a *Punch* XI as well as playing for Authors teams at Esher and Lord's for a number of years during the 1900s.

He was not yet well known enough, at least by Barrie, to be invited to the Allahakbarries games that summer. The next game took place on 1 June against Pasture Wood near Dorking in Surrey, not far from where George Meredith lived at Box Hill. It was a two innings game and the Allahakbarries fielded thirteen players for it. It proved to be an unlucky number when, batting first, five of their number – Birrell, Seaman, Barrie, Mason and Meredith – were all out for ducks and they scored just forty-seven in total. Pasture Wood, at perhaps a slight disadvantage with just twelve batsmen, made seventy-four in reply with Cotterill taking six for thirty-two. Pawling was playing for the opposition in this game, and he scored seven, batting at number four. In the second innings five members of the Allahakbarries were again out for ducks, though Barrie managed to score five. The treacherous Pawling took six Allahakbarries wickets and Pasture Wood rattled off the forty-seven runs required for the loss of just three men.

Exactly a month later the team assembled once more at Black Lake Cottage, though this time the event was extended from a weekend to a week, perhaps to make up for the fact that the previous year it had not taken place at all. Many of the regular characters were there including Mason, Gilmour, Henry Ford, Charles Turley Smith, Owen Seaman and E. V. Lucas. In amongst the usual obsessive bouts of golf-croquet on the lawn, the team played two games of cricket against familiar opponents: the first against Shackleford and the second against a team of artists which was played at Frensham.

The game against Shackleford on 4 July 1903 is the last game that the Allahakbarries played where there can be any great degree of precision about what actually happened, as it falls on the last pages of the Allahakbarries' only known scorebook. Lucas showed that he was more than just an avid spectator of cricket by making sixty-seven runs and the Allahakbarries were comfortable winners. According to Mackail they were not so fortunate against the Artists a few days later, but apart from the fact that they lost, there is nothing else known about this game. But there were speeches back at Black Lake Cottage and Barrie told for the first time a joke that he repeated many more times about the player who scored a single in his first innings, 'but in the second innings was not so successful.' And another joke, though like the first it certainly had a basis in truth, that the Allahakbarries' opponents had once made fourteen, 'but we nearly won'.

The Llewelyn Davies family arrived later in the month to stay in Tilford as they did the previous summer and on 24 September Barrie's latest play, *Little Mary*, was performed for the first time at Wyndham's Theatre. The play contained within it a line that Barrie had copied from the eight-year-old Jack Llewelyn Davies who, when his mother had warned him 'You'll be sick tomorrow' after he had been stuffing himself with cake, merrily replied, 'I'll be sick tonight' and carried on eating. Barrie drew up a comic mock-formal contract with Jack whereby he would get a half-penny ever time the play was performed: in all, Jack made more than eight shillings from the arrangement. It meant that the other Llewelyn Davies boys were keener than ever to watch all of Barrie's future plays in case they might be able to profit from them.

The play that Barrie later admitted to the boys was most 'streaky' with them, though, was yet to be written. But on 23 November 1903 Barrie sat down and wrote on a piece of paper 'Anon: A Play'. Over the next few months he transformed it into his most popular and enduring piece of work: *Peter Pan*.

❧ III ❧

TAIL-ENDERS

# 7

## THE REAL-LIFE PETER PANS

All children, except one, grow up.

J. M. Barrie, *Peter Pan*

———

It was the double-edged curse of a number of members of the Allahakbarries to be remembered principally for just one of their works or characters. Double-edged in the sense that they set out to achieve success and found it, yet their most celebrated creations also came to overshadow all their other work. For Conan Doyle it was Sherlock Holmes, for Jerome it was *Three Men in a Boat*, for Milne, Winnie-the-Pooh, for Barrie, *Peter Pan* and for Hornung, Raffles.

In the 1920s Conan Doyle said that he often wished he had never invented Sherlock Holmes at all. Jerome felt similarly burdened by the success of *Three Men in a Boat* and Milne came to vehemently resent Pooh. But Barrie did not have the same attitude towards *Peter Pan*, the work through which his name has remained well known more than a hundred years after the play was first performed in December 1904. All the other plays and novels of Barrie have faded into relative obscurity, yet *Peter Pan* quickly became a popular myth which has endured throughout the twentieth century and beyond. One of the reasons that Barrie could not despise his creation was that it was so closely based on his personal experiences, especially those with the Davies boys, such as those in the summer of 1901 at Black Lake Cottage. And according to Andrew Birkin in *J. M. Barrie and the Lost Boys*, 'it is Barrie himself who pervades every character and situation to a degree unparalleled in all his other plays.'

At the start of 1904 Barrie was busy writing the play at the same time as Conan Doyle was completing the final four Sherlock Holmes stories of the series of twelve that had been commissioned to mark the return of the amateur detective. Barrie had finished his first full draft of *Peter Pan* at the beginning of March, though he continued to revise it for many years after. At this stage he still hadn't decided what to call it, though for the time being it was referred to as 'Peter and Wendy' in his note-books.

Towards the end of the month, at the traditional time of year for thinking about the cricket matches to come that summer, he wrote to his friend H. B. Marriott-Watson in Shere to try and arrange a game against the old enemy.

> Let us say June 18, as that is the date they prefer and I shall try and get an XI for that day. The main fun of the thing, not to speak of the sentiment, would lie in their being the old team as much as possible, and the same with ours. I count upon yourself and will try to get Gilmour, Reid and Partridge – a really weak team.

Soon after, at the start of April, Barrie showed his new play to the London actor-manager Herbert Beerbohm Tree. Tree had a reputation for putting on extravagant productions and there was no doubt that *Peter Pan* fell into this category with a large cast of over fifty, including pirates and redskins as well as animals such as a dog, a crocodile, an eagle and a jaguar. Some of the cast were also required to fly. It is likely that Barrie had taken the play to Tree because he thought that he might take it if Frohman rejected it. If that was the case, his plan back-fired spectacularly as Tree not only didn't like the play himself but also wrote to Frohman to warn him about it.

*Barrie has gone out of his mind . . . . I am sorry to say it, but you ought to know it. He's just read me a play. He is going to read it to you, so I am warning you. I know I have not gone woozy in my mind, because I have tested myself since hearing the play; but Barrie must be mad.*

It was an extremely unconventional piece of theatre for the time with its animals, a fairy and an eternal boy who lived in a fantastical place called Neverland. Yet there were also parts of the play that did not fit in with the most obviously suggested genre of a children's pantomime or fantasy: the dialogue was quite adult and the mood was a strange mix of adventure story, whimsical comedy, sentimentality, farce and melodrama. '*Peter Pan* has never, in any easy way, been a book for children at all', according to the critic Jacqueline Rose, who asks whether it is actually: 'a spectacle of childhood for us, or [a] play for children?' George Bernard Shaw certainly believed that it was a play 'foisted on children by the grown-ups' and it is an interesting point to determine how far the play is merely Barrie's own exploration of a fantasised notion of childhood. In the play a little boy, Peter, accompanied by the fairy Tinker Bell, breaks into the nursery of the Darling family and takes the children, including Wendy, away to an island called Neverland, which contains redskins, pirates and a wild menagerie of exotic and anthropomorphic animals. There they indulge in the kind of adventures which the Darling children would only have read about in books, like learning to fly and fighting pirates, before safely returning home at the end. It combines the adventure story of which Barrie had always been so fond, with the fairy tale that he had more recently become obsessed by.

Barrie met Frohman at the Garrick Club after having arrived in London from New York at the end of April, and the story of their famous meeting has been retold many times. Barrie was evidently cautious, as he took two plays with him: the second, *Alice Sit-by-the-Fire*, was meant to compensate Frohman for any loss that he might make on 'Peter and Wendy', which Barrie had now renamed 'The Great White Father'. But Frohman immediately loved the play and gave directions for a performance of it to be given that Christmas. The only change he suggested was that the name be changed to *Peter Pan*. Frohman was a successful businessman but he was also an adventurous spirit: George Bernard Shaw described him as 'the most wildly romantic and adventurous man of my acquaintance.' He is said to have acted out scenes from *Peter Pan* to friends in the street soon after reading it for the first time, such was his enthusiasm for the play, which, whether he realised it then or not, would ultimately make both he and Barrie an enormous amount of money.

That spring the Llewelyn Davies family had left their home in Kensington to live in a larger house in Berkhamsted. Sylvia and Arthur now had five children: George, Jack, Peter, Michael and Nicholas, and Barrie had by this time forged friendships with all but the youngest of them, Nicholas, who came to be known as Nico. The friendship was reciprocated by the boys: in a letter in 1903, for example, Jack, then eight, wrote to Barrie that 'I've put Black Lake Cottage in capital letters because wherever you are must be a very celebrated place.' Barrie had played with George, Jack and Peter in the woods around Black Lake Cottage and created the book about their exploits *The Boy Castaways of Black Lake Island*. And George had also been fictionalised as David in *The Little White Bird* but *Peter Pan* seemed to celebrate Barrie's relationship with all of them. In 1928 Barrie wrote a dedication to the Davies boys, which offers an explanation of how *Peter Pan* came to be written.

What a game we had of Peter before we clipped him small to make him fit the boards. He was the longest story on earth, and some of you were not born when that story began and yet were hefty figures before we all saw that the game was up. [...] Do you remember Marooners' Hut in the haunted groves of Black Lake, and the St Bernard dog in a tiger's mask who so frequently attacked you, and the literary record of that summer, The Boy Castaways, which is so much the best and rarest of this author's works? What was it that eventually made us give to the public in the thin form of a play that which had been woven for ourselves alone? Alas, I know what it was, I was losing my grip. One by one as you swung monkey-wise from branch to branch in the wood of make-believe you reached the tree of knowledge. [...] That was quarter of a century ago, and I clutch my brows in vain to remember whether it was a last desperate throw to retain the five of you for a little longer, or merely a cold decision to turn you into bread and butter.

Barrie played games with the boys wherever he could: on holidays by the sea at Rustington in Sussex, in Kensington Gardens and at Black Lake. As well as playing at adventures about shipwrecks and pirates, they played sports too, which included improvised games of cricket. The boys were too young, for now, to play in the Allahakbarries games, but Michael was photographed with the team in 1905 as its mascot and by 1913 George, who by then had proved himself an exceptional cricketer at Eton, was actually playing for them. Barrie's marriage, which was now ten years old, was childless and increasingly unhappy. Was his friendship with the boys an opportunity to experience fatherhood without the more onerous obligations and responsibilities of being a father? After all, he only indulged in the lighter sides of a paternal relationship. But he was also their captain, in the same way that he was the captain of his cricket team – the instigator and the director of adventures – and also in the same way that Peter is the captain of the Lost Boys. It's one of many points that makes inevitable the direct comparison between the character of Peter Pan with Barrie himself. At the end of the written version of the play, called

*Peter and Wendy*, which was first published in 1911, Peter Pan looks through the window as the Darling children are reunited with their parents:

> He had ecstasies innumerable that other children can never know: but he was looking through the window at the one joy from which he must be for ever barred.

Does this describe Barrie's own feelings as he returned the Davies boys to their parents after their adventures together? If so, it paints the picture of a character who is a bit more than the boy who wouldn't grow up: Peter is also a representation of Barrie, the sometime father of other people's children. Peter is also a character who steals other people's children away. 'Pan, who and what art thou?' asks Hook, and the answer does not appear to be a straightforward one. In 1922, though, Barrie himself suggested in one of his notebooks that it was actually he who was the child who would never grow up: 'It is as if long after writing *Peter Pan* its true meaning came to me – desperate attempt to grow up but can't.'

This is the conventional wisdom on Barrie. He is the energetic sprite who never fully engaged with adulthood. The man who loved the company of children more than other men and who transformed his adult friends into children for his own amusement. He wasn't 'grown up', not because he chose to be like that but because he could not be anything else. And there's no doubt that his friends saw this in him. When Barrie took a box of fireworks with him to the Davies's house for Guy Fawkes Night, Sylvia wrote to her sister-in-law Margaret. 'I shall have a good look at them before they are lighted,' wrote Sylvia, 'Jimmy is sure to light them at the wrong end.' The implication is that he was too irresponsible and childish to be trusted with fireworks. Cynthia Asquith, though, who was his secretary from 1917, disagreed with the idea that Barrie was himself childlike:

As for the legend of his being himself 'The Boy Who Wouldn't Grow Up', I see no evidence whatsoever of this. On the contrary he strikes me as more than old. In fact, I doubt whether he ever was a boy. But then, for the matter of that, Peter Pan isn't a boy is he? He's a wish fulfilment projection in fable form of the kind of mother – Barrie's an expert at her – who doesn't want her son to grow up.

Elsewhere she wrote about a photograph of Barrie aged six that:

His face continued to impress me as the most adult, the most experienced, I had ever seen, and each glance at the photograph of that six-year-old boy in braided and frogged velveteens, noticed on my first visit to the Adelphi flat, confirmed my suspicions that the creator of Peter Pan had been a case, not of arrested, but of precipitated development. The precocious concern on that shockingly thoughtful countenance made it pitiably plain that the little boy, at whom life had too early bared its teeth, had never enjoyed his share of that irresponsibility which, for a few years at least, should be every child's birthright.

So rather than continuing his childhood, Asquith by implication suggests that Barrie used his adult life to try to experience that 'share of irresponsibility' that had been taken from him by the death of his brother at so young an age. But is childhood necessarily about irresponsibility or even about play? There are, after all, plenty of serious children and plenty of silly adults, yet the general assumption is that frivolity is a childish characteristic and responsibility an adult one. Even if it is assumed that irresponsibility is a distinguishing characteristic of childhood, Asquith's theory is not entirely sound as Barrie enjoyed a playful childhood despite his brother's death and the impact it had on his mother in particular. Yet he recognised that in youth there was an essential creative energy. 'What is genius?' asked Barrie in *Tommy and Grizel*; 'it is the power to be a boy again at will.'

There has always been speculation that one of the Davies boys in particular was the inspiration for the character of Peter Pan, and because of the coincidence of name, it was generally believed to be Peter. Yet there is nothing to suggest the link and in as much as one individual did form the inspiration for Peter (actually, like most fictional characters, he is an amalgamation of traits from a number of real-life people, including Barrie himself) it is probable that it was George who most resembles him. 'There never was a cockier boy,' wrote Barrie about George in *The Little White Bird*, and if one characteristic marks Peter out more than any other, it is cockiness. In the preface that Barrie wrote to *The Boy Castaways of Black Lake Island* he wrote that 'George was a fine, fearless youth' – just as Peter is.

But Peter Pan's courage, his sureness in the face of adversity, is also reminiscent of Barrie's career as much as other aspects of the play direct attention to his relationship with specific children and childhood in general. Against all the odds, Barrie had succeeded with his career as a writer. This Scottish lad with a relatively humble background, who had come to London with almost nothing, had become one of the most popular playwrights of his time, and one of the wealthiest too. He had battled to establish himself in the publishing world with his unique style, which, in its own way also betrayed a kind of cockiness: a certainty in his own abilities as a writer and an unwillingness to conform.

The Allahakbarries are not left out of *Peter Pan* either. Allahakbarries Charles Turley Smith and A. E. W. Mason are both pirates in the play: Chas. Turley and Alf Mason, respectively. Hook is a cricketing stroke and he and Peter Pan opposing captains. In the final sword battle between the two, they might just as easily be batsmen: 'Hook, scarcely his inferior in brilliancy, but not quite so nimble in wrist play'. And there is the same reference to breaking ducks which appeared in Barrie's letter to Mary de Navarro: 'I'm the little bird that broke out of the egg', says Peter, whereas Barrie in 1897 had written that 'Knighthoods are in the air for everyone who breaks their egg.' The Allahakbarries are as much a part of *Peter Pan* as the Davies boys, for they are the original lost boys, the first group that Barrie successfully corralled and badgered into playing games with him.

―――――

Barrie was saddened by the move of the Davies family away from Kensington in the spring of 1904: he had seen them every week while he was in London and now they were twenty-five miles away at Egerton House in Berkhamsted. It may be that Arthur Llewelyn Davies desired to put this distance in between his family and the strange Scottish writer who had taken such a fancy to them, but Barrie's determination meant that he was soon paying visits. And Arthur's attitude to Barrie also softened, largely due to a set of terrible circumstances that changed his family's lives – and that of Barrie's – for ever.

On 18 May 1904, the *New York Times* ran a story called 'Conan Doyle at Cricket', which gave the view from the crowd as the great man stepped out to bat at Lord's.

> There was a long interval of waiting before the man who was to take his place put in an appearance. Then he came sauntering out of the pavilion, bat in hand, and moved leisurely across the beautiful lawn towards the wickets.
>
> 'That's Sir Arthur Conan Doyle,' a man with a score card remarked. 'Know who he is don't you?' he asked, and then without waiting for an answer, he went on: 'He's the writer, the man who wrote all those stories about Sherlock Holmes. Maybe you've read some of them.'
>
> 'Does Conan Doyle play cricket?' queried a person near by, who looked as though he might have been born and reared in Boston City.
>
> 'Why shouldn't he play cricket?' demanded the man with the score card, bristling up and showing his teeth.

'Oh, my,' the Bostonian answered, 'I didn't mean it that way. I didn't know that such a famous man would take a hand in a field game like this. I sort of fancied he wouldn't care to appear in public without his starched shirt, frock coat, creased trousers and patent leather shoes.'

'Doyle's human,' laughingly responded the man with the score card, 'and really he doesn't play the game well enough to hurt him.'

By this time the new batsman had advanced close to the wickets. He was altogether the biggest man on the field, a handsome fellow, but a little too much inclined to curves to pass muster according to athletic standards.

On 30 May, Barrie was the chairman at a celebration dinner given by the Author's Club at Whitehall Court on the Thames for P. F., or Plum, Warner who had been the captain of an MCC-organised England team in an unexpected triumph against Australia that winter. At another celebratory dinner for Warner and his Ashes team given by the MCC a month earlier, at which Conan Doyle was present, an old foe of the Allahakbarries, the artist G. H. Swinstead (who Warner described as 'himself no slight cricketer') was not only in attendance but had also designed the menu cards which depicted a lion with a bat trampling on a kangaroo. A similar scene was published a few years later in *Punch*.

Warner, a journalist as well as an amateur cricketer, wrote a book about the series called *How We Recovered the Ashes*. He was rewarded at the dinner with a number of Barrie's curious jokes about cricket, which he had first told the previous summer at his Black Lake Cottage cricket week. In Warner's book *My Cricketing Life* he writes that Barrie proposed his health by saying 'The first time I saw Mr Warner play he made one, the second time he was not quite so successful'. The *Express* also reported Barrie suggesting that perhaps Shakespeare had invented cricket: 'He

DOWN UNDER.

The Kangaroo. *"No matter! We meet again in England."*
The Lion. *"Yes, but let's be photographed like this first."*

thought the man who invented cricket did a bigger thing than
the man who wrote *Hamlet*. Indeed, he was not quite sure that
the same man had not done both.' This is an interesting aside,
because two things that might be most readily identified as being
at the very heart of English national identity are literature
(particularly Shakespeare) and cricket, a potent combination that
formed the basis of Barrie's own side.

*The Times* meanwhile, reported Barrie as saying that

> it was not merely as a cricketer that they were doing honour
> to Mr Warner, it was also as a captain of cricketers, one of the
> gayest and gallantest captains that ever led a team of heroes
> across the seas, in an attempt to bring back an article which
> he would not particularise. Mr Warner doubtless had it at the
> present time in his back garden, and they were all delighted
> that he succeeded in bringing it back. Mr Warner had done

something far greater than merely winning the rubber. They had entrusted to his hands the reputation of the game of cricket for honesty, manliness, fair play, and courtesy, and he brought that back to England unsullied. That was to his mind worth a hundred rubbers.

There is more than a hint here that Barrie, for the evening at least, has decided to endorse the more Newboltian idea of 'the game' than the rather more irreverent view of it which was traditional for the captain of the Allahakbarries to take. He is saying that beyond the fact that Warner won the Ashes, the most important thing is that he upheld the spirit of the game, in a way that suggests that it is the England team's special duty to do so. But then perhaps this is not surprising considering that Barrie was more and more becoming an establishment figure himself.

On 18 June the match between the Allahakbarries and Shere took place, though there is no record of either who played or who the victors were that day. Soon after the match, though, Barrie left the country for Paris at the invitation of Charles Frohman. Frohman 'wanted to give Barrie the time of his life', according to his biographers, and so he spared no expense in providing the best hotel suite, the finest dinner and the best theatre tickets in town. Barrie was stunned by the suite at the Hotel Meurice but turned down a banquet in favour of a quiet dinner at the hotel. And when Frohman asked him what he would like to do that evening, Barrie replied that he would like to go to a country fair 'where they have sideshows and you can throw balls at things'. So Frohman kept the expensive theatre tickets in his pocket and the two men instead went to throw balls and rings at a fair at Neuilly on the outer reaches of Paris. Barrie could not have enjoyed the evening more and on 25 June he wrote to Peter Llewelyn Davies, in a letter reprinted in *J. M. Barrie and the Lost Boys*, to tell him about it.

*My dear Peter,*
*This is where we are holding out. One day we went to the fair*
*and played at flinging rings on to pocket knives. If you get*
*them on you get the knife. We have won eleven knives and if*
*we go back we shall win some more. . . .*

Barrie arrived back in England just in time for his cricket week at Black Lake Cottage in the first week of July. P. G. Wodehouse turned up with Owen Seaman, who was also playing Wodehouse in the *Punch* XI, and beginning to commission pieces from him. Wodehouse opened the batting for the Allahakbarries in the two games that they played that week against the now traditional opponents of Edgar Horne's XI at Shackleford and the Artists at Frensham. But Wodehouse does not seem to have inspired the team for they lost both games. It's not known what the scores were.

Wodehouse had first taken his own XI back to his old school, Dulwich College, in 1904, and they continued to play annually until 1908. He also appeared at least four times with the Old Alleynians – the Dulwich College alumni team. And there were three other invitation teams as well: the F. P. Knox XI, the J. M. Campbell XI and the F. D. Browne XI. He also participated in the Authors v. Actors games at Lord's which began in 1905.

They played the usual games in between the cricket matches but by 9 July the party had broken up and Barrie and his wife were left at Black Lake Cottage on their own. It was their ten-year wedding anniversary and Barrie scribbled some notes that expressed his feelings about the state of his marriage, though quite typically he did this in the form of notes for a play.

Idea – Husband and wife story, scene caused by husband –
evidently they don't get on very well together – his fault – she
violent . . .

It was Barrie's way to turn all of his real-life experiences into material for plays or books, or at least potential material in the form of notes, which showed that his 'professional' brain was rarely, if ever, disengaged. Even, or perhaps especially, when what was happening in real life exerted a strong emotional impact on him: the death of his mother, for example, or in this instance, the breakdown of his marriage. He always thought about life *as a writer* and by extension about himself as a character acting out an identity. As Mackail wrote in comment on Barrie's notes on his tenth wedding anniversary: 'The border-line between truth and imagination never existed, or each must always overlap. His own life was a play, in a sense, but whether he were author or actor he never knew. So painfully vulnerable at one moment. So utterly remote and impassive the next.'

This is far removed from the spontaneity and apparent lack of self-analysis of the character of Peter Pan. Would Peter write everything that he saw down in a notebook? Of course he wouldn't: that would be boring. That's why he is also an anti-dote to Barrie the writer; he's not Barrie himself but Barrie's fantasy, just as Peter in turn is a fantasy of childhood rather than what childhood *really* is. Just as, in real life, Barrie idolised men of action, particularly explorers and cricketers, because they represented to him such an escape from the stymieing ennui of his own obsession with recording, choreographing and construct-ing narratives. They went out and *did* things while he merely sat in his study and wrote about them. 'Everybody should do some-thing once,' he wrote in a letter to the explorer Robert Falcon Scott, 'I want to know what it is really like to be alive.' Barrie developed an idealised and romantic version of childhood as a state of innocence in the same way that he saw nature as being, as Jacqueline Rose puts it, 'knowable in a direct and unmediated way'. Peter Pan is both 'the eternal child' of Barrie's play and a gross caricature of childhood, just as nature is constantly char-acterised as an idealised Garden of Eden in his writing. And cricket, the game that Barrie saw as befitting to this garden, was a potent symbol for expressing both this view of childhood and nature together: it represents 'the regressive desire for a pre-industrial, rural world' but this idea of an innocent world was also compatible with the project of Barrie and his fellow writers to indulge in what Wullschläger calls the 'identification of the child with purity, a pre-sexual life, moral simplicity'. This last point is an interesting one as all the major writers in the Allahakbarries are not only notable for the absence of sex in their work, but for their pronounced evasion of the subject, such as in *The Little White Bird* where Barrie suggests that all children were once birds – a very marked and conscious avoidance of the question of where children really do come from, as though this question was painful for Barrie to discuss.

Barrie's own sexuality has been the subject of enormous amounts of speculation but this book does not intend to add to it. He was not typical, certainly, and Birkin, probably the most well-informed and convincing of authors on this subject, suggests that Barrie was asexual. Indeed, there is very little evidence to suggest that he had any sexual relationship in his life, even, and perhaps especially, with his wife, which was almost certainly a contributing factor in the downfall of their marriage. There is little reason to comment further; other than to remark that the relationships he had with children may have been unusual but they were almost certainly not sexual, as attested to most notably by Nico Llewelyn Davies who said that: 'I don't believe that Uncle Jim ever experienced what one might call a stirring in the undergrowth for anyone – man, woman or child.'

Barrie might not have been having the happiest of summers as relations with his wife got worse and worse, despite the forthcoming production of *Peter Pan* and his adventures in Paris, but one of his star fast bowlers, Hesketh Prichard, was having the best cricket season of his life. He had great success with his county side of Hampshire but he also played a significant role in one of the most prestigious fixtures of the year, the Gentlemen v. Players match of 1904, a three-day match played at Lord's from 4 to 6 July. Prichard actually played in this fixture in 1903 and 1905 as well, but he put in a particularly distinguished performance in the 1904 game. The Players won the toss and made 327 in their first innings with Prichard taking three wickets for 102. In reply the Gentlemen struggled, and were 112 for nine when Prichard was the last man in. He stubbornly hung on at his end while the captain F. S. Jackson scored heavily at the other. This final stand made fifty-nine runs in all, which still left the Gentlemen a long way behind, but gave them some hope that they could win the game. Prichard bowled quickly on a fast and bouncy pitch in the Players' second innings, making the ball rear up to the batsmen, and he took five for eight runs, restricting the opposition to 255. But it still meant that the Gentlemen had to make an enormous 412 runs in the final innings to win the match. Ranjitsinhji (nicknamed 'Run-get-Sinhji' in *Punch*) and Jackson, two of the greatest batsmen of the era, both played excellent innings taking the score from 108 to 302. Jessop described Ranji's innings of 121, which contained fourteen fours, as 'an absolutely perfect exhibition of batsmanship'. But when the eighth wicket fell there were still twelve runs needed and actually only one batsman left, as H. C. McDonell, batting at number ten, was injured. It meant that the number eleven, Prichard, came out of the Lord's pavilion to face the aggressive bowling of Worcestershire and England's Ted Arnold. He survived, though, and his partner, A. O. Jones, hit the winning runs for the Gentlemen to win the game by two wickets. Prichard had contributed eight wickets in all and two extremely import-ant not outs. It was a spectacular victory and no doubt if Barrie was there, as he may well have been, he must have considered it a victory not just for the Gentlemen of England but for the Allahakbarries as well.

In October 1904 one of the Allahakbarries, the artist and sometime wicket-keeper, Charles Furse, died at his home in Camberley, Surrey. He was thirty-six. Furse had been suffering from tuberculosis for a number of years and despite travelling to the Alps and the south of France to try and regain his health he had become progressively weaker, though he had still been producing successful paintings, such as the *Return from the Rise*, up until 1903.

Barrie was concentrating most of his energy in the autumn on the production of *Peter Pan*, which was due to open at the Duke of York's theatre on 22 December. One of his Allahakbarries, the artist Henry Ford, provided the costume drawings for Peter Pan's own costume. The Davies boys went to see the play in rehearsal at the start of December but otherwise the preparations for its opening had been shrouded in secrecy. The director, Dion Boucicault, had assembled the cast together after the first day of rehearsals to say that 'I would like to swear you all to keep everything you see and hear in this play an absolute secret. Nothing must leak out as to what the play is about.'

The preparations were besieged with difficulty and the opening date had, by mid-December, to be moved back to 27 December. The script was revised, again and again, and on Christmas Day Barrie was still working on the ending to the play as the scenery for the final scene, which was meant to take place in Kensington Gardens, had still not been finished and the stage hands refused to work over the Christmas holiday. On Boxing Day the cast rehearsed for most of the night and went to bed shortly before dawn. According to Andrew Birkin:

> Barrie was now quite convinced that Beerbohm Tree's estimation of his sanity had been accurate. 'The Greedy Dwarf' had been one thing, a hugely enjoyable amateur entertainment for children, but no more a contender for the West End stage than the Allahakbarries were for the Test Match.

When the curtain finally rose on 27 December it was not an audience of children who were sat watching *Peter Pan* but the same regular (and almost wholly adult) theatre-goers who had been watching Barrie's plays for the past few years: 'the elite of London's society' according to Birkin. But most of them loved it. When the actress who played Peter Pan, Nina Boucicault (the sister of the director, Dion) called out to the audience to ask whether they believed in fairies, the overwhelming, affirmative response so astounded her that she burst into tears.

The critics, on the whole, were similarly impressed though some thought it ludicrous as well. '*Peter Pan* is from beginning to end a thing of pure delight,' was the verdict from *The Times*. And Max Beerbohm, writing in *The Saturday Review*, set off the speculation that it was in fact Barrie who was the boy who would never grow up and that *Peter Pan* was his defining work in as much as it perfectly captured the playwright's character:

> Undoubtedly, *Peter Pan* is the best thing [Barrie] has done – the thing most directly from within himself. Here, at last, we see his talent in full maturity; for here he has stripped from himself the last flimsy remnants of a pretence to maturity. . . .
>
> Mr Barrie is not that rare creature, a man of genius. He is something even more rare – a child who, by some divine grace, can express through an artistic medium the childishness that is in him. . . . . Mr Barrie has never grown up. He is still a child, absolutely.

Frohman was cabled in America to let him know how the play had gone: 'Peter Pan all right. Looks like a big success', ran the telegram.

'Have you seen *Peter Pan*? It's too wonderful to love,' wrote A. A. Milne rather breathlessly in a letter to his old teacher and now literary mentor, H. G. Wells, in 1905. Robert Baden-Powell meanwhile, visited the Duke of York theatre on consecutive nights – 10 and 11 February 1905 – because he found *Peter Pan* so moving. The first night he went with a friend, the second on his own. The obsession remained with him, too: in an early letter to his future wife in 1912 he suggested that they go and watch

*Peter Pan*. He also asked whether she was 'perhaps Wendy', though elsewhere, to a previous marriage prospect, he had written that he ideally wanted 'a sort of girl Peter Pan' (of course Peter Pan is always played by a girl). The combination of youth and adventure in the play was a potent one for Baden-Powell, and it fitted in with what Jackie Wullschläger called his 'imperial boy-man idealism'.

'A clean young man in his prime of health and strength is the finest creature God has made in the world', Baden-Powell wrote later and, indeed, Peter Pan himself was the kind of heroic youth that Baden-Powell, along with much of the rest of Edwardian society, was so enamoured with. The cavalier amateur cricketing heroes were readily adopted as part of the same belligerently militaristic and imperialist mythology that was becoming such a significant part of life in Britain. Which is one of the reasons why, according to Derek Birley, when the war came 'the rush to the colours was led by the sports-mad leisured classes', or what Kipling had famously called the 'flannelled fools and muddied oafs'. The scout movement itself was military in ethos and origin when it was founded by Baden-Powell, who later expressed his admiration for Hitler's *Mein Kampf*. (C. B. Fry, that exemplar of the Newboltian British sporting hero, also expressed his esteem for Hitler when he visited Germany in 1934 to try and build better links between the Boy Scouts and the Hitler Youth. He later wrote in his autobiography that 'Berlin in 1934 gave me the feeling of a world swept clean by a fresh wind which had left it stimulated, energetic, and ready to work without losing its capacity to enjoy itself . . . . The fact that we have come to look upon the Nazi system as hostile and dangerous to our interests does not prove that the means whereby Germany has reformed itself into such a capacity are not worth our close attention.')

Baden-Powell was promoted to Major-General after his heroism at the Siege of Mafeking in 1900. He wrote a military handbook called *Aids to Scouting for NCOs and Men*, which was subsequently adapted to become the seminal text of the scouting movement in 1908, the rather ambiguously named *Scouting for Boys*, published by Hesketh Prichard's mentor, and the owner of the *Daily Express*, Arthur Pearson. Both of these books had drawn attention to the observation skills of Sherlock Holmes and his real-life inspiration Dr Joseph Bell. According to Conan Doyle's biographer Andrew Lycett, 'Sherlock Holmes became something of a literary mentor to the Scouts, encouraging them to use their deductive powers by looking for clues and exercising their visual imagination.' In his final letter to the Scouts, Baden-Powell wrote that: 'One step towards happiness is to make yourself healthy and strong while you are a boy, so that you can be useful and so you can enjoy life when you are a man.'

In April 1905 Barrie invited Sylvia Llewelyn Davies, who he nicknamed Jocelyn, to Dives in northern France, though his wife Mary was not there and neither had he invited Sylvia's husband Arthur. Sylvia took Jack and Michael, now almost five years old, with her and Barrie photographed her leaning over the hotel balcony while below Michael, dressed as Romeo, reached up imploringly to his Juliet mother.

This year E. V. Lucas joined with Conan Doyle, Barrie, E. W. Hornung and Andrew Lang in starting a fund for the three poverty-stricken granddaughters of John Nyren — the writer of one of the first classic cricket books, *The Young Cricketer's Tutor*, which was published in 1832. Perhaps as a consequence of his involvement in this good cause, in 1907 E. V. Lucas produced a new edition of Nyren and a year later contributed a piece to *The Times* in which he wrote that: 'Any step that can bring sentiment again into first-class cricket is to be welcomed: for a hard utilitarianism and commercialisation have far too long controlled it.'

Lucas argued, in the bucolic tradition in which the Allahak-barries liked to view themselves, that 'an occasional pastime, marked by geniality and rapture' had tragically become 'a more

Newspaper boys in London give notice of Baden Powell's double century in South Africa in May, 1900.

Charles Turley Smith fastens on his armour in a tented field.

*Right*: E. V. Lucas with his wife Elizabeth, daughter Audrey and their Chihuahuas, a love of which they shared with P. G. Wodehouse and Denis Mackail.

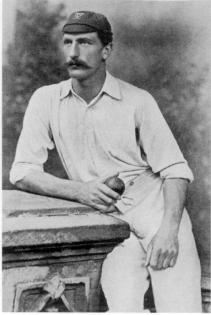

Charles Burgess Fry in 1899, 'Probably the most variously gifted Englishman of any age'.

Charles Aubrey Smith, actor, cricketer and founder of the Hollywood Cricket Club with P. G. Wodehouse in 1932.

Hesketh Vernon Hesketh-Prichard used his six foot, four inch height and long arms to great effect as an outstanding fast bowler in the early 1900s.

'It's rather fun seeing an enemy skulking along about 500 yds off, and potting at him'.
George Llewelyn Davies with the Eton Officer Training Corps in 1912.
He is first on the right in the front row.

Eton (wearing plain blazers without trim) v Winchester, 1912.
George is in the back row, furthest on the left.

'He is walking back, bat in hand, to the pavilion. An unearthly glory has swept over the cricket ground.' Michael Llewelyn Davies in cricket whites, 1916.

Barrie's flat: a picture of George with his cricketing cap hung beneath is on the left, Michael in the centre, Nico on the right.

*Right*: George takes a catch at Lord's in the Eton v Harrow game of 1912. He did not take it cleanly at first, but ultimately hung on.

'15,000 tall hats – one cad hat (mine); 15,000 stiff collars, canes, shiny faces — one soft collar, cudgel, dreary face (mine).' The crowd promenading at Lord's in their finery in 1909.

Barrie shapes to crack one through the covers at Stanway in 1926, while Charlie Macartney keeps wicket. Jack Ellis and Arthur Mailey seem to have given up all hope of taking his wicket.

*Above*: 'An incomparable Captain. The life and soul of his side. A treat to see him tossing the penny.' Barrie tosses the coin in a game billed as the Allahakbarries v West of Scotland, 1930.

Percy Jeeves inspired the name of Wodehouse's incomparable valet. He played for Warwickshire and was killed in action fighting for the Royal Warwickshire Regiment in 1916.

Barrie bowls an 'insidious left-hand good-length ball' at Dundee
University College on 5 May, 1922, while (right) . . .

... Douglas Haig prepares to recieve Barrie's ball. Barrie succeeded in taking the wicket.

The final game of the Allahakbarries, 28 July, 1913, at Downe House School against E. V. Lucas's XI.
Back row (left to right): George Llewelyn Davies, T. L. Gilmour, Will Meredith, George Meredith jnr., Denis Mackail, Harry Graham, Dr. Ernest Goffe. Centre row (left to right): A. A. Milne, Maurice Hewlett, J. M. Barrie, George Morrow, E. V, Lucas, Walter Frith. Front row (left to right): Percy Lucas, Audrey Lucas, T. Wrigley, Charles Tennyson, Willie Winter.

or less mechanical trade' and that 'a three-day match today can be a scene of little joy and little enthusiasm'. Such sentiments are in stark contrast to those expressed by writers who later romanticised this entire period as being the golden age of cricket. At the time, though, the self-styled cricketing purists, as they have continued to do ever since, felt that the old-days were best and that cricket would soon be toppling over the edge of a precipice to be broken into a thousand tiny pieces. William Rees-Mogg writing in *The Times* in 2008, for example, lamented that 'the culture of cricket now seems to be going the way of Troy, or indeed of the Roman Empire.' He no doubt would have written the same thing a hundred years previously had he been alive.

While Mary Barrie went on a motoring holiday in France with her friend Molly Muir in June, Barrie headed down to Black Lake Cottage with E. V. Lucas, his wife Elizabeth and their daughter Audrey. Sylvia and Michael also went along and it seems that Michael being there – his first visit to the cottage and the surrounding woods and lakes – inspired Barrie to write a new third act for *Peter Pan* in which Peter and Wendy are marooned on a rock. Barrie is photographed with Michael on the south lawn of the cottage and he also appeared in the midst of the Allahakbarries team photograph in July wearing a floppy white sunhat with the brim turned up at the front with E. V. Lucas handing him a cricket ball: he had become their mascot. At this age, certainly, he looks like he could be either a girl or a boy with his long hair and loose-fitting smock: an ideal Peter Pan.

Barrie's cricket week in 1905 was the last of his festivals of cricket. Henry Ford, A. E. W. Mason, Charles Tennyson and Charles Turley Smith arrived at the very end of June, some of them staying nearby in Farnham. On 30 June they played a golf-croquet tournament on the south lawn of the cottage as well as other competitive games. The day before, Wodehouse, Snaith, Conan Doyle and Hornung were all playing for the Authors against the Actors at Lord's. Wodehouse and Conan

Doyle, who captained the Authors, opened the batting together, but both failed: Wodehouse got a duck, perhaps just to prove that he was, indeed, quite bad enough to play for the Allahakbarries, and Conan Doyle scored just two. Philip Trevor top-scored for the Authors with forty-four. The actors, captained by Aubrey Smith, were convincing winners by seven wickets, but Wodehouse did get a notable scalp when he took Smith's wicket. The two men later collaborated in the 1930s when they founded the Hollywood Cricket Club in California: Smith became its first president, Wodehouse one of the vice-presidents and secretary.

On 1 July, the Allahakbarries made the traditional trip to Shackleford to play Edgar Horne's team, though they lost once more. On Monday, 3 July, though, the Allahakbarries had a great triumph against the Artists at Frensham by making 250 runs, declaring and then bowling the Artists out for 101. The Allahakbarrie Henry Ford had switched sides to play for the Artists on this occasion and, considering the scores, probably wished that he hadn't. According to the *Farnham, Haslemere and Hindhead Herald* 'At the luncheon interval the score was 195 for 3 wickets. After lunch Pawling hit out freely, getting one 6 and several 4's and Mr Barrie was able to declare at 247 for 5 wickets, Pawling being 47, not out.' Barrie was meant to play with a bat given to him by the great all-round cricketer and sportsman C. B. Fry, though in the end he did not get to block, cut or pull a single ball – the declaration came too early. If he had known that it was his last proper opportunity to do so for eight years he might have waited a little longer to declare. So perhaps it was fitting that he took the catch that ended the match.

After a banquet back at the cottage, the party broke up on Tuesday, 4 July. Barrie did not know that it was the last such parting or that eighteen summers of cricket with his beloved team, almost uninterrupted, since 1887, had suddenly stopped. Denis Mackail wrote that but for the captain's extraordinary and persistent enthusiasm, nothing could possibly have kept [the Allahakbarries] alive. Yet it wasn't because Barrie was forty-five now, or had lost any of his love for these boyish days in the country, that the series had come to an end. Tragedy, destiny, and a special and vindictive Nemesis would dissolve the Allahakbarries, though sparing all their lives. These were waiting in the wings now, and wouldn't be satisfied until they had struck not once, but again and again. No wonder those old photographs make us sad and uneasy in more ways than one. For the little central figure, in his white cricketing cap and snake-linked belt, is to know something worse and far more relentless, before long, than the mere bludgeoning of chance.

Aubrey Smith appeared in Barrie's play *Alice Sit-by-the-Fire* that summer, which did well, but was not nearly as successful as *Peter Pan*, and closed at the end of July. In November, *Peter Pan* opened for the first time in New York. Mark Twain, with no obvious irony, wrote that 'It is my belief that *Peter Pan* is a great and refining and uplifting benefaction to this sordid and money-mad age; and that the next best play is a long way behind it.' The irony, of course, is that *Peter Pan* became one of the most commercially successful plays of all time. A second season in London began at the same time and was immensely popular. Early in 1906, on 20 February, there was an altogether more unique production of the play when Barrie and Frohman took the younger members of the cast to Berkhamsted, complete with scenery, and in 'an array of vehicles almost as glorious as a travelling circus', to put on a performance for Michael, who was ill and confined to his bed. Barrie later reported that Michael 'looked on solemnly from his bed and never smiled once'.

It was early in the year too, that two of the Allahakbarries were elected as part of the large Liberal majority in the general election of 1906: A. E. W. Mason became the Liberal MP for Coventry and Augustine Birrell the MP for Bristol North. Birrell also became a member of Henry Campbell-Bannerman's cabinet, as president of the Board of Education, though he was forced to resign from this post the following year, when he became Chief Secretary to Ireland.

Barrie was also developing a new friendship with the explorer Robert Falcon Scott, who had returned from a successful expedition to the Antarctic with Ernest Shackleton among others, aboard the *Discovery* in September 1904. Scott had made the crucial assertion on this trip that 'our experience has led me to believe that for sledge work in the Antarctic Regions there is nothing to equal the honest and customary use of one's own legs.' Relying on so-called man-hauling of sledges as opposed to using dogs was later seen to be one of the main downfalls of the *Terra Nova* expedition which ended in tragedy for Scott and his companions a few years later.

A. E. W. Mason had introduced the two men. He had also been on Scott's boat the *Discovery* shortly before it set sail in

THE BIRRELLIGIOUS TRAVELLER.

Minister of Education. *"Thank you; but I'm going my own way."*

August 1901. Mason and Scott were good friends and according to Scott's biographer David Crane, Mason even based a fictional character, Henry Rames, on Scott in his novel *The Turnstile*. Crane writes of the character that 'what we have here . . . is the Scott of modern myth, a man of ambition without direction, of aspirations without vision, of will without conscience, of charm without kindness, of character without *centre*.' Scott, aged thirty-seven at the start of 1906 and a naval officer as well as an explorer (in January he had been appointed to the post of assistant to the director of naval intelligence at the Admiralty), gave Barrie the book he had written about his expedition, *Voyage of the Discovery*, and Barrie, in turn, took him to a rehearsal of *Peter Pan*, introduced him to Frohman and his other friends and invited him to Black Lake Cottage. Scott flirted with Pauline Chase, one of the actresses in *Peter Pan*, for some time after first meeting her at the rehearsal. The introduction to Charles Turley Smith in particular proved to be a significant one, as Smith later wrote the book *The Voyages of Captain Scott* and subsequently two books about other famous explorers: *Nansen of Norway* and *Roald Amundsen, Explorer*. If a strange entry from Turley's diary in 1905 is to be believed then adventure was also being considered by Barrie, Mason and himself. 'We fixed up that J. M. B., Mason and I should go to America in September and live backwoods-men's lives. I think of the passage with fear and trembling, but there is no question that I should be much sicker staying at home than I should be at going, great as are my capabilities in that direction.'

Barrie's friendship with Scott was one of a number that Barrie developed with explorers, which had started with Joseph Thomson and also included Paul du Chaillu and Hesketh Prichard. They were all heroes to him as men of action, something which Barrie himself implicitly recognised. 'On the night when my friendship with Scott began,' Barrie wrote, 'he was but lately home from his first adventure into the Antarctic, and I well remember how, having found the entrancing man, I was unable to leave him. In vain he escorted me through the streets of London to my home, for when he had said good-night, I then escorted him to his, and so it went on long through the small hours. Our talk was largely a comparison of the life of action (which he pooh-poohed) with the loathly life of those who sit at home (which I scorned).' Barrie carried in his pocket the last letter that Scott had written to him for many years after he had received it. Scott, though, never played for the Allahakbarries, like all these other explorers had done.

There was a problem with one of the Allahakbarries in May that seemed to mark the beginning of a whole series of tragedies in Barrie's life. Barrie's dramatic agent Addison Bright, who had played for the team and starred alongside Barrie in 'The Greedy Dwarf', had admitted to embezzling a large amount of money from his clients. In all he had appropriated £28,000 of box office returns from fellow Allahakbarries: a remarkably large amount of money at this time; £16,000 of it was from Barrie, £9,000 from Conan Doyle and a small amount from Hornung, whose stage version of Raffles had recently been successful in America and which had opened at London's Comedy Theatre on 12 May with Gerald du Maurier in the starring role. Bright had been a friend of Barrie's for many years and was part of the gang of young bachelors which included Jerome K. Jerome and Bernard Partridge who dined, smoked and talked together in the late 1880s. The news came as a shock. But Barrie was not angry. He blamed himself to a large extent as from the beginning of his career he had always been extremely vague about his business dealings. And this, combined with the fact that he was making phenomenal sums of money, had inevitably provided Bright with a great temptation. According to Mackail, Barrie hoped that there did not have to be a prosecution: the money could be repaid in full and the matter forgotten about. But it was too late: Bright shot himself in Lucerne on 29 May and Barrie, along with Bright's younger brother, Golding, travelled to Switzerland in order to identify the body. In a small obituary he wrote for *The Times*, which was published on 1 June, Barrie wrote that 'For many years he had been my most loved friend.' Barrie said that he didn't want the money returned to him but it was, and later that year Golding Bright became Barrie's theatre agent and remained so for the rest of Barrie's life.

Only the day after the obituary was published in *The Times* there was more gloomy news. Arthur Llewelyn Davies had a lump on his face that was diagnosed as being a sarcoma of the jaw. He needed to have an operation to remove half his upper jaw and his palate. He wrote to his sister, Margaret, on 2 June: 'After the operation I shall be incapacitated for about 6 weeks, and unable to speak properly for 3 or 4 months – and there will always be an impediment in my speech. I think of our future and the boys.'

Barrie took charge of the situation and met the expenses for the best possible medical treatment, as well as staying with Arthur in his hospital room and talking to him. Arthur, who it seems had previously been irritated by Barrie, softened his attitude towards him considerably. After his operation, Arthur wrote to Peter on 14 June:

> Mr Barrie is now sitting here with me reading the newspaper, and Mother has gone for a little drive in the motor with Mrs Barrie. Don't you think Mr Barrie is a very good friend to all of us?

The previously good-looking Arthur had been disfigured. He went home to Berkhamsted at the end of June and in August the family went on their annual Rustington holiday, staying at Cudlow House, which had been rented by Sylvia's mother Emma du Maurier for the month.

Barrie had stayed at Black Lake Cottage during July but there was no cricket this year in the heart of the pine woods, despite the fact that it was ideal cricketing weather and one of the finest summers of the decade. There was a further reminder of mortality when normally the Allahakbarries would be sipping lemonade and playing golf-croquet when Conan Doyle's wife, Louise, who had been suffering with tuberculosis for more than a decade, finally succumbed on 4 July. Conan Doyle was not playing two weeks later when the Authors took on the Actors in their annual fixture at Lord's on 19 July but Wodehouse, Hornung, Prichard, Pawling, Philip Trevor and the historian, author and competent wicket-keeper Cecil Headlam (who had also played for the Allahakbarries on a few occasions) all were. Gerald du Maurier was also playing for the Actors who were once again captained by the talismanic Aubrey Smith. Pawling took six for fifty-nine in the first innings and Wodehouse three for thirty-seven in the second and the Authors won by thirty-four runs. One of the umpires that day was called Mycroft, which is also the name of Sherlock Holmes' brother. He had previously played first-class cricket as a wicketkeeper for Derbyshire before he became an umpire.

Kent were the victors in the county championship that year, and the West Indies were touring, though at this time they did not have test status (the only team other than England to do so was Australia, though in 1907 it was also given to South Africa for the first time). However, the finest individual performance this season was from a Yorkshire professional called George Hirst, who at thirty-five managed the unprecedented feat of taking more than 200 wickets and scoring more than 2000 runs in a first-class season. When he was asked if he thought whether anyone would repeat the feat he is said to have replied 'I don't know, but whoever does it will be very tired.' No one ever has. In 1921 he became a cricket coach at Eton and it's likely that he coached the youngest of the Davies boys, Nico, for a term there.

Barrie went to Rustington with the Davies family in August and Peter Davies later wrote that

> The presence of J. M. B. at Cudlow House through these holidays was a queerish business, when you come to think about it: as odd a variation of the *ménage a trois* as ever there was, one would say. I think by now Arthur had surrendered utterly

and was reconciled, for all sorts of reasons. But how strange the mentality of J. M. B., whose devotion to Sylvia seems to have thriven on her utter devotion to Arthur, as well as on his own admiration for him.

Barrie had a Peter Pan outfit specially made as a gift to Michael, and he and the boys played cricket in the garden of the house. The photographs that Barrie took of Michael wearing his costume were later used as the inspiration for the statue of Peter Pan erected in secret in Kensington Gardens in 1912. At the end of August Barrie invited the family to stay with him in Fortingall in Scotland where he and the boys went fishing in Glen Lyon. While he was in Fortingall Barrie received a letter from Captain Scott, asking whether he knew any boy who might be suitable to study at Osborne Naval College on the Isle of Wight. He immediately nominated Jack, who was coming up to twelve years old, writing to Scott that

> from his earliest days he has seemed to all of us cut out for a sailor, he is really a fine intelligent quick boy with the open fearless face that attracts at first sight and in view of the future he already assumes a rolling gait. His people were meaning to try and get him a nomination for the exams next March (he is the right age) and so you can imagine how grateful they are to you.

Scott had invited Barrie to go with him on a naval manoeuvre but Barrie felt the need to decline: 'I can't, I mustn't, I have been doing practically nothing for so long. But I know it means missing the thing I need most – to get into a new life for a bit . . . . Altho', mind you, I would still rather let everything else go hang and enrol for the Antarctic.'

Back in London in mid-September, Arthur was given the bad news that the cancer had spread and that he might only live for another six months to a year. He wrote to his father to prepare him for the worst.

*Whatever may be in store for me, I hope I shall bear it as befits the son of a brave & wise man. I am troubled for myself, but much more for Sylvia. She is brave to a degree that I should have thought hardly possible, busy all day with endless activities & kindnesses for me and the boys, & all the time the burden is almost heavier than she can bear.*

He added that 'Barrie's unfailing kindness and tact are a great support to us both'. Yet tact was not very much in evidence when *Peter Pan in Kensington Gardens*, the chapters about Peter Pan in *The Little White Bird* had been taken to form a book of their own with illustrations by Arthur Rackham, was published in December with a dedication from Barrie:

*To Sylvia and Arthur Llewelyn Davies and their boys (my boys)*

Arthur struggled on through the winter months, needing morphine to help him manage his pain. *Peter Pan* was now in its third season but Barrie's thoughts were clearly with Arthur: his pain and suffering made Barrie yearn for a paradise in which there is no pain or death more keenly than ever; a place where time can stand still, as seen in this fragment from his notebook in January 1907.

The Lovely Moment. The Finest Dream in the World. That it is early morning & I am out on a highland road – dew, &c. – it is time before I knew anything of sorrow pain or death. Everyone I have loved is still alive – it is the morning of life – of the world.

But of course it could not be. It was another Neverland – merely a fantasy. After a great deal of pain Arthur died on 18 April 1907. Yet his death was not the end of the suffering for his family; it was actually more like the beginning. And as Barrie became more and more closely involved with the remaining members of the Llewelyn Davies family, cricket continued to take a back seat. The ageing Allahakbarries were forced to look after themselves; Barrie was too busy looking after the lost boys.

# 8

## THE LAST MAN IN

*O Batsman, rise and go and stop the rot,*
*And go and stop the rot.*
*(It was indeed a rot,*
*Six down for twenty-three.)*
*The batsman thought how wretched was his lot,*
*And all alone went he.*

Siegfried Sassoon, 'The Extra Inch'

———

In February 1906, aged just twenty-four, A. A. Milne was asked by Owen Seaman to become the assistant editor of *Punch*. Seaman had just been appointed as the editor of the magazine after the veteran F. C. Burnand had been forced to resign: Burnand had spent more years in the top job (twenty-six) than Milne had been alive. The young A. A. Milne had been contributing to publications including *Punch* as a freelancer, with all the unpredictability that involves, and he was excited by this unexpected opportunity which was set to earn him £500 a year. 'I was so certain that I should get everything I wanted in the end,' he wrote, 'Hadn't I always said that I would be editor of *Punch* one day?' He was an ambitious, rather eager young man; slender and athletic, blond and blue-eyed (his wife and son simply called him 'Blue') and his writing was full of the same kind of carefree spirit that his appearance seemed to embody. Within a few years he received another exciting and unique opportunity when Barrie invited him to be 'the last member' of the Allahakbarries.

Alan Alexander Milne had enjoyed an untroubled upbringing and a happy childhood. In his autobiography, *It's Too Late Now*, his childhood and university career occupy more than 150 pages of a 270 page book. He was a Londoner, born in Kilburn in 1882, the third son of J. V. Milne and his wife, Maria. J. V. Milne ran a small independent school called Henley House in south Hampstead less than a mile away from Lord's, and very close to the home of the fashionable Victorian painter William Frith, whose son Walter played for the Allahakbarries. He was far from being a stern headmaster: Alan's brother Ken said that he had 'too much laugh' for a school teacher and Alan wrote that he was both 'funny' and 'shy'. For Alan that meant that 'it was natural to be interested; it was easy to be clever.' In a photograph taken with their father in 1886 all three brothers are dressed in Little Lord Fauntleroy suits and collars with matching long blond hair, in imitation of the character in the book which was published that year. All three were educated at Henley House and H. G. Wells taught there for a while and later became Milne's friend and mentor; a kind of benevolent uncle figure. The school's most famous pupil, other than Milne, was Alfred Harmsworth, later Lord Northcliffe, the newspaper tycoon who while he was at Henley House had edited the school magazine. (Later Northcliffe considered buying *Punch* at one point and suggested to Milne that he become editor.)

Milne loved reading adventure stories as a child, such as *Treasure Island* and the *Swiss Family Robinson*, though mathematics became his subject: he gained a scholarship to Westminster School in 1893 and later read mathematics at Trinity Hall, Cambridge. It was at Westminster that he first developed his love of cricket. 'I was a taught batsman rather than a natural one,' he observed later, and it was thanks to the cricket coach at Westminster that he gained any sort of proficiency at the game. 'Come out to it' the coach instructed Milne, who recollected that 'I could come out to anything that was straight and not too high; the difficulty lay in staying in.' Cricket became one of Milne's great loves in life and not long before he died he declared that watching cricket had given him 'more happiness than any other inactivity in which I have been engaged'. It even influenced the name that he gave to his son, Christopher Robin, when he was born:

> I had decided on two initials rather than one or none, because I wanted him to play cricket for England, like W. G. Grace and C. B. Fry, and if he was to play as an amateur, two initials would give him a more hopeful appearance on the score-card. A father has to think of these things. So, one of us liking the name Christopher, and the other maintaining that Robin was both pleasing and unusual, we decided that as C. R. Milne he should be encouraged to make his name in the sporting world.

He played for Westminster in his last two years there and recorded a highest score of thirty-eight, but in an important two-day game against Charterhouse he scored a duck. He later wrote to his granddaughter to tell her about another incident from the game, involving the batsman at the other end of the wicket from him.

> Playing against Charterhouse in 1899 (the year Canute died, if your history book goes as far as that) I was in with a boy called Plaskett. And he hit his first ball in the air towards the bowler, and we ran; and in comes the bowler in the middle of the pitch just as he was getting ready for this c. & b.; and Plaskett was so nervous and excited that he leaped in the air, rather as if he was up at the net, and knocked the ball away. He didn't wait for an appeal, but ran straight back to the pavilion, and hid in a locker. Luckily for him he took six wickets for 58 in the next innings, and we won the match. Otherwise he would have had to emigrate. Now you know all about Obstructing the Field.

He started writing when he was at Cambridge, and edited *Granta*, the university magazine. He wrote funny pieces and light, comic verse. 'I see no one among the young people with so light and gay and happy a touch as you show,' wrote Barrie to Milne some years later in 1910, though to modern tastes his writing might appear to represent what Jackie Wullschläger has called 'mawkishness . . . a desperation to be flippant, unchallenged, intellectually and emotionally cosy'. There was cricket at Cambridge as well, though it was clear that Milne was never destined for cricketing greatness himself, though he could still hit the odd boundary and wasn't a complete duffer. His biographer Ann Thwaite writes:

> One tends to think of far-off summers as always glorious. Milne's first summer at Cambridge, 1901, had been pretty good. There is a glimpse of him trying to write a sonnet on Clare Bridge but it is too hot to think of rhymes for ducks and panamas and weeping willows. There is some good cricket. Fifty years later he can still hear the rattle of his ball against the spokes of a bicycle someone had left leaning on a fence, just beyond the boundary. He said it was the zenith of his cricketing career: a fast bowler, half a dozen slips, and he had found the only small gap.

Milne left Cambridge with a third-class degree in 1903, which meant that his father didn't speak to him for a week. Like many other recent graduates Milne was not sure what he wanted to do with his life immediately after university. He considered the civil service and his father, when he spoke to him again, suggested that he might want to become a schoolmaster like him. But by September 1903 he had resolved to become a writer and in October his first piece was published by *Vanity Fair*; it was a parody of Sherlock Holmes. He had a number of contributions accepted by other publications in his first few months including the *St James's Gazette*, the *Daily Chronicle* and the *Daily Express*. His first piece for *Punch*, a poem, was published on 18 May 1904. Another of his early pieces for *Punch* was on the subject of cricket; it begins:

> Of Tomkins as a natural cricketer
> It frequently has been remarked — that IF
> He'd had more opportunities of bowling
> And rather more encouragement in batting;
> And IF his averages so disclosed,
> Batting and Bowling, had been interchanged;
> And IF the field as usually set
> Contained some post (at the pavilion end)
> Whose presence rather than a pair of hands
> Was called for, then, before the season finished,
> Tomkins would certainly have played for Kent.

R. G. G. Price in his *History of Punch* noted that 'It is the Milne of the Saturday afternoon on the cricket field who is remembered. The characters of the house party were reflected in their cricket and their conversation. The match was both negligible and all-important. References to mid-week work were flippant or incredulous. The narrator was not much of a cricketer but he earned his place in the team by his repartee.'

It is exactly this version of Milne which was attacked in the post-war years as the modernists took over the literary centre-ground and many of the Edwardian writers were seen to represent an unpalatable version of literature. Joseph Connolly wrote witheringly of Milne that:

> He reminds me of Noel Coward, a pre-war Noel Coward springing from the same unexpectedly lower-middle-class stock, but moving with pre-war acceleration into a smooth heaven of light verse, cricketing weekends, good society, whimsical taste and money, money, money.

Milne had already written his first book by 1905, called *Lovers in London*, though like Barrie's opinion of his own first book, it was not an effort that he cared to remember afterwards. Just ten years later in 1915 he said that 'It is out of print fortunately; I haven't even got a copy myself. But I read my brother's copy the other day with mixed feelings; gladness that it was out of print, shame that I once thought it so good, pride that I had advanced so much since then.'

He was regularly getting pieces published in *Punch* but the offer of a job at the magazine in 1906 was still a relief as he was far from having a secure income. He remained assistant editor until the First World War, though his relationship with his boss, Owen Seaman, was often strained. According to Price 'the two men were temperamentally opposed'. But it was most likely the political differences between the two that meant that Milne was not elected to the *Punch* Table until 1910.

The appointment gave Milne money and a certain amount of freedom and confidence in the future ('How delightfully extravagant one could be with £500 a year', he wrote later): it meant that he could head out into the countryside for weekends with friends rather than staying in his London rooms writing and worrying about money. He remembered these trips, and life in general at this time, with great affection, and some bitterness, many years later:

> The world was not then the damnable world which it is today; it was a world in which imaginative youth could be happy without feeling ashamed of its happiness. I was very young, very light hearted, confident of myself, confident of the future. I loved my work; I loved not working; I loved long weekends with the delightful people of other people's delightful houses.

From 1908, E. V. Lucas and his family had a house in the country just outside Lewes called Kingston Manor and on weekends guests visited from London. Lucas was one of Milne's great friends, and a useful ally at *Punch*, and so Lucas's house became one of a number of 'other people's delightful houses', that Milne visited during the summer months. Many of the Allahakbarries also visited Lucas at Kingston Manor at various times, such as Barrie, A. E. W. Mason, Maurice Hewlett and Charles Turley Smith, though there is no suggestion that Milne met Barrie before 1910. Elizabeth Lucas, writing in the portrait of her father, remembered Milne fondly:

> Alan, very fair and handsome, knowing exactly how to talk un-patronisingly to a child, was, with one great exception, my favourite among all the visitors. This exception was Maurice Hewlett, who I loved, in spite, perhaps because of, his diabolical habit of teasing me.

Milne may not have known Barrie yet but he did know Charles Turley Smith, who wrote reviews for *Punch* and who he had met at a weekend party given by Philip Agnew, one of the proprietors of *Punch*. Turley Smith had 'an innocent goodness with a keen sense of humour, and intelligence and a boyish devotion to games.' Elizabeth Lucas described him as the 'most delightful and elusive of men'. He lived in Cornwall and Milne visited him there to play golf. But these years after 1905 were barren ones for the Allahakbarries and so despite all Milne's connections to the team, he did not get to play for them for a number of years to come.

He was playing for the first time in the annual Authors v. Actors game at Lord's on 15 August 1907 alongside Conan Doyle, Wodehouse, Hornung, Guggisberg, Philip Trevor and Cecil Headlam. But despite fielding a strong team they lost by six wickets. Milne only managed to score five, though he did better than Wodehouse, who scored only a single run, and Conan Doyle, who scored four. The previous day, however, Conan Doyle had scored fifty-six playing for MCC against the Royal Academy. Another of the Allahakbarries, Henry Ford, had played for the

Royal Academy and was bowled by Conan Doyle for forty-four. Prichard, meanwhile, was chosen by the MCC to captain a tour of America that summer. His side included Major E. G. Wynward, his captain at Hampshire and a close personal friend, and Gregor MacGregor, the Middlesex captain.

South Africa played their first test series against England in 1907 but in a wet summer the most outstanding performances were delivered by bowlers. Wodehouse did some ghost-writing for his fellow bowler from his Dulwich days, N. A. Knox, who played twice for England in this series. The article, 'On Fast Bowling', was published in the *Daily Mail* on 17 May. Colin Blythe, known universally as Charlie, was a slight and sensitive left arm spinner who played for Kent. He was a professional but had an artistic temperament and was a good violinist. On 1 June, against Northamptonshire, he took seventeen wickets for forty-eight runs, the most that any bowler has ever taken in a day in first-class cricket. These figures included the ten for thirty that he took in the first innings. That same summer he took fifteen for ninety-nine against the South Africans at Headingley. 'Blythe's spin was something quite out of the ordinary', according to his obituary in *Wisden*, 'On a sticky wicket or on a dry pitch ever so little crumbled he came off the ground in a way that beat the strongest defence.'

Albert Trott, nicknamed 'Albatrott', also gave an astonishing performance in his benefit match for Middlesex in 1907 when he took four wickets off four balls and later in the same innings took a hat-trick. He was considered to be well past his best at this point after illness and an addiction to alcohol – often taken on the boundary edge from adoring spectators – had ruined his physique, but this performance was a glorious reminder of his past greatness. In view of his later financial difficulties it was even said that he shot himself in the foot on this day, bringing the match to a premature end by bowling the opposition out, while there were more queuing spectators ready to pay to come into the ground.

Barrie and the Davies boys sat out the wet summer in Dhivach Lodge near Loch Ness, which Barrie had rented. It was so wet that Luath, the Barries' enormous Newfoundland dog, almost got swept away by a burn in spate. Barrie wrote in a letter on 26 August that 'I do nothing up here but fish & fish & fish, and we ought all to be fishes to feel at home in this weather.' But as ever he was also writing and scribbling notes into his little notebooks. He was working on the play *What Every Woman Knows*, which was first performed in 1908, and writing the book version of *Peter Pan*, *Peter and Wendy*. After a visit from Captain Scott, he also started sketching out an idea for a new play: 'North Pole (or South)', though this is one of many ideas of Barrie's that fell by the wayside.

Arthur Conan Doyle married his second wife, Jean Leckie at St Margaret's Church in Westminster on 18 September, at the end of the cricket season in which he played his last first-class game (he was now forty-eight years old). They had waited more than a decade for this occasion: the two had first met on 15 March 1897, though they decided that the honourable thing to do was to wait for the death of Conan Doyle's first wife, Louise, who had at the time already been ill for some years. One of the guests at the wedding was George Edalji, who, in a plot that could have come straight out of one of Conan Doyle's own Sherlock Holmes stories, had been wrongfully convicted of maiming animals in a Staffordshire village. Conan Doyle had successfully intervened in the case and in so doing had pointed out the stupidity of the Staffordshire police in a way that also imitated Sherlock Holmes's criticism of Scotland Yard. Barrie too was railing against perceived injustice in 1907, by becoming a member of the newly founded committee seeking the abolition of the office of Censor after Harley Granville-Barker's play *Waste* had been refused a licence. The secretary of this committee was Gilbert Cannan, a young lawyer, author and playwright, with 'corn coloured hair and a crooked smile', and the man who played the decisive role in the split between Barrie and his wife in 1909.

On the same day as Conan Doyle's wedding in September, George Llewelyn Davies sent his first letter home to his mother from Eton where he had begun his first term just a few days earlier. Sylvia and the boys had moved back to Kensington with Barrie's help after the death of her husband. George's letters are awash with the public school slang of the time: everything is 'ripping' and 'topping' and George is 'bucked' when the mother of his 'fagmaster' came for tea and gave him 'ten bob'. He wrote letters to Barrie too and so began Barrie's powerful fascination – almost an obsession – for the English public-school system (and, indeed, for the higher reaches of English society in general), which found its way into later versions of *Peter Pan*: soon it became known that Captain Hook himself went to Eton. In a later speech Barrie revealed that for all his English mannerisms and connections, public schools still managed to make him feel like an outsider:

> Your great English public schools! I never feel myself a foreigner in England except when trying to understand them. I have a great affection for one at least of them, but they will bewilder me to the end; I am like a dog looking up wistfully at its owner wondering what the noble face means, or if it does have a meaning. To look at, these schools are among the fairest things in England; they draw from their sons a devotion that is deeper, more lasting than almost any other love.

The public schools were developing many fine amateur cricketers and at the same time preparing their charges for military service as well.

The end of the year meant the latest season of *Peter Pan*, which was now in its fourth year, and had a gang of fervent admirers who booked their seats months in advance and hurled thimbles onto the stage during the performance. The play was now so successful that the London company was going to theatres across the country and beyond. The following year, in 1908, Barrie and Frohman took *Peter Pan* to Paris, printing a twelve-page 'history' of *Peter Pan* (in French) to help the French audiences discover what the play was about. The French newspaper *Le Figaro* described Peter Pan in the most romantic terms imaginable:

> If we look deep down in our memories, we will find Peter Pan: he is our fine hopes as we start forth, our certainty that we shall triumph, our complete confidence in ourselves, which for a moment lifted us on high, only to throw us to the ground later on. It was that prodigious hour when destiny hovered above an immense joy, before crushing it.

For Barrie the company of *Peter Pan* actors were starting to act as some form of substitute in place of the Allahakbarrics. In 1906 Barrie and Frohman had founded the *Peter Pan* Golf Club for members of the touring company (they played for a cup called the Frohman Trophy) and once every tour they had a dinner. In Paris they also played cricket with two teams taken from the cast. Barrie was still in France for Michael Llewelyn Davies's eighth birthday on 16 June but he arranged for a redskin costume and all the trimmings (wigwam, bows and arrows, etcetera) to be delivered to the Davies home on Campden Hill Square in Kensington. 'I wish I could see you putting on the redskin's clothes for the first time,' wrote Barrie to Michael, 'Won't your mother be frightened.'

Barrie was back at Black Lake soon after and it was there that Kathleen Bruce announced that she was engaged to be married to Captain Scott. She had also been courted by Gilbert Cannan and now he had lost that battle he began to spend more and more time with Mary Barrie, which included a holiday in Switzerland that December with Barrie as well as Sylvia and the Davies boys. It's not clear whether Barrie understood what was happening right in front of him and perhaps he was in denial about the situation or felt powerless to do anything about it, but the slow disintegration of his marriage had now reached a critical point.

He was busy for much of the rest of the summer with rehearsals for his latest play, which, perhaps rather ironically given the circumstances, was called *What Every Woman Knows*, and once again starred Gerald du Maurier. It opened at the Duke of York's Theatre on 3 September, the day after Scott's wedding to Kathleen Bruce.

The Olympic Games were held in London that summer and Conan Doyle again demonstrated his love of the underdog. He pledged his support for the unfortunate marathon runner Dorando Pietri (who looked like a Mediterranean version of a younger Barrie – small, thin, dark and moustachioed), who had been leading the race on 24 July as he entered the stadium but had to be helped to the finishing line after collapsing a number of times. Pietri was disqualified and the gold medal awarded to the American athlete Johnny Hayes instead, to the disgust of many members of the public, including Conan Doyle, who reported on the race for the *Daily Mail* and made an appeal for donations. On 31 July he and his wife Jean presented the Italian runner with a gold cigarette case (that essential accoutrement for all successful marathon runners) and a cheque for £308 10s.

Yorkshire remained unbeaten all season in the County Championship of 1908, thanks to the combined heroics of George Hirst and Wilfred Rhodes. The annual Authors and Actors game was rained off and it was also the last season where a first-class eleven from Philadelphia toured the country, this time to disappointing attendances. But the big cricketing story of the summer was the return of one of the most dazzling cricketers of recent years, the great batsman Ranjitsinhji, who had recently become His Highness the Jam Sahib of Nawanagar. He rented a large country house in Sussex called Shillinglee Park and according to W. G. Grace's biographer Simon Rae, 'embarked on a Wodehousian summer of country-house cricket and creditors' summonses.' Grace took a team of twelve to play the host's side at Shillinglee and joined in the fun by wearing a turban. There was a farewell dinner at Ranji's university town of Cambridge in October as he prepared to head home once more, where Conan Doyle spoke on the subject of the relationship between Britain and India. Grace also spoke: in response to the toast 'Famous cricketers and county cricket', a subject on which he was clearly an expert.

Gerald du Maurier and Sylvia Llewelyn Davies's elder brother, Major Guy de Maurier, wrote a play called *An Englishman's Home* which, with some help from his brother and Barrie, was first performed at the end of January 1909. It was intended as a wake-up call to Britain to do something about the German naval expansion, which it suggested would inevitably lead to an attempt at invasion by the Germans. The Germans had gained victory in the original ending of the play but Barrie's amended version gave triumph to the British. 'Of course the ending does rather spoil the lesson', wrote George Llewelyn Davies, who was sixteen that summer, to his mother who was ill in bed. 'It makes one think that even if the Germans did have a high old time for a bit, England would win in the end alright.'

George was soon after on exercises with the Eton College Officer Training Corps (O.T.C.), which he viewed as another great game. 'It's rather fun seeing an enemy skulking along about 500 yds off, and potting at him,' he wrote. And later that year, in June, George was awarded his 'Sixpenny' at Eton: the colours given to the best eleven cricketers at the school under the age of sixteen. 'Perhaps no one who has never got a colour of some sort at Eton can comprehend the satisfaction it gives', his brother Peter later wrote; 'a successful love affair is possibly the only comparable triumph in after life.'

George Meredith died after a brief illness on 18 May and

Barrie campaigned, unsuccessfully, for his ashes to be buried in Poets' Corner at Westminster Abbey. Not long after, on 1 June, Barrie and Frohman took *Peter Pan* back to Paris again. *The Stage* magazine published an account of some of the cast's extra-curricular activities at St Cloud, a town just west of Paris:

> Mr J. M. Barrie invited the whole company to St Cloud where they all played cricket. One match was between the company and staff, and in another the ladies participated. 'Our day', says Mr George Shelton [who played Smee, the pirate] in writing to us on the outing, 'commenced at ten in the morning, and we arrived at Paris about seven in the evening, all feeling very pleased with our day's experience, which Mr Barrie had so generously given us. Our party numbered seventy-five.'

It must certainly have been an unusual sight for the locals of St Cloud to see seventy-five members of an English theatrical company playing cricket and all of them being corralled and directed by a five foot-tall man with a dark moustache.

Despite this and other events (such as the knighthood which he was offered and which he refused, and the fact that the Authors had eked out an undeserved draw against the Actors in what was the last of these annual fixtures at Lord's) that no doubt made Barrie smile this summer, though, it was to be a wretched few months for him. He was staying on his own at Black Lake Cottage on 27 July and expecting his wife to come and join him the following day when the gardener there, Mr Hunt, told him that Mary Barrie had spent a night with Gilbert Cannan at the cottage the previous November. Hunt might not have told Barrie but for a slight that he felt he had received from Mary Barrie about his work. Barrie went to London immediately and telegraphed his wife to tell her that he wanted to meet her. At their meeting he confronted her and Mary admitted that the incident had indeed taken place. However, Barrie's report that she had told him that it was the only time was later denied by her in a letter to H. G. Wells, who sided with Mary over the incident, along with some other of Barrie's friends. A. E. W. Mason looked after him, though, and Barrie stayed in Mason's London flat and afterwards went to Switzerland with him and another trusted old friend, Gilmour: Mason climbed mountains while Gilmour and the abject Barrie walked. Even those who did not exactly support Mary claimed to understand her actions. 'The whole truth is that Mrs B is a woman – with a woman's desires – which for many years she had controlled', wrote Barrie's friend Will Meredith, for example. She had fallen in love with Cannan and Barrie's efforts to get her to renounce him were futile. Divorce was inevitable and on 13 October, at an uncontested hearing, it was over. Barrie never returned to Black Lake Cottage again and the following year Mary married Cannan. 'J. M.'s tragedy', she later wrote to Peter Llewelyn Davies, 'was that he knew that as a *man* he was a failure and that love in its fullest sense could never be felt by him or experienced, and it was this knowledge that led to his sentimental philanderings. One could almost hear him, like Peter Pan, crowing triumphantly, but his heart was sick all the time.'

There was a connection between Captain Scott's marriage and Mary Barrie's infidelity, however tenuous (Cannan had only turned his attention to Mary Barrie once Scott had been engaged to Kathleen Bruce), and almost to emphasise the connectedness of these two events, Barrie became one of the godfathers of Scott's son, Peter, the same day that he got divorced.

Two days after the divorce case, Sylvia Llewelyn Davies collapsed at her house on Campden Hill Square and was diagnosed with an inoperable cancer close to her heart. It remained a secret from the boys, though as she was prescribed a long rest in bed and had been unwell for some time, they no doubt realised that she was in poor health. Barrie meanwhile had taken a flat at Adelphi Terrace just off the Strand, which is where he remained (later moving upstairs to a penthouse apartment) for the rest of his life. This first apartment overlooked George Bernard Shaw's residence and Gerald du Maurier later joked that 'Everyone's famous for something, and you're famous for living opposite Shaw.'

If Barrie had been in better spirits he might have enjoyed P. G. Wodehouse's book *Mike*, which consisted of two public school stories with cricket at their core, published on 25 September. But he was flat and dejected as George noticed when Barrie went to visit him at Eton in November. 'He was very sad, of course', he wrote to his mother, 'but he seemed to buck up at times.' By contrast, the work of another of the Allahakbarries which was published this year, if he had read it, may have compounded his misery rather than alleviated it. Hornung had attempted for the first time to make a novel out of his Raffles character with the book *Mr Justice Raffles*, after improbably reviving the amateur cracksman as his brother-in-law had done with Sherlock Holmes. But even ardent devotees of Raffles found it to be a weak effort compared to earlier stories, with poor plotting coupled with venomous anti-Semitism, though this was hardly unique at the time: Maurice Hewlett, for example, had written in a letter to Mary Barrie around the time of her divorce that Barrie's lawyer, Sir George Lewis, was a 'loathsome Jew'.

The official end of the Edwardian era was in 1910, when King Edward VII died in the same place that he had been born, at Buckingham Palace, on 6 May, three days before Barrie's fiftieth birthday. That spring Barrie had played with Michael, Nico and Captain Scott in Kensington Gardens, which Barrie later described as 'our Antarctic exploits'. Scott left for the real Antarctic in July that year on his ill-fated *Terra Nova* expedition in an attempt to reach the South Pole. Conan Doyle had helped Scott to raise funds for the expedition, though Scott's efforts to get more funding continued right up until the moment that their boat, the *Terra Nova*, left Auckland in New Zealand for the final journey to the Antarctic. The *Terra Nova* first set sail from

London, before picking up Scott at Weymouth on the south coast and then journeying to Cardiff before the immense journey south, as part of a long goodbye to the country from the intrepid explorers. One of the crew members described that at Weymouth they saw evidence of the huge naval fleet which had been built up over the past few years; 'the funnels of a fleet the like of which I have never seen, & I am sure the world has never seen such a squadron. Every "Dreadnought" and Dreadnought-cruiser was there & the splendid King Edward Class. We were given the honour of steaming through the lines. I must say I was never so impressed in my life with hideous strength. The new monsters are ugliness itself but for sheer diabolical brutality in shipbuilding some of the Dreadnought Cruisers take the cake.' Britain was preparing for war.

All the Davies boys were beginning to call Barrie 'Uncle Jim' rather than just plain old 'Mr Barrie' and with Sylvia still unwell he was playing a more significant role in their lives. This included trips to Eton to see George who was soon joined there by Peter after he won a scholarship to the school (which he was told about by his headmaster during a game of corridor cricket). Barrie watched George playing cricket and even helped to organise his school uniform for him. George was an exceptionally popular pupil at Eton and a very sporty one too (the two facts inevitably related), though he was not yet in the school's first XI. However, the Eton first XI had a famous triumph this summer against their old adversaries Harrow in what has been called 'the most dramatic school game of all time.' The game was played at Lord's on 8–9 July, though it was scheduled to last for a further day, and Eton were inspired to victory by their captain Robert St Leger Fowler; so much so that it has been known ever since as 'Fowler's match'. The fixture was treated as a major sporting event as well as a school rivalry, and many thousands attended the game. Barrie went to a number of these games and he wrote a letter describing one of them.

I went with N [ico] to the Lord's match. 15,000 tall hats – one cad hat (mine); 15,000 stiff collars, canes, shiny faces – one soft collar, cudgel, dreary face (mine). The ladies comparatively drab fearing rain but the gents superb, colossal, sleek, lovely. All with such a pleased smile. Why? Because they know they had the Eton something or the Harrow something. They bestowed the something on each other, exchanged with each other as the likes of me exchange the time of day. I felt I was nearer to grasping what the something is than ever before. It is a sleek happiness that comes of a shininess which only Eton (or Harrow) can impart. This makes you 'play the game' as the damned can't do it; it gives you manners because you know in your heart that nothing really matters so long as you shine with that sleek happiness. The nearest thing to it must be boot polish.

Harrow, who were undefeated all season, batted first and made 232 in their first innings with Fowler adding four wickets to the eleven that he had taken in the same fixture during Eton's victory the previous year. Eton were bowled out for just sixty-seven in their first innings with Fowler the only player to make double figures, scoring twenty-one. They were forced to follow on and in their second innings were faring little better at forty-seven for four when Fowler came to the crease to top score again for his side with sixty-four. They made 219 in all but still looked as though they would lose the match after leaving Harrow just fifty-four to win the game. But Fowler, bowling off-spin, took eight Harrow wickets for just thirty runs in ten overs and Eton won the game by nine runs. George may have been among the reported 10,000 spectators who were there at the end to cheer Eton off the pitch.

Soon after Sylvia decided that the family should spend the rest of the summer in the country, despite her illness. Barrie rented the remote Ashton Farm, which was sandwiched between the rugged,

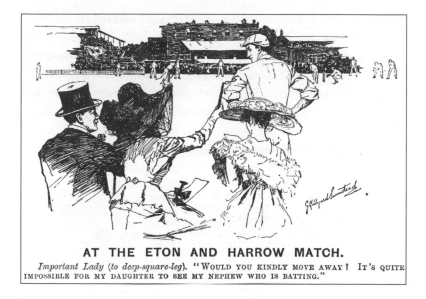

**AT THE ETON AND HARROW MATCH.**

*Important Lady (to deep-square-leg).* "WOULD YOU KINDLY MOVE AWAY? IT'S QUITE IMPOSSIBLE FOR MY DAUGHTER TO SEE MY NEPHEW WHO IS BATTING."

heathery wilds of Exmoor to the south and east, and the north Devon coastline to the north and west, fourteen miles from the nearest railway station at Minehead. The journey there, with Barrie, the boys, their nursemaid, Mary Hodgson, and Sylvia's nurse, Nurse Loosemore, was exhausting for Sylvia and she spent much of the holiday resting on either the sofa or her bed while the boys went fishing during the day. Peter later remembered that:

> From now onwards, while we fished and golfed and walked furiously, or made expeditions to Lynton and ate huge cream teas with bilberry jam and Devonshire cream, or on idle days watched the buzzards circling slowly, high above the valley of the Lynn – while, in fact, we went our boyish ways – Sylvia weakened rapidly, and I think she never again left her room.

She knew that she was desperately ill and made a second version of her will, which specified that Barrie should be a trustee and guardian to the boys, along with other family members including her mother, Emma du Maurier, who had been staying at the farmhouse from the start of August. She also asked that the boys should not see her after she died.

Sylvia died at approximately two o'clock on the afternoon of 27 August, lying in her bed with her mother and Barrie, as well as Nurse Loosemore and a local doctor in attendance. Jack was out playing golf and Peter and George were fishing on this grey, damp day, and when Peter came home on his own the first person he saw was Barrie: 'a distraught figure, arms hanging limp, hair dishevelled, wild-eyed'.

> In what exact words he told me what I had no need to be told, I forget; but it was brokenly, despairingly, without any pretence of philosophy or resignation or the stiff upper lip. He must have been sunk in depths far below that, poor Jimmy; I think it was I who propelled him, as much as he me, into the room on the left of the little entrance hall, where we sat and blubbered together.

Despite the wishes expressed in Sylvia's will, which was only found months later, at least some of the boys went into the room and saw her body, which was soon after taken back to London by train to be buried in Hampstead.

Barrie was shattered by Sylvia's death; she had been a joy to him for many years and he had clearly worshipped her as well as her family. But he now realised that he had a responsibility to care for the boys: he was *in loco parentis*, and so he took on the responsibilities of a father, though he was never seen as a replacement to Arthur. Instead he remained 'Uncle Jim' and was later given other nicknames such as 'Sir Jazz Band Barrie', but never 'father'. In one of the more bizarre and tragic instances of life imitating art, Barrie, as Peter Pan, was now the captain of 'the lost boys', though the experience was far from resembling the exciting adventures of escape to Neverland.

Jack, aged sixteen, went back to naval college in September

and was the least close of all the boys to Barrie, while George, his senior by a year, was joined at Eton by the more introvert Peter, aged fourteen, who was bullied so much for being 'the real Peter Pan' in his first term, that he came to despise the play and his connection to it for the rest of his life. Michael, aged ten, and the ebullient Nico, who was now almost seven years old, remained living at Campden Hill Square under the care of their nursemaid Mary Hodgson, who according to Andrew Birkin, 'looked upon herself as the boys' substitute mother.' (On a holiday to a remote part of Scotland in 1912 when E. V. Lucas and A. E. W. Mason were guests, Hodgson, who was never on friendly terms with Barrie, wrote to her sister, Nancy, that 'We have had . . . the pick of the literary genius's of England, but alas – either my liver is out of order, or my ideals too high, for at close quarters they are but mortal – & very ordinary at that.') Barrie meanwhile did his best to spoil the boys with the things that he knew would delight them, such as fishing rods, theatre trips, bicycles and fishing holidays. Over the next few years the relationship between Barrie and Michael, who Denis Mackail called 'quick, sensitive, attractive and gifted', developed to the extent that Michael became what Barrie called, with some seriousness, 'the sternest of my literary critics'. 'He was the cleverest of us, the most original, the potential genius', wrote Nico in 1975, and Barrie not only considered him to be a brilliant mind but had a special emotional closeness with him as well.

In October 1910 A. A. Milne was invited by Barrie to become the last member of the Allahakbarries – a cricket team that by now had not played for five years. The introduction came about because of their mutual friend, E. V. Lucas. Milne, who had finally been elected to the *Punch* Table that year, found Lucas to be a great ally in his battles against Owen Seaman and he enjoyed the contrasts between the two personalities, as he recounted in his autobiography:

> When Owen went off to the Riviera or Scotland, E. V. Lucas came into the office as acting editor. He had as many concerns outside *Punch* as Owen had few, and consequently was as quick as Owen was slow. After the paper was put to bed on Friday night, Owen had nowhere to go but home, and a lonely home at that. E. V. had a hundred mysterious activities waiting for him.

Lucas, the urbane clubman with a weakness for alcohol, was exceptionally well connected and he suggested to Milne when his book *The Day's Play* was published in 1910, that he should write a letter to Kipling, whose title *The Day's Work*, Milne had mischievously adapted.

> When I said that I didn't know Kipling, and couldn't imagine the author of the famous and recently published line 'The Flannelled fool at the wicket, the muddied oaf in the goal' being interested in a book full of cricket and lesser games, E. V. assured me that Kipling was 'not like that'.

*The Day's Play* was a collection of Milne's articles in *Punch*, which featured a number of Milne's pieces about The Rabbits, a series of witty (or, perhaps, just plain irritating, depending on your point of view) dialogues on the leisure pursuits of the upper middle class, which ran from June 1909 until the start of the war in 1914. Milne started his letter to Kipling with the greeting 'Sir' but he felt that his letter was more appropriate for Barrie, 'The only writer whom I did admire at all like that in those days.' It was an astute move as not only did Barrie turn out to be a fan but his young charges were also: when Milne sent his following book in 1912 Barrie had to fight with the boys in order to read it.

This is the reply that Barrie sent to Milne on 13 October, 1910:

*Dear Mr Milne*

*I see no one among the young people with so light and gay and happy a touch as you show in this book,* The Day's Play, *and as I read it last night I was putting on my guards once more and taking centre for the last time. You have given me one day more. It set me looking for a little booklet of my cricket club to send you but I seem to have no copy. We were all mad and glad. I elect you the last member.*

*The gaiety and irresponsibility of your work (I know it in* Punch) *are rarer gifts than you wot of know. When you know you won't be so gay. So don't know as long as you can. Something else will take their place by and bye – something very good I hope, but don't be in a hurry. Hide and seek with the angels is good enough for anyone.*

*I feel an affection for the man behind your book, and hope all will always be well with you – or thereabouts Perhaps someday you will lunch with me. I wander about alone.*

*Yours sincerely,*

*J. M. Barrie.*

'I wander about alone.' Barrie was clearly unhappy and it is perhaps telling that he wrote these words on 13 October, which was the first anniversary of his divorce. As for the invitation to join the Allahakbarries, Milne may have wondered if the team would ever play another game, something which his rather morbid election as 'the last member' seemed to reinforce. 'Even after twenty-five years', Milne wrote, 'I wished that I had not forced myself on him, but had been introduced in the ordinary way.'

The Allahakbarries did play again, and that was also because of E. V. Lucas. Barrie was so much preoccupied with looking after the boys that he had little time for writing, let alone cricket. One of the oldest members of the team, Augustine Birrell, though, would have struggled to play cricket even if Barrie had asked him to after he was attacked by suffragettes on 23 November 1910.

**THE SUFFRAGETTE THAT KNEW JIU-JITSU.**
THE ARREST.

The following day, also Nico's seventh birthday, the *New York Times* reported that 'Augustine Birrell, the veteran Chief Secretary for Ireland, as a result of injuries from the blows and kicks of the Suffragettes yesterday, is today confined to his bed and under the care of physicians.' When on the same day the women had tried to disrupt a speech that Lloyd George was giving in St Pancras, Lloyd George had told his audience to 'take no notice of these cats mewing'.

The following year's cricket season began with a bang on 20 May when Ted Alletson, playing for Nottinghamshire, struck one of the most ferocious and brilliant innings of all time – an hour-and-a-half of superlative batting. It was all the more remarkable as he never scored another first-class century and in his first-class career he averaged less than twenty. But on this occasion, playing against Sussex at Hove, he hit 189 in ninety minutes, 142 of which came in just forty minutes after lunch. The innings also included eight sixes, one over in which he scored thirty-four (a record at the time) and seven overs in which he individually scored 115 runs (more than sixteen an over).

That summer Barrie took the Davies boys, except for Jack who was at sea, to Scourie Lodge, a small manor house owned by the Duchess of Sutherland in a remote corner of north-west Scotland. It perfectly fitted the criteria that Barrie had set out in a letter to the Duchess:

> I bring four boys with me; what they yearn for is to be remote from Man and plenty of burn trout fishing, of which they never tire from the rising to the setting of the sun.

Was it the boys who wanted to be remote from man, or Barrie? Was his emotional torment driving him to find places of greater and greater isolation (the following year they journeyed even further: to stay at Amhuinnsuidhe Castle in the Outer Hebrides), as Neverland became harder and harder to recreate within a train ride of London? He described the surroundings in idyllic, though typically humorous, terms in a letter he sent in September:

> It is a remote place, nearly 50 miles from a railway, and when you want food you have to kill a sheep. It is very beautiful with sea and lochs, all blue as the Mediterranean, and in the course of their wanderings the boys see eagles, otters, whales, seals &c.

In a far more remote place, at the very end of the earth, meanwhile, Scott and his team had spent the southern winter on Cape Evans in near-constant darkness making preparations for their journey to the pole. To the east of them, at the Bay of Wales, a Norwegian team led by Roald Amundsen were also planning their trip in direct competition to the Scott expedition.

Significantly, they were a full sixty miles closer to the pole and were using dogs to propel them there whereas Scott was mainly relying on ponies, untried motorised sledges and arduous man-hauling. As the days were getting lighter and the weather beginning to improve, both teams were readying themselves for the final trek. The Norwegians started first, setting out on

19 October, whereas Scott's team set out on 1 November. They eventually made the South Pole itself on 18 January 1912, and erected their 'poor, slighted Union Jack' there, for Amundsen had beaten them to it, by slightly more than a month. 'Great God', wrote Scott at the Pole, 'this is an awful place . . . Now for the run home and a desperate struggle. I wonder if we can do it.'

Despite their best efforts, though, they could not. By the end of March, Scott and the four other men he had taken with him on the final push to the southernmost extremity were all dead. However, the rest of the world only discovered their fate in February 1913, after the *Terra Nova* had returned to port with news that after the Antarctic winter had finished, a party had reached the final resting place of the three men, including Scott, who had nearly made it back to safety.

There was a far greater loss of life just over a fortnight after Scott and his men had perished in a polar blizzard, when on 15 April 1912 the *Titanic* sank after striking an iceberg: more than fifteen hundred people were killed. Among them was the American artist Frank Millet, who had played for Broadway against the Allahakbarries in the series of 'test matches' between the two sides from 1897–1899. 'What? Spoil my painter's hands for a dirty leather ball?' Millet had shouted at one of the Broadway games. Barrie wrote a letter in May to Charles Turley Smith, who had played alongside Millet in these matches (it was only later that he played for Barrie's side) to commiserate him. 'I have thought a good deal lately of how Frank Millet's death must have saddened you. . . . We used to discuss whom we should prefer to be wrecked with. Here was a man one would choose to be on a liner with when it was going down. Tho' I had seen nothing of him for years I have always had this same feeling about him, that he was brave and true and loyal.'

Barrie's alluring unorthodoxy expressed itself again quite publicly and to most people, quite unexpectedly, on 1 May when, as dawn broke, a statue of Peter Pan which had not been there a day earlier, appeared in Kensington Gardens as though by magic. Barrie had commissioned the statue from George Frampton, and had given him the photographs of Michael dressed as Peter Pan, which he had taken in 1906. But Frampton had based the statue more on a life model than on Michael and Barrie was dissatisfied with the result, writing that 'It doesn't show the devil in Peter.'

George was in the first XI for Eton in summer 1912 and it gave Barrie the cricket bug again: 'This confounded excitement about the XI has rather caught me and I have begun to dream about it', he wrote to George on 29 May, and a few days later he was playing cricket in the small and steeply sloping gardens at the centre of Campden Hill Square with Nico and Michael, where the ball must always have been running away down towards Notting Hill Gate. King George V became the first reigning monarch to watch a test match this summer, though he perhaps strangely chose to watch Australia v. South Africa, who were both playing in a damp and unexciting triangular tournament along with England. Wodehouse played his last match at Lord's this summer, also, playing for the Authors against the Publishers, the last match of its kind to be played there.

But for Barrie at least the highlight of the cricket season took place at the beginning of July, when George played a starring role for his school in the match against Harrow at Lord's. He was selected as a bowler but as well as taking the leading Harrow batsman's wicket, he scored fifty-nine in the first innings and also snatched a stunning high left-handed catch fielding at square leg. The photograph of him reaching skywards for the ball, the tips of his toes just leaving the ground, was splashed across a number of newspapers the following day. The ball threatened to spill out of his grasp but he hung on to it as though his life depended on it. Eton won the match comfortably, by six wickets.

Barrie wrote to George to congratulate him on his performance. 'I am greatly delighted and rayther [sic] proud,' he wrote on 8 July; 'your mother used to speak of the possibility [of playing at Lord's] with shining eyes.' Michael, too, was showing himself to be a promising athlete at his preparatory school, Wilkinson's, where he was captain of football and in the cricket first XI. He was now twelve years old, and in his final innings before going up to Eton, he scored twenty-six runs against 'Juddy's'. With his own statement about childhood, 'Nothing that happens after we are twelve matters very much' in mind, Barrie soon after wrote about Michael in a piece he called *Neil and Tintinnabulum*:

> A rural cricket match in buttercup time with boys at play, seen and heard through the trees; it is surely the loveliest scene in England and the most disarming sound. From the ranks of the unseen dead, forever passing along our country lanes on their eternal journey, the Englishman falls out for a moment to look over the gate of the cricket field and smile. Let Neil's 26 against Juddy's . . . be our last sight of him as a child. He is walking back bat in hand to the pavilion, an old railway carriage. An unearthly glory has swept over the cricket ground. . . . I never know him quite so well again. He seems henceforth to be running to me on a road that is moving still more rapidly in the opposite direction.

Although this was written in 1912, some of Barrie's language, like 'the ranks of the unseen dead' already seems to unconsciously anticipate war, now just two years away.

# ❧ IV ❧
## STUMPS: DEATH AND ENNOBLEMENT

# 9

## GALLANT GENTLEMEN

But think of the poor batsman. He goes in first, big with high thoughts of 'all the centuries yet to come' – and out first. His companions build up a huge score; but there he sits, not conquering but conquered, under the cool shade of the pavilion, musing over a mis-spent existence. What can he do? No one cares to hear his explanations.

J. M. Barrie, 'The feelings of a batsman'

---

When in *Peter Pan* the Lost Boys seem doomed to walk the plank of Captain Hook's pirate ship, Wendy is given the opportunity to speak a few last words to them.

> 'These are my last words, dear boys. I feel that I have a message to you from your real mothers, and it is this: "We hope our sons will die like English gentlemen."'

These lines were cut from the play for the duration of the First World War, though A. A. Milne wrote a poignant account of his journey to the front line in July 1916 which suggests that even if this was not what mothers really did want (surely they actually wanted their sons to live), the sentiment that there was something deeply honourable about dying as an. 'English gentleman' was widespread. A. E. W. Mason, for example, wrote about it in 1902 in his most famous novel *The Four Feathers* as 'to die decently was worth a good many years of life.'

Milne was travelling to France with a quiet young man who was joining the same battalion of the 11th Royal Warwickshire Regiment. He was the younger of two sons and his elder brother had already been killed a few months earlier. His parents had provided him with:

> an under-garment of chain mail, such as had been worn in the Middle Ages, to guard against unfriendly daggers, and was now sold to over-loving mothers as likely to turn a bayonet thrust or keep off a stray fragment of shell; as, I suppose, it might have done. He was much embarrassed by this parting gift, and though, true to his promise, he was taking it to France with him, he did not know whether he ought to wear it. I suppose that, being fresh from school, he felt it to be 'unsporting'; something not quite done; perhaps, even, a little cowardly. His young mind was torn between his promise to his mother and his hatred of the unusual. He asked my advice: charmingly, ingenuously, pathetically. I told him to wear it; and to tell his mother that he was wearing it; and to tell her how safe it made him feel, and how certain of coming back to her. I do not know whether he took my advice . . . Anyway it didn't matter; for on the evening when we first came within reach of the battle-zone, just as he was settling down to his tea, a crump came over and blew him to pieces . . .
>
> *Dulce et decorum est pro patria mori* [It is sweet and fitting to die for one's country]
>
> But just why it was a pleasant death and a fitting death I still do not understand. Nor, it may be, did his father and mother; even though assured by the colonel that their son had died as gallantly as he had lived, an English gentleman.

'Dulce et decorum est' was also the title of one of Wilfred Owen's most famous poems, about a gas attack in the First World War – a poem which savagely tears apart the myth that there is any glory in war. But at the start of 1913, with the war more than a year away, Wendy's message was thought about not in terms of soldiers dying on the front line, but of Captain Scott and his men, whose fate became known on 10 February when the expedition's ship, the *Terra Nova*, arrived in New Zealand. The news reached Britain soon afterwards and the fallen polar explorers, who had already been dead for more than ten months, instantly became national heroes, providing the opportunity for a great deal of nationalistic fervour. This was further encouraged by Scott's *Message to the Public* which he had written as he waited for death alongside his comrades in an isolated tent besieged by wind, ice and snow. 'Had we lived,' he wrote, 'I should have had a tale to tell of the hardihood, endurance, and courage of my companions which would have stirred the heart of every Englishman.' Robert Baden-Powell saw it as a great example of the natural heroism of the British people: 'Are Britons going downhill? No! . . . There is plenty of pluck and spirit left in the British after all. Captain Scott and Captain Oates have shown us that.' The artist John Charles Dollman's painting of Captain Oates, who had stepped out of the tent into a blizzard in order to save the others in the party, was entitled *A Very Gallant Gentleman*.

Gallantry was also meant to be an integral part of cricket and cricket's moral outlook, and Barrie himself had praised the then-England captain, Plum Warner in 1903 as 'one of the gayest and gallantest captains that ever led a team of heroes across the seas'. He had told Warner then that the most important thing he had done was not to win the Ashes but to uphold the values and traditions of cricket. Similarly, Scott may have lost, but the consensus at the time was that he had done so heroically, with courage, valour and gallantry.

Barrie joined in the nationalistic fervour surrounding their deaths, though his intention, in a letter to *The Times* in February and as godfather to Scott's only son, was to try and raise funds for the families of the men who had died. 'Almost every Briton alive has been prouder these last days because a message from a tent has shown him how the breed lives on', he wrote, before urging readers to dig deep into their pockets. Barrie's efforts are in the spirit of what were probably the very last words that Scott wrote.

> I do not think we can hope for any better thing now. We shall stick it out to the end, but we are getting weaker, of course, and the end cannot be far.
> It seems a pity, but I do not think I can write more.
> R. Scott.
> For God's sake look after our people.

It was not until April that Barrie actually received the letter that Scott had personally written to him in the final days of his life. Scott wrote that he was 'pegging out in a very comfortless spot'. There had evidently been some sort of misunderstanding between the two men before Scott had left Britain ('It hurt me grievously when you partially withdrew your friendship or seemed so to do') but he writes that:

> My attitude towards you and everyone connected with you was always one of respect and admiration – Under these circumstances I want you to think well of me and my end and more practically I want you to help my widow and my boy your godson – We are showing that Englishmen can still die with a bold spirit fighting it out to the end.

He signed off the letter but then later added a postscript:

> *Later*. – We are very near the end but have not and will not lose our good cheer – we have four days of storm in our tent and now have no food or fuel – We did intend to finish ourselves when things proved like this but we have decided to die naturally in the track.
> As a dying man my dear friend be good to my wife & child

– Give the boy a chance in life if the State won't do it – He ought to have good stuff in him – and give my memory back the friendship which you inspired. I never met a man in my life whom I admired and loved more than you but I never could show you how much your friendship meant to me – for you had much to give and I nothing.

Barrie carried this letter in his pocket for many years and often read excerpts from it to friends and sometimes in speeches, such as his famous address, 'Courage', to the students of St Andrews University in 1922, though he did not allow the more personal parts of the letter to be published. He told the undergraduates that 'I have the little filmy sheets here. I thought you might like to see the actual letter; it has been a long journey; it has been to the South Pole. It is a letter sent to me from Captain Scott of the Antarctic, and was written in the tent you know of, where it was found long afterwards with his body and those of some other very gallant gentlemen, his comrades. The writing is in pencil, still quite clear, though towards the end some of the words trail away as into the great silence that was waiting for them.'

––––––––––

Michael Llewelyn Davies started at Eton in April but he hated it and could not settle there. He was depressed and lonely. Barrie wrote to Charles Turley Smith to tell him that he was 'foolishly taken up about it. It rather broke me up seeing him crying and trying to whistle at the same time.' So Barrie decided to write to him every single day that he was at school, without exception, and Michael replied every day as well: a truly copious correspondence.

In June 1913 Barrie became a baronet and so, in society, he began to be known no longer as 'J. M. Barrie' or 'Mr Barrie' but 'Sir James Barrie, Bart.' instead. He had turned down a knighthood in 1909 but felt that he could not turn down a baronetcy when it came along. Was it a further sign of his growing obsession with the aristocracy and the ruling classes, which in some places earned him a reputation as a snob? Or did one element of this obsession – the particular fascination with Eton that had developed since he became more involved with the Davies boys – mean that as the guardian (or perhaps, in his mind, putative father) of the boys he felt that he should have a title that favourably compared to the other fathers of Etonians? He may have simply thought that he deserved the recognition for his hard work and success, though this appears rather out of character. But whatever the reason, at the very end of the belle époque in Europe, that period of pre-welfare state (and pre-income tax) upper-class good-living which had lasted for at least as long as the Allahakbarries had been playing cricket, Barrie the baronet appeared to pitch his hat in with the privileged, but increasingly besieged rich. Many of the Allahakbarries joined him – in all six of them received knighthoods.

In a letter to Charles Turley Smith on 4 July 1913 about the test match at Lord's, Barrie showed that he still had time for cricket. 'My best memory is Barnes bowling', he wrote. 'He took no wickets but it was the most "classic" sight I have seen since Richardson. What do I mean by classic? Well thus I feel the Greeks would have bowled.' Unlike the old days, though, Barrie did not plot and harry and instruct his friends and acquaintances to attend a brief resurrection of the Allahakbarries later on that month. It was thanks to E. V. Lucas, that 'the Bart' had an opportunity to appear for his cricket team for the final time, as both the captain and a baronet as well. But there is also no record of Barrie's excitement about the game, which is in great contrast to the earlier days of his side and he announced that it was definitely the very final outing for his team.

The venue for the game was the grounds of Downe House School, in Kent, where Lucas's daughter Audrey was a boarder, and the match was the Allahakbarries v E. V. Lucas's XI. It had previously been Charles Darwin's house and in 1907 the school – a girl's independent boarding school – was founded there. The game was organised for 28 July and A. A. Milne and George Llewelyn Davies got their first, and only, 'caps'. Only Barrie, who wore the cap with the colours he had had designed for the 1899 Broadway match, and the genial Gilmour, were survivors from the original members of the club who had first turned out twenty-six years earlier. They were both fifty-three now and had been in their twenties when they played their first match against Shere in 1887 when some members of the team had turned out without even knowing which side of the bat to use. But Will Meredith (who played alongside his teenage son George), Maurice Hewlett, Walter Frith and Charles Tennyson were all longstanding members of the team which made it, if not quite the occasion of old, at least a genuine revival of the team rather than the totemic resurrection which took place in 1930 with Barrie as twelfth man, aged seventy. In spirit it was a resumption of the early days in terms of there being no first-class cricketers there, but rather a collection of good friends and their relatives: most not particularly distinguished as cricketers. The previous Allahakbarries match had taken place eight years earlier, in Surrey, in 1905 and there was little sign then that Barrie's team would be hanging up their boots so soon. But there had been so many terrible events in Barrie's life in the intervening years that the Allahakbarries had ceased to be important to him; and what he may have previously regarded as the enervating responsibilities of adulthood had become an ever-present reality to him in the form of five 'lost' boys who were growing up as surely as Peter Pan didn't.

Denis Mackail, who as a child twelve years earlier had sat in the audience as some of the Allahakbarries had performed 'The Greedy Dwarf' in Barrie's Kensington home, was now a theatre set designer, working with Barrie on his play *The Adored One*, which opened (disastrously) in September 1913. Like Milne

and George Llewelyn Davies, this was his only game for the Allahakbarries. And playing on E. V. Lucas's side were the *Punch*
cartoonist George Morrow, who had joined the magazine in 1906,
the librettist Harry Graham, and E. V.'s brother Percival.

Mackail later described how 'the time and scene were still
so Arcadian that it was a long journey, with a change on the
way, from Charing Cross to Orpington, and a horse-brake still
transported the players through narrow lanes to the school.
Glorious summer weather.' Mackail was remembering the
game from a distance, not just after the First World War, but
during the Second, and the tinge of romantic nostalgia in his
account is unmistakeably present in Audrey Lucas's recollections as well.

> The weather was gloriously fine; a delightful sort of garden-
> party atmosphere prevailed; there was a wonderful cold lunch
> out of doors; and, of course, no lessons of any kind.
>
> Which side won I cannot remember; I should imagine the
> one lucky enough to have George Llewelyn Davies, captain of
> the Eton eleven, who, in his perfect flannels and pale blue cap,
> looked the most accomplished and handsome cricketer of
> them all.

Schoolgirls watched as cricketers young and old, skilful and un-
skilled, famous and unknown, battled with varying degrees of
success against one another. The school magazine recorded that
'Sir J. M. Barrie and Mr E. V. Lucas brought two elevens to play
a cricket match. They said it was to be their last, but they proved
themselves far too agile and keen to think of giving up the game'.
Mackail notes, however, that not all of the schoolgirls stayed
until the end of the game, which ended as a final triumph for the
Allahakbarries: even the lure of watching some of the country's
most famous authors and the handsome young George was not
enough to keep them enthralled. They trailed away to chatter
and play amongst themselves.

There was laughter in that last match, and superb exhibitions of incompetence; but henceforth there would only be memories in the summers that still remained.

Stumps. The bails were lifted and the stumps pulled from the ground for the final time. There was a photograph taken in the sunshine with Barrie in the centre staring unsmilingly at the camera, and Milne, at the end of the same row wearing a white scarf and stretching his flannelled legs out on to the turf to one side. After the match, both teams returned to London by train and ate a final banquet at the Savoy Hotel, which was now Barrie's regular dining place, since he had moved to nearby Adelphi Terrace. It was certainly more luxurious than the team's first dinner at The White Horse in Shere but there is no record as to which establishment Barrie preferred: the snob, of course, would have said the Savoy, and the sentimentalist most probably the country inn.

It was the end of the Allahakbarries. And it was also the final years of what later became known as the golden age of cricket. It is a curious coincidence that the dates of the golden age – 1890 to 1914 – are almost entirely the same as those of the Allahakbarries. The popular concept of the 'golden age' suggests a romantic vision of a tranquil and untroubled era that was suddenly blown apart by the war and everything that the war brought with it. The Allahakbarries' own history suggests that this was true up to a point, though the team had begun to unravel far before the notional end of the golden age and its final game was really an anomaly and a misrepresentation of its true history. But the golden age is also something of a myth. Derek Birley, in his authoritative *A Social History of English Cricket*, notes that many of the same cultural values that led to the First World War were a deeply embedded part of British culture and, indeed, of cricket itself. Britain was in large part at least as belligerent, nationalistic, competitive and aggressive as Germany in the years leading up to the war. And cricket was for the political establishment at least, the sport that most defined Britain. If 'the Battle of Waterloo was won on the playing fields of Eton', then Britain's long preparation for the First World War could similarly be said to have started on the cricket pitches of Britain's public schools. Cricket was a vital part of the cultural indoctrination of young men with concepts which miraculously transposed aspects of the game into a moral outlook: 'playing with a straight bat' being the most obvious one of these, representing the 'British belief' in fairness and decency. This was most memorably captured in Newbolt's poem 'Vitai Lampada', with the motif of 'Play up! Play up! And play the game!' running through it. The all-white dress of cricketers confirmed their status as angels of the empire. They became 'inspirational stereotypes embodying self-sacrificing service, personifying national nobility, justifying the grandeur of imperialism', something which was easily translated from the sports ground to the battlefield. And this was played out, by the rush to sign-up to the army at the onset of war from the young, leisured, cricketing classes, who in many cases saw the war not as something to be feared but instead as a great and joyous opportunity in the Newbolt tradition.

Cricket's pre-war age was also not viewed with quite such an uncritical gaze by those living at the time, including, as we have already seen, E. V. Lucas, who thought that the sport was suffering a terminal decline. Cricket has always been regarded with nostalgia ever since people began to write about it at the beginning of the nineteenth century: according to Birley, John Nyren and other traditionalists, for example, thought that cricket had been ruined by allowing round-arm bowling, while contemporary purists mourn the death of quality cricket due to the invention and popularity of the twenty-over game. It is a game in which people have always been particularly excited to talk about great past deeds than possible future ones; in Britain at least.

The golden age was a retrospective title given to the 1890s

and 1900s in the post-war years when cricket was part of a more general wistfulness about the period before the war. The cricket writer Neville Cardus, writing in the 1920s, was at the forefront of this fondness for romantic reminiscence; his account of the 1904 Gentlemen v. Players match a fine example of his style:

> Never since has such batsmanship been seen as this for opulence and prerogative; it was symbolical of the age's prestige. It occurred a year after the Coronation of Edward VII; and it was indeed coronation cricket, yet one more swaggering pageant reaching to a glittering horizon.

Cardus aligns cricket with wealth, luxury and the monarchy, exposing his characteristic weakness for sentimentality and journalistic cliché, as well as focusing attention on the fact that a 'golden age' is really about a celebration of the success of the wealthy rather than, say, the fact that cricket was 'better' at this time than any other. And the golden age is as much a fond memory of the gentleman amateur's predominant role in the cricket, as any comment on the quality of sport, which has had as many great heroes coming from brilliant teams in numerous decades since.

But the more long-lasting nostalgia about the game represents cricket as the game of a pre-lapsarian rural idyll, an idealised England of old, and the game is difficult, therefore, to conceive of being in the present or the future. The ideal (and stereotypical) English village always has a cricket green in the centre of it, with what Barrie called 'white figures on reasonable terms' knocking a leather ball with a willow bat. Barrie bought into and contributed to this cultural myth, and this sense of timelessness, of cricket always being in the past, is the precise same sentiment that runs through *Peter Pan*. Cricket for Barrie represented an earlier time where man was in harmony with nature, where there was all the time in the world for languidness on the boundary-edge, removed from the pressures of life and the particular burdens of modern post-industrial society. Cricket is the game of Neverland, the game which can never grow up, just as Peter is not only the child who can never grow up but an earlier version of mankind in the Garden of Eden. But that's why it's called Neverland, which marks Barrie out as more of a realist than he is often given credit for – it can never be; just as Utopia literally means 'nowhere place'. In real life, the Llewelyn Davies boys were growing up and cricket, far from being the fixed and idealised harmony of man and nature, was also growing up and had been doing so throughout its so-called golden age. By 1914 the age of the privileged gentleman amateur was waning and Neverland was giving way to No-Man's Land, from where cricket before the war could hardly be more golden.

# 10

## HAPPY DAYS LONG DEAD

*No Lord's this year: no silken lawns on which*
*A dignified and dainty throng meanders.*
*The schools take guard upon a fierier pitch*
*Somewhere in Flanders.*

*Bigger the cricket here: yet some who tried*
*In vain to earn a colour while at Eton,*
*Have found a place upon an England side*
*That can't be beaten*
                    E. W. Hornung, 'Lord's Leave'

Barrie and the boys filled out the pages of 'My Confession Book' at the start of 1914 which asked a series of questions intended to elicit answers of a personal nature. George, who had gone up to Cambridge in autumn 1912, was in a strange mood. To the question 'Your ideal man?' he answered 'The Kaiser'; to 'the most suitable place for a flirtation' he answered 'a lunatic asylum'; and to 'the most unselfish thing you could do', he wrote 'suicide'. Michael seemed in better spirits: he answered the question 'do you believe in spiritualism?' with 'Rather!' Barrie, meanwhile, when asked for his 'opinion on motor cars in general', wrote 'horrible'.

He had disliked motorised vehicles for many years, in keeping with his love of peaceful countryside and sentimentalism about the past, but this view did not extend to all modern technology. He was experimenting with cinema in the spring and summer of 1914 and he was transformed into an excited, and even rather naughty, schoolboy by the possibilities of this new medium. In July 1914 he did something which was more like the prank of a teenager than that of a baronet in his fifties. Five days after the assassination of Archduke Franz Ferdinand in Vienna on 28 June, a select, invited audience attended an evening of entertainment organised by Barrie which he called 'The Cinema Supper'. The guests were made up of the elite of London society including the prime minister, Herbert Asquith, and his wife. But what none of them knew is that Barrie had arranged to secretly film them and afterwards use the film as the back-drop to a music hall production he was intending to produce starring an erotic dancer from Paris called Gaby Deslys. 'A thirty-foot close-up of Prime Minister Asquith would, Barrie felt, make an original back-drop to one of Gaby's erotic dance routines', wrote Birkin. Of course, when Barrie's scheme was discovered, he soon received an angry letter from Downing Street and the idea had to be abandoned. Was madness creeping into Barrie's mind? Or perhaps it showed that the wildly imaginative, irreverent and juvenile spirit lived on in Barrie still; his age and the adversity he had faced had not knocked this out of him, yet.

Another of the Allahakbarries was knighted this summer: Milne's sometime nemesis, Owen Seaman, who during the war as Sir Owen Seaman, wrote patriotic poetry, 'reflecting the optimism and devotion to his native land rather than the stirrings of poetic genius', according to one critic.

Barrie, the boys – George, Peter and Michael – and Frohman went to Paris in July to see out the final days of the belle époque in a city that has always done decadence with more style and panache than London. They stayed at the grand Hotel Meurice, where Frohman had taken Barrie in 1904, and wore tail coats and white ties as they enjoyed fine dining and theatre as well as Barrie's personal favourite: going to the fairground to fling rings over hooks for prizes.

Later on in July, Barrie took the boys to the wilds of Scotland again for fishing and walking at Auch Lodge just north of Loch Lomond. Peter arrived later as he was on an Eton Officer Training Corp summer camp, while Jack, who was now a sub-lieutenant in the Royal Navy, was at sea.

On 30 July the great all-rounder Albert Trott shot himself aged forty-two at his lodgings just over two miles away from Lord's Cricket Ground where he had in 1899 hit the ball clean over the pavilion. Since his retirement from cricket he had been living in poverty, had continued to have problems with alcohol and was suffering with oedema (then called dropsy). Before he killed himself he wrote a will on the back of a laundry ticket, leaving four pounds and his wardrobe to his landlady.

A few (very wet) days later, on 4 August, Barrie had an inkling of what was about to happen when he wrote to his friend Lord Lucas (no relation to E. V.) from Scotland:

> We are so isolated from news here, that when I wrote last I was quite ignorant that Europe was in a blaze. . . . It seems awful to be up here at such a time catching fish, or not catching them, for it has rained four days and nights and is still at it, and all the world is spate and bog. . . . We occasionally get the morning paper in the evening and there may be big news to-day.

There was big news: Britain declared war on Germany that night. Denis Mackail wrote in his biography of Barrie that 'We know now that it was the end of a world which can never return again.' And just two days later, George, aged twenty-one, and Peter, aged seventeen, headed south to sign up. Barrie, left behind, wrote in his notebook:

> - The Last Cricket Match. One or two days before war declared – my anxiety and premonition – boys gaily playing cricket at Auch, seen from my window – I know they're to suffer – I see them dropping out one by one, fewer and fewer.

Rudyard Kipling's son John, the same age as Peter and known as Jack, left school to fight and E. W. Hornung's son, Oscar, signed up early too. He had left Eton at Easter, aged nineteen, and had been improving his knowledge of history before going up to Cambridge in the autumn. But very soon after war was declared he became a second lieutenant in the 2nd Essex Regiment, attached to the 3rd. He wrote to his uncle, Arthur Conan Doyle: 'I am waiting to go off any night now – I am longing to go – it is a chance for us chaps, isn't it? It is the one good thing the war has done – to give public school fellows a chance – they are the one class who are enjoying themselves in this war.' When he was out in the trenches he compared the fighting to 'putting your left leg to the ball at cricket'.

Peter later wrote of his experience of signing up with George. They went to Cambridge first where they were advised to go to Winchester to sign up for the King's Royal Rifles. They had just arrived at the barracks when

George had one of those queer turns, something between a fainting fit and a sick headache, to which he had been prone since childhood, and had to sit for a few minutes on a seat outside the barracks. I would willingly have turned tail and gone back to London humiliated but free. George however, the moment he recovered, marched me in with him through those dark portals. . .

Once inside they found their way into the office of a busy Lieutenant Colonel, who was commanding the 6th (Reserve) Battalion of the King's Royal Rifles, and who looked up from his papers and asked them, 'rather gruffly' what they wanted.

'Well – er – Sir, we were advised by Major Thornton to come here to ask about getting a commission – Sir,' said George.

'Oh, Bulger Thornton at Cambridge, eh? What's your name?'

'Davies, sir.'

'Where were you at school?'

'Eton, sir.'

'In the Corps?'

'Yes, sir, Sergeant.'

'Play any games? Cricket?'

'Well sir, actually, I managed to get my eleven.'

'Oh, you did, did you?'

The Colonel, who had played for Eton himself in his day, now became noticeably more genial, and by the time he had ascertained that George was the Davies who had knocked up a valuable 59 at Lord's (which knock he had himself witnessed with due appreciation) it was evident that little more need be said.

'And what about you, young man?' he asked, turning to me.

'Please, sir, I'm his brother' was the best I could offer in the way of a reference.

And so, after filling in a couple of forms, they were enlisted, though they had to wait to be gazetted and in the meantime went back to Scotland to do some more fishing with Barrie and their younger brothers.

Milne, in his autobiography, wrote that 'I should like to put in asterisks here, and then write: "It was in 1919 that I found myself once again a civilian." For it makes me almost physically sick to think of that nightmare of mental and moral degradation, the war.' He was not as enthusiastic to sign up as those such as Oscar Hornung, but then he was also not as young. Milne wrote:

To people like myself the Great Sacrifice was not the sacrifice of our lives but of our liberties. Ever since I had left Cambridge I had been my own master. I fixed my own hours, I was under no discipline; no bell rang for me, no bugle sounded. Now I was thirty-two, married, with a happy home of my own and engaged happily in work which I loved. To be a schoolboy again, to say 'Yes, sir' and 'No, sir' and 'Please, sir' and 'May I, sir?' was no hardship to schoolboys, no hardship to a million men in monotonous employment, but it was hell itself to one who had been as spoilt by good fortune as I.

First-class cricket had carried on during August but *The Times* stopped printing cricket scores and on 27 August a letter from W. G. Grace was published in the *Sportsman*:

> *Sir,*
> *There are many cricketers who are already doing their duty, but there are many more who do not seem to realise that in all probability they will have to serve either at home or abroad before the war is brought to a conclusion. The fighting on the continent is very severe, and will probably be prolonged. I think the time has arrived when the county cricket season should be closed for it is not fitting at a time like the present that able-bodied men should play day after day and pleasure-seekers look on. There are so many who are young and able, and yet are hanging back. I should like to see all first-class cricketers of a suitable age, etc., set a good example, and come to the help of their country without delay in its hour of need. – Yours, etc,*
> *W. G. Grace*

After the great man had spoken, Surrey were soon declared champions with two games still to play, and the season was wound up early, though it was not until January 1915 that the following season was cancelled. Plenty of first-class cricketers had already signed up and some senior members of the cricketing establishment, such as Plum Warner, helped to support the recruitment drive. Michael and Nico continued to go to school and they both played cricket there; in 1915, Michael batted nineteen innings and scored 304 runs of which fifty-four was his highest score, and had an average of 17.88. He was becoming a far better bowler, however, and that season his figures were: 230 overs, thirty-six maidens, 606 runs, sixty-nine wickets with an average of 8.78. In spite of everything else that was going on at the time, Barrie must have been delighted.

The government clearly felt that writers had a part to play in the war effort too. Barrie was invited to Wellington House in London, the headquarters of the new Propaganda Bureau, on 2 September 1914 along with many other writers including no less than six other members of the Allahakbarries: Conan Doyle, Maurice Hewlett, E. V. Lucas, A. E. W. Mason, Gilbert Murray and Owen Seaman. Thomas Hardy, G. K. Chesterton, H. G. Wells and John Buchan were among the others who turned up. Kipling and Quiller-Couch could not make it but expressed their willingness to help in whatever way they could. Conan Doyle, whose brother-in-law Malcolm Leckie had already gone missing (later confirmed killed) in the first battle of the war at Mons, was typically industrious and committed to the national cause and he quickly wrote *To Arms!* — a full-length statement of Britain's case for going to war, which was published as a penny pamphlet by Hodder and Stoughton at the end of September. In it he wrote: 'Happy the man who can die with the thought that in this greatest crisis of all he had served his country to the uttermost, but who could bear the thoughts of him who lives with the memory that he had shirked his duty and failed his country at the moment of her need?'

Ever since the Second Boer War he had insisted that Britain needed to be better prepared for future hostilities and wrote an article in 1912 entitled *Great Britain and the Next War* in response to General Friedrich von Bernhardi's book *Germany and the Next War*. In 1914 he was also determined to write a history of the war, which he hoped would become the officially sanctioned record of the conflict, though he had competition in the form of John Buchan, who had just written *The Thirty-Nine Steps*, and shared the same ambition as Conan Doyle. (In 1917 Buchan became the head of the newly created Department of Information and

Gilmour worked under him with special responsibility for cables, wireless, newspapers, magazines and the cinema.)

Barrie, meanwhile, had ideas other than writing and on 12 September he secretly and rather impetuously set off for America, with Mason, Gilmour and his manservant Harry Brown on what seemed to be a mission to persuade America to join the allies. But by the time he arrived in New York the secret had already leaked out, and he was rather humiliatingly forced to abandon his mission under pressure from the British Ambassador in Washington. He told reporters there that he had only gone to New York in order to see his friend and business associate Charles Frohman. Wodehouse was also in New York at the time, where he had been going regularly since 1909 when he had managed to sell two stories for the then remarkable sum of $500. He arrived on American shores on his latest visit on 2 August, two days before Britain declared war, and remained there for the rest of the conflict. According to his biographer Frances Donaldson, Wodehouse had such poor eyesight that 'there was no question of Plum being able to serve in any combatant force'. The only thing which appears to throw this statement into any doubt is Wodehouse's cricketing record: in 1911 playing for the Authors against the Publishers at Lord's he had managed to take four wickets and score sixty runs, and the following year he scored twenty-seven before rain stopped play. Donaldson writes that 'there was some criticism of Plum's conduct in not returning to England, and, although in retrospect it may seem a minor offence not to have abandoned his extraordinary career in the theatre if he could not serve, there is a censorious streak in Englishmen which dwells with satisfaction on other people's failure in war.' It certainly didn't help his cause when he courted controversy and faced allegations of being a traitor years later during the Second World War.

Barrie was back in London by the end of October and was working on a propaganda play called *Der Tag*, though when it came to be performed it was actually both rather dull and too sympathetic to the Germans for the taste at the time. 'Barrie's patriotism,' wrote Mackail, 'already and always, a bit too subtle and broad-minded – shall we say? – for the music-halls.' Barrie himself wrote that 'It was received with much applause, but it struck me that in their hearts the Coliseum audience thought it heavy food.'

After training with the 6th Battalion at Sheerness, George was posted to the 4th Battalion of the Rifle Brigade at the start of December. He took with him a copy of the book that he had helped to inspire as a young boy more than twelve years ago: *The Little White Bird*. Barrie wrote to him on 21 December: 'I'll write often and will be so glad of any line from you'. A whole series of letters between the two of them was first printed in Andrew Birkin's *J. M. Barrie and the Lost Boys*.

On 13 January 1915 George wrote to Barrie that 'The fear of death doesn't enter so much as I expected into this show' and later in the letter reassured him: 'Don't you get worried about me. I take every precaution I can, & shall do very well.' He was laid low by an illness in the following days but by 22 January he was writing to Barrie that 'I am now a young bull once again, & ready for our next show. We shall be in the trenches again either tomorrow night or the night after.' His uncle, Guy du Maurier, who was a Lieutenant Colonel, was stationed just a few miles away and in a letter to his wife, he mentioned some of the horrors of the war.

> All the filth of an Army lies around rotting. . . . The stink is awful. There are many dead Highlanders just in front – killed in December I think – and they aren't pleasant. . . . When we've done our four days I'll try and go over and see George who I think is only two miles off.

Barrie sent more than just letters. On 14 February he wrote to George, who was heading back to the trenches, to tell him that a hamper from Fortnum and Mason was on its way to him and that Mary Hodgson was sending him some fresh underwear too. 'I can understand that getting ready to go back is uncommonly like "putting on your pads"', he wrote. Pads wouldn't have helped. George sustained a minor wound to his leg that night though he did not mention it to Barrie in his next letter. On 20 February the hamper arrived and George sent his thanks: 'We are a grateful party of officers, & shall be in clover for the six days' rest that is coming. It is good of you.' Barrie's reply, written on 28 February, promised books and a further hamper and ended with the line: 'The one great doing for me is when we are all together again. Loving J.M.B.'

George wrote on 7 March to tell Barrie that he had seen a 'violent death within a yard of me', and by the time Barrie replied to him on 11 March he had the unpleasant duty of relaying to George the fact that Guy du Maurier had been killed. Barrie described him as 'One of the most attractive personalities I have ever known'. (A couple of years later he cruelly described his death to Jack's wife, Geraldine, in his Adelphi flat saying that du Maurier had 'wandered about the battlefield for half-an-hour with his stomach hanging out, begging somebody to finish him off.') Now more anxious than ever about George's welfare, he poured his heart out to him in this, the final letter from Barrie which George read:

> I don't have any little iota of desire for you to get military glory. I do not care one farthing for anything of the kind, but I have the one passionate desire that we may all be together again once at least. You would not mean a featherweight more to me tho' you came back a General. I just want yourself. There may be some moments when a knowledge of all you are to me will make you a little more careful, and so I can't help going on saying these things.
>
> It was terrible that man being killed next to you, but don't be afraid to tell me of such things. You see it at night I fear with painful vividness. I have lost all sense I ever had of war being glorious, it is just unspeakably monstrous to me now. Loving J.M.B.

George replied to the letter. He tried to cheer Barrie up as he could see that he was terrified. 'Keep your heart up, Uncle Jim, & remember how good an experience like this is for a chap who's been very idle before.' But by the time his letter reached London, George was already dead. He was killed on 15 March 1915. Aubrey Tennyson wrote to Peter with all the details he could find out about his death.

*The battalion was advancing to drive the Germans out of St Eloi . . . Stopford Sackville was marching alongside of George part of the way up, & he says he fancied George had a sort of premonition that he was going to be killed & said that he hoped that they would not take him back into one of the villages behind but would bury him outside his own trench, & that he considered it was the finest death one could die & he wished to be buried where he fell. He was the first officer to be shot that night. The Colonel was talking to all C Company officers before the attack was made, & George was sitting on a bank with the others, when he was shot through the head, & died almost immediately, so that he can have felt nothing. It was impossible to comply with his wishes & bury him there, [so] they took him back and buried him in a field on the left of the road . . . outside Voormezeele . . . and they took a lot of trouble making the grave look nice and planting it with violets.*

George was twenty-one years old and Barrie, of course, was completely shattered by the news. 'This dreadful war will get them all in the end', he cried when he heard of George's death. Two days after finding out the news he had the added torture of receiving George's last letter to him, in which he urged Barrie to 'carry on with your job of keeping up your courage'.

A fortnight later, he wrote to his friend Charles Turley Smith.

*Just a word to say what you will like to know, that George*
*was killed instantaneously. It was a night attack. I had a letter*
*from him two days after I knew he was dead. This is now the*
*common lot. I feel painfully for Peter between who and George*
*there was a devotion not perhaps very common among brothers.*

It was indeed the common lot. Tens of thousands of dead
young men were piling up in the muddy trenches. Thirty-three
men from the tiny villages of Shere and Gomshall in Surrey,
where the Allahakbarries had first played, died in action during
the war. In July, Oscar Hornung was killed in action near
Ypres, and in October Kipling's son John fell at the Battle of
Loos. The following year Richard Marriott-Watson, the only
son of one of the founding Allahakbarries, H. B. Marriott-
Watson, was killed, along with Gilmour's eldest son and E. V.
Lucas's brother, Percival, who had played in the final game in
1913. Barrie wrote to Turley Smith: 'You may have seen that
E. V.'s brother Percival, who sometimes played cricket with us,
was killed in the "push". He had George's revolver and field
glasses which are again without an owner. In a recent letter to
E. V. he said he didn't see how one could escape. Peter is out
there in the thick of it. Life is forlorn despite the gaiety of the
newspaper press.'

Barrie's grief must have been further deepened by a number
of other significant deaths in 1915. Many of the major figures in
his life before the war were now falling around him. On 4 April
the great Middlesex and England captain of the 1890s, and
sometime reserve batsman for the Allahakbarries, A. E. Stoddart,
shot himself at his home near Lord's after struggling with debt
and poor health for a number of years. He was fifty-two.

At around the same time Barrie was trying to persuade his
great friend and theatrical mentor Charles Frohman to come to
London. He agreed and set off from New York on board the
*Lusitania*. But the boat never arrived: on 7 May it was torpedoed

by a U-boat and sank. One hundred and twenty-four people died, including Frohman. A survivor said that his last words had been: 'Why fear death? It is the greatest adventure in life', which struck Barrie, and many others, as being a paraphrase, deliberate or otherwise, of Peter Pan's famous words: 'To die will be an awfully big adventure.' In an article he wrote about Frohman in the *Daily Mail* a few days later Barrie referred to him as 'The man who never broke his word'.

And in October W. G. Grace also died. He had suffered a mild stroke at his home in Mottingham, south-east London, on 9 October, but while in bed recuperating he became increasingly upset by the German Zeppelin raids which were by now taking place over the city (Conan Doyle called them the 'Zeppelin murderers'). The ex-Surrey and England captain Henry Leveson-Gower visited him and joked about how the Zeppelins were nothing compared to the generations of fast bowlers that Grace had dispatched to the boundary time after time. 'I could see those beggars,' W.G. replied, 'I can't see these.' In a fit of agitation during a raid on the night of 13 October he fell heavily and ten days later died of a heart attack. Conan Doyle wrote in his obituary in *The Times* that 'The world will be the poorer to many of us for the passing of the greatest of cricketers'.

Conan Doyle romanticised Grace as not just a great cricketer but as a personification of British chivalry and decency.

> Those who know him will never look at the classic sward of Lord's without an occasional vision of the great cricketer. He was, and will remain, the very impersonation of cricket, redolent of fresh air, of good humour, of conflict without malice, of chivalrous strife, of keenness for victory by fair means, and utter detestation of all that was foul. Few men have done more for the generation in which he lived, and his influence was none the less because it was a spontaneous and utterly unconscious one.

Amongst all the deaths there was also a discordant, comic birth of sorts: P. G. Woodehouse's character Jeeves, the highly knowledgeable and infinitely resourceful manservant, made his first appearance in September 1915 in the story 'Extricating Young Gussie', first published in the American *Saturday Evening Post* and later in the *Strand* magazine. Wodehouse had taken his name from the Warwickshire all-round cricketer, Percy Jeeves, who also died in action the following year.

Almost surprisingly there was genuine heroism and bravery too amongst all the demoralising death and quagmire of front-line despair. Hesketh Prichard, the writer, explorer, big-game hunter and cricketer who had played for Barrie's side, felt sure that he could be of use in the war effort, but was not accepted for combat duty because he was seen as being too old at thirty-seven. He eventually secured the post of assistant press officer at the War Office and then in February 1915 he was sent to the front lines as an 'eyewitness officer', looking after war correspondents. While he was there he used his considerable expertise with rifles to improve the standard of weapons and sights being used by snipers. He begged and borrowed weapons from friends at home. And he began to improve marksmanship and campaign for more to be done. By September he had taken on a role training snipers and by November he was in high demand from many units who had heard about his work. He not only improved marksmanship but also trench defences. The British trenches were cut with a straight line but Prichard realised that this made it easy for soldiers' heads to be spotted by enemy snipers looking over the parapet. So he recommended irregular parapets instead. He developed 'dummy heads' with periscopes to make it easier to spot enemy snipers and he picked snipers off himself with the same skill that he had staked out and shot moose and caribou before the war. By December he had been made a captain and in August the following year he founded the First Army School of Sniping in the village of Linghem, Pas-de-Calais. In October he was awarded the Military Cross and in November 1916 he was promoted to major. The citation for his medal read: 'For conspicuous gallantry and devotion to duty. He has instructed snipers in the trenches on many occasions, and in most dangerous circumstances, with great skill and determination. He has, directly and indirectly, inflicted enormous casualties on the enemy.' Prichard, as a talented amateur, had made a huge impact on a professional army in a way which was inconceivable in future conflicts, cutting down the deaths from snipers from five a week per battalion to forty-four in six months, across sixty battalions. He worked hard and found it exhausting but he still tried to play cricket when he could. He organised a match between the sniping school and the signalling school in France on 12 July 1917, the anniversary of a famous Gentlemen v. Players match at Lord's in 1904. Prichard had played that day but in 1917 he pretended to the opposition that he did not have the slightest idea about how to play cricket. His side were bowled out for forty-two but thanks to his bowling they still managed to win by three runs. 'The little officer, whom, by the way, I asked which leg to put the pad on, was flabbergasted!'

Milne had a relatively easy and carefree start to the war in the manner of his life so far. In August 1915 he was sent to Weymouth in Dorset to the Southern Command Signalling School, and then to the Isle of Wight where he lived with Daphne, his wife. It was a long way from the front line. But in the summer of 1916 he went to the bloody Battle of the Somme and remained there until he was invalided home in November with a fever. As a signals officer he did not, as he put it, have to 'fire a shot in anger', and he did not return to the front for the rest of the conflict: he became an instructor on the Isle of Wight, and lived with his wife once more. He later worked in the War Office, writing propaganda. But despite the fact he had seen relatively little action, the war had an impact on him nonetheless: he became a far more bitter man than he had been before, as shown in his poem 'O.B.E.':

I know a Captain of Industry,
Who made big bombs for the R.F.C.,
And collared a lot of £ s. d. –
And he – thank God! – has the O.B.E.


I know a Lady of Pedigree,
Who asked some soldiers out to tea,
And said 'Dear me!' and 'Yes, I see' –
And she – thank God! – has the O.B.E.


I know a fellow of twenty-three,
Who got a job with a fat M.P.
(Not caring much for the Infantry.)
And he – thank God! – has the O.B.E.


I had a friend; a friend, and he
Just held the line for you and me,
And kept the Germans from the sea,
And died – without the O.B.E. Thank God!
He died without the O.B.E.


But in April 1917, largely thanks to Barrie, Milne successfully set out on what for the next ten years or so was the main
work of his writing career, as a dramatist, when his two-act
comedy play *Wurzel-Flummery* appeared on a bill with two
one-act plays of Barrie's. The play revolves around the idea that
in order to inherit £50,000 the inheritors must change their
name to Wurzel-Flummery. How far will people go for money?
Milne got thirty pounds a week for the eight weeks of its West
End run.

Elizabeth Lucas founded an orphanage and hospital with
Barrie's financial help at the Chateau Bettancourt, near Reims in
France, in 1915 in order to give a home for the lost French boys
and girls who were emerging from the debris of the war. Barrie

contributed £2,000 to start the scheme and visited it that summer, writing to Gilmour on 26 July 26 that:

> You can hear the guns from Reims direction in the north. . . . One boy had a leg blown off by a shell at Reims. His parents wept to see him but they bored him – so he wandered off to play. A significant note – The drummer went round the other night to warn the villagers all dogs must be chained up at nights. This because the dogs have developed a grim hunt for bodies which they scrape up in the night.

Turley Smith worked there as an orderly for a few months in 1916 and recorded a perhaps surprising but surely not untypical experience of the consequences of war: 'never since the war began have I been so near to happiness and the reason is that I have never had time to think, and have been at work all of every day.' However, Bettancourt closed in 1917; Lucas had fallen ill from exhaustion caused by looking after the orphanage and could no longer run it.

Peter Llewelyn Davies became eligible to fight after he had turned nineteen in February 1916 and that summer he took part in the Battle of the Somme. He was invalided home after two months suffering from eczema and shell-shock. He wrote to Barrie that:

> Not long ago I can remember rather looking forward to taking part in a fight. My curiosity has been satisfied, and I shall never have any such desire again. Honestly, Uncle Jim, I can't write about it – I don't believe anyone could, and I'm not particularly anxious than anyone should. There isn't a single attractive feature from beginning to end.

After he had recovered he went back to the front again; he gained a Military Cross and survived the war, though the memories of it lasted for the rest of his life. The poet Siegfried Sassoon later lived in the same house in Campden Hill Square in Kensington, number 23, which had been the home of the

Llewelyn Davies boys from 1910 to 1918, when Nico and Michael went to live with Barrie in his Adelphi flat. Sassoon did write about the very horrors of war which Peter was unwilling to, and he also helped his friend Wilfred Owen with one of the most famous war poems, the 'Anthem for Doomed Youth', written in 1917, which begins with the lines:

> What passing-bells for these who die as cattle?
> Only the monstrous anger of the guns.

Doomed youth is remembered in another famous poem, by Laurence Binyon, called 'For the Fallen', an extract from which, 'The Ode of Remembrance', has been used for remembrance days ever since. There is something of *Peter Pan* in the most regularly quoted lines from the poem, something of Barrie's attempt to find solace in life from the idea of eternity. The young soldiers who died in the war were also boys who could not grow up.

> They shall grow not old, as we that are left grow old:
> Age shall not weary them, nor the years condemn.
> At the going down of the sun and in the morning
> We will remember them. We will remember them.

Conan Doyle was exhausted by his vigorous efforts in writing his history of the war – an epic six volume tome – as well as his increasing forays into spiritualism and other activities. By the summer of 1917 he was in bed with a serious case of flu, which was probably the same pandemic strain that went on to kill millions. He soon after started recording his dreams and in one of them he was opening the batting in an important cricket match: Catholics v. Protestants. He was playing for the Catholics and batted well, though he was eventually run out in strange circumstances. He had to run up a hill slowly and awkwardly and he told the wicketkeeper that this was wrong. There was no umpire and the wicket was marked on a wooden cross that stood at right angles to the pitch. All the old certainties of cricket had been replaced by what Andrew Lycett called 'a mad Alice in Wonderland-type game'.

Conan Doyle's brother, Innes, and his son, Kingsley, both survived the fighting but both succumbed to the Spanish flu pandemic which swept across the world in 1918–19 and killed three times as many people as had died as a direct consequence of warfare in the past four years.

'We jog along here, not very gaily', wrote Barrie to Turley Smith in March, 1918. 'Peter has just gone back from a fortnight's leave. Michael is editing the *Eton Chronicle* and contributing leaders and poems galore.' The following month Barrie also wrote something which sounds as though it came from a dream in a letter to his Godson, and son of Captain Scott, Peter Scott, who was at school in France. It is a nightmare about being literally the very last person left in London, and consciously or not is full of anxiety, though it was clearly also intended to be funny (Peter was just nine years old).

> My dear Peter,
> Your mother thinks I do not write clearly, but I expect this jealousy. It is funny to think of your being at a French school, parelez-vous-ing with big guns firing and bells ringing and hooters hooting. What a lot you will have to tell me when we meet again. Michael and Nicholas are here just now, and tomorrow we are going to Wales for ten days. Michael won the competition at Eton for flinging the cricket ball farthest. Peter is where the fighting is heaviest, near Amiens. I think Brown [Barrie's manservant] will have to go and be a fighter now as he is under fifty. It will be queer if I am the only person left in London and have to cook the food and kill the cow and drive the bus. It will be rather difficult for me to be the engine-driver and guard at the same time and also take the tickets and sweep the streets and sell balloons at every corner and hold up my

*hand like a policeman to stop the traffic every time a taxi comes
along. Then I shall also have to be the person inside the taxi at
the same time as I am sitting outside driving it, and if I run
over anybody it will have to be myself, and I will have to take
my own number and carry myself on a stretcher to the hospital
and I will need to be at both ends of the stretcher at once. Also
I will have to hurry on in front of the stretcher so as to be the
doorkeeper when the stretcher arrives, and how can I be the
doorkeeper when I have to be the doctor, and how can I be the
doctor when I have to be the nurse? You see I am going to have
a very busy time, and I expect that a letter from you would
cheer me up. I will have to be the postman who delivers it.
Your loving Barrie.*

His fear of being left alone was exacerbated by the fact that
Michael, who was eighteen on 16 June 1918, would soon be
eligible to enlist. But Barrie was actually in Paris with Gilmour
and surrounded by cheering, happy people on the streets when
the Armistice was signed on 11 November 1918, the day before
Michael was due to join up: 'I don't think he will be wanted for
the army now', he wrote in a letter with obvious relief.

At the start of December Barrie sent a letter to the actress
Maude Adams, who had played Peter Pan in America between
1905 and 1915:

I was in Paris at the time the Armistice was signed, and one
thing I shall never forget. It was not the celebrations, it was
the change that had come on all faces. On the 10th they were
as heavy with care as in all the four years, and on the morning
of the 11th they were all happy faces. The universal cry was
not 'We have won,' but 'It is finished!' . . .

I don't tell you what a melancholy person I grow lest it
should disturb your kind heart. I feel very much like drift-wood
flowing on the bank with one foot only in the water. But I
have had a good time – long ago.

# 11

## A FINAL INNINGS FOR
## THE ALLAHAKBARRIES

Courage is the thing. All goes if courage goes . . . Be not
merely courageous, but light-hearted and gay.

> J. M. Barrie, 'Courage', 1922

———————

B arrie was agonisingly aware that it was his generation which
had started the war but it was their children who had died
fighting it: fifteen million of them altogether, across all nations.
And all, so it seemed, for very little positive result ('The war has
done at least one big thing,' said Barrie, 'it has taken spring out
of the year'). In November 1919 he had been elected as the rector
of St Andrews University, and was obliged to give an address to
the students at some point during his three-year tenure. He
started scribbling notes in his notebooks on the subject of his
talk. 'Age (wisdom) failed', he wrote, 'Now let us see what youth
(audacity) can do.' Elsewhere he wrote that 'New may be better
than Old. We can't be sure that they are wrong and we are right
– *we who seem to have made the greatest mess of things that has ever
been made in the history of the world.*'

This notion was not just being developed in Barrie's mind. In
literature the old was certainly giving way to the new in the post-
war years and already, and increasingly so over the next two decades
of jazz, trades unionism and economic depression, writers such as

Barrie and Conan Doyle, and even the much younger A. A. Milne, came to be seen not just as old-fashioned and sentimental but utterly irrelevant too. In Jerome K. Jerome's biography, Joseph Connolly wrote that 'In the twenties, it was felt, his [Barrie's] particular brand of artifice was no longer required.' James Joyce's *Ulysses* and T. S. Eliot's *The Wasteland*, generally considered to be two of the most important modernist works in English, were both published in 1922. The new writers also included D. H. Lawrence and Virginia Woolf and they in turn looked for inspiration not among authors such as those members of the Allahakbarries, but in Dostoyevsky, Proust, Ibsen and Nietzsche. Literary modernism was already sweeping away the work of what came to be seen as those rather whimsical, parochial and self-indulgent Edwardian writers. It is a trend that has continued ever since and an image that persists. None of the work of the Allahakbarries forms the mainstay of academic study though much of it, and particularly Sherlock Holmes and *Peter Pan*, as well as Jeeves and Winnie-the-Pooh, has remained extraordinarily popular. Academic literary departments have instead been dominated by what have been seen as more serious and influential writers from the period such as Conrad and Forster. In his notes, though, Barrie appears happy to be a target to be knocked down by the younger generations.

> Great thing to form own opinion, don't accept hearsay. Try to get at what you really see in it all. Question authority. Question accepted views, values, reputations. Don't be afraid to be among the rebels. . . . Speak scornfully of the Victorian age. Of Edwardian age. Of last year. Of old-fashioned writers like Barrie, who accept old-fangled ideas.

It was difficult to be alive after the First World War; those young men who survived had to confront their own guilt about the fact that they had lived where so many others had died. And tens of thousands of families had to cope with the loss of their sons, brothers and fathers. Many of the Allahakbarries were old now, most of them had lost people they loved, and few had any appetite for playing cricket, though with time those days where they did enjoy playing in cricket matches became the subject of fond reminiscence for some of them. But the world had changed.

In 1918 Barrie wrote a one-act play called *A Well-Remembered Voice*. In the play a mother, Mrs Don, arranges séances in order to speak to her son, Dick (based on George Llewelyn Davies), who had recently died in the war. One night, after another attempt to speak to her son has not worked, she goes off to bed disappointed and full of grief, but Mr Don (based on Barrie) remains, sat on a hard wooden settle in the inglenook fireplace, trying to read his newspaper. However, he soon hears the 'well-remembered voice' of his son, who talks to him about 'the veil' that is what seems to hang between life and death, obscuring the one from the other. (In a letter to Elizabeth Lucas, Barrie wrote that 'the veil that separates the survivors and the killed must be getting very thin'.) These types of reunion were becoming a more and more regular feature of Conan Doyle's waking life, and during 1918 and 1919 he claimed to have communicated with his dead brother, Innes, and son, Kingsley, via a medium. The American John Dickson Carr, in his biography of Conan Doyle, suggests that people were almost universally surprised by Conan Doyle's commitment to spiritualism. 'This fellow had bowled W. G. Grace. He had bowled W. G. Grace: which, in America, corresponded to striking out Ty Cobb with three pitched balls. He could make a three-figure break at billiards, or hold his own against any amateur heavyweight. He had created Sherlock Holmes. For a quarter of a century he had loomed thick-shouldered as the sturdy Briton, with no damned nonsense about him. What was wrong? What ailed the man?'

Carr is being deeply ingenuous here for dramatic effect as he knew that Conan Doyle had been interested in spiritualism for many years, though after the First World War it did become nothing less than his greatest mission in life to bring spiritualism to as many people around the world as possible. But Carr does also capture what many people thought about Conan Doyle: how could a man of such clear reason hold such irrational beliefs? However, particularly with so many recently bereaved people, there was a huge amount of interest in the possibility of communicating with spirits. 'The war has brought so many tragedies to our doors that those waiting to hear the fatal knock sometimes forget that the other partings are going on also', wrote Barrie to a bereaved friend in 1919. Conan Doyle gave a talk on the subject of spiritualism to six thousand people in Glasgow, though his wife noted that another six thousand would have listened if there had been room for them. Of course, despite its popularity, spiritualism was also extremely controversial, but Conan Doyle was determined to win over sceptics, most notably the escapologist Harry Houdini, and in order to do so he toured Britain, America and Australia, and wrote extensively on the subject. This obsession also explicitly demonstrated the strange and complex double sidedness of Conan Doyle's character. On the one side: a qualified medical doctor, the creator of the brilliantly logical Sherlock Holmes, a belligerent propagandist for the war and a knight of the realm. On the other: a man of unconventional spiritual beliefs, who fell for the Cottingley fairies hoax in 1920 (a reminder of Peter Pan's question to the audience: 'Do you believe in fairies?'), and railed against all kinds of orthodoxies and rational materialism. He ultimately recommended that all police forces should have a psychic working for them. In 1926 *Punch* published a cartoon of Sir Conan Doyle drawn by Sir Bernard Partridge, with an accompanying poem:

> Your own creation, that great sleuth
> Who spent his life in chasing Truth –
> How does he view your late defiance
> (O Arthur!) of the laws of science?

Barrie may have been willing to use séances as a dramatic device, but he did not believe in the possibility of communicating with the dead. When he and Conan Doyle were together, which

was infrequently (though they remained on friendly terms) Barrie's friends feared that Conan Doyle might suggest to Barrie that he could help him to speak to some of his (many) dead loved ones. They feared this even more after the death of Michael in 1921, just a few weeks before his twenty-first birthday.

Michael had always had a close relationship with Barrie and was becoming an exceptional writer himself. Ever since Barrie first made his promise to Michael that he would write to him every day after Michael had been homesick in his first term at Eton, the letters had continued, and carried on even when Michael went to Oxford. The number of letters between the two eventually ran into the thousands, though almost all of them were later destroyed by Peter Llewelyn Davies, who wrote that he found them unbearable. In the summer of 1920, Barrie had rented an entire island off the Scottish west coast, called Eilean Shona, and took Michael and Nico, some of their friends from Eton and Oxford, and Elizabeth and Audrey Lucas (E. V. had by this time split from his wife) for the traditional long summer holiday. Eilean Shona was, according to Barrie in a letter to his secretary, Cynthia Asquith, 'A wild, rocky, romantic island.' Michael wrote an extraordinarily accomplished sonnet while he was there before returning to Oxford in the autumn. The writer Lytton Strachey called Michael 'the only young man at Oxford or Cambridge with real brains.' But he had a dark side too, which Barrie recognised when he called him 'the dark and dour and impenetrable', and he also acknowledged, in a letter to Elizabeth Lucas, that 'few have suffered from the loss of a mother as he has done.'

The following year, on the evening of 19 May 1921, a date which would once have meant that the cricket season was about to begin for the Allahakbarries, Barrie had written his daily letter to Michael and was on his way to post it when he was approached by a newspaper reporter who asked Barrie for some further facts about the drowning. But Barrie didn't know anything about any drowning. He didn't know that Michael and his friend Rupert Buxton had sunk beneath the surface of Sandford Pool on the River Thames just south of Oxford earlier that day. This was the way that he found out the terrible truth. After the realisation had sunk in he staggered back to his flat, shocked to the core by the news, and was later joined by Peter, Gerald du Maurier and Cynthia Asquith after he had telephoned them all to tell them what had happened. Barrie was utterly distraught, was drowning in sorrow, and could not be comforted. This was the worst of all the many tragedies he had to face in his life. According to Denis Mackail, 'He never got over it. It altered and darkened everything for the rest of his life . . . The wound that was dealt him on that fatal day was one that could never heal.'

The inquest recorded a verdict of accidental drowning though the suspicion remained that it had been a suicide pact (Nico said that 'I've always had something of a hunch that Michael's death was suicide'). Jackie Wullschläger compared Michael's life with that of Alistair Grahame, the son of *The Wind in the Willows* author Kenneth Grahame, who she grouped with Barrie, Milne and others as being a 'fantasy writer' (Milne later adapted *The Wind in the Willows* into a successful play).

> Kenneth Grahame's twenty-year-old son Alastair, who made his suicide look like an accident on a railway line, died exactly a year before Michael, also at Oxford. Each was born in 1900, each had been the centre of hope and love of a great children's writer, and each had grown up in the shadow of masterpieces for and about childhood which had fixed the mood of the Edwardian age. In a sense, they were as much victims of the cult of glorious youth as the wartime casualties; young men

suffused in a personal sense by the dream of eternal boyhood, boys to whom Barrie and Grahame transferred their own ideals of childhood, and for whom adulthood seemed impossible to face.

This seems a rather glib conclusion, but there is clearly more than an element of truth to the fact that the idea of eternal boyhood had been a part of Michael's life for as long as he could remember (*Peter Pan* was first performed when he was four years old). The belief in youth, though, as we have clearly seen, was not just expressed through Barrie's memorable play but through a whole culture, of which cricket was a major part, which praised boys and young men in particular before they were carelessly tossed to their deaths in the First World War. Wullschläger seems to suggest that Michael committed suicide because he could not bear to grow up, or perhaps because he had seen the terrible results, or the hypocrisy therein, of a culture that had sent his older brother, so inescapably linked with the character of *Peter Pan*, to his grave. That may well be true but the suggestion that Michael was a victim of 'the cult of glorious youth' when the precise circumstances of his death are not entirely clear, makes this seem a rather polemical twisting of facts to suit an argument.

Cynthia Asquith came to Barrie's rescue in the days and weeks following Michael's death, helping him when he needed it most and was actually at greatest risk of committing suicide himself. He had no appetite for organising a summer holiday that year so Asquith suggested that he go to her childhood home (her father was the 11th Earl of Wemyss), Stanway House, a grand, gabled Jacobean mansion in the Cotswolds with a spectacular Inigo Jones gatehouse, just a few miles from Broadway. Nestled just below the Cotswolds escarpment and built in warm, honey-coloured Cotswold limestone, with two large lawns suitable for croquet and informal games of cricket, and 'the restful shabbiness, dignified dilapidation of a quite unmodernised, much lived-in family home', it was a place which became a much-loved hideaway of Barrie's over the summer months for the following decade. Asquith's parents went to Scotland every summer and so left the house free, but even she was not prepared for the alacrity with which Barrie not only became a visitor to the house but the host there as well, inviting many friends, old and new. That first year Charles Whibley and E. V. Lucas were the only two members of the Allahakbarries to visit, but over the following ten years various others followed including Conan Doyle, Birrell, Gilmour, Seaman and Mackail. John Galsworthy and H. G. Wells were among the other guests, Wells sporting a particularly natty croquet outfit which consisted of a stripy 'zebra' T-shirt (very outré in the 1920s) and a beret.

Although Barrie always thought of Michael and dreamt and wrote about him, and although he was never quite the same man again, he did begin to slowly emerge from his torment. He began to play and have fun again, though it is likely that this was more from memory and even habit than anything else, and with the abandon of a man for whom nothing matters very much anymore ('*Peter Pan* is rather bleached bones to me in these twilight days', he wrote to Turley Smith in his later years). This was play as a diversion from grief, rather than as a celebration and enjoyment of life. There was a new game at Stanway, which he fell in love with, though, called shuffleboard or shovelboard: an elaborate version of shove ha'penny. Stanway House had an eight-yard-long antique shuffleboard: a vast, ancient and highly polished oak table marked with two lines which players aimed to propel their brass discs across without falling off the sides or into the gutter at the end. Barrie very quickly became an expert at it and according to Asquith he 'enjoyed many exultant hours at the long disused shovelboard. I heard it said that he looked younger and younger, and, in truth, with each disk sped on its triumphant way he did seem to throw off a year or two.'

There was cricket too, both on the lawn and at the village cricket pitch just across the lane from the house. It must have felt, particularly being so close to Broadway, that it was a throw-back to the old days, yet Barrie does not once seem to have contemplated a reprise of the Allahakbarries. Perhaps because George had played in that last game before the war and how could the team possibly play again after what had happened to him, and others? The spell that had made the venues of the Allahakbarries games into a Neverland had been broken. Instead he played informal lawn cricket (of a standard far lower, even, than that of the Allahakbarries) with scratch teams of whoever could be persuaded to play: children of all ages from the local village, guests and members of staff at the house. Even Millie the nursery maid was called on to play; in fact Asquith calls her 'the keenest of all our players.' She was an intrepid fielder and would stop the ball with whatever part of her body seemed most appropriate at the time. Asquith recalls a conversation between Barrie and Millie where he asked: 'Why didn't you stop that ball with your hand, Millie, instead of with your head?' To which she replied that 'My head seemed to come more handy, sir.'

Charles Whibley was one of the few who could not be coerced into playing cricket this time; he felt his time of running after cricket balls had gone. Instead he appointed himself scorer and match referee and sat in the shade of a tree and watched the others. Asquith recalled that Barrie 'would bowl the gentlest, most enticing daisy-cutters' to small children, but 'to their elders he would send down those wily googlies for which as Captain of the Allahakbarries he had been renowned.' She writes that in 1924 these cunning deliveries of Barrie's enabled him to achieve something which he hadn't done with the Allahakbarries: he took a hat-trick, that is, three wickets in consecutive deliveries. However, a letter that Barrie wrote to Mary de Navarro in Broadway suggests that this actually took place in 1923. Since he started spending summers at Stanway, Barrie had started to see his old foes again from the Broadway 'test matches' of 1897–99, the de Navarros. In 1922 they had sent him a copy of his old cricket book from

1899 (he had lost his copy many years previously) and he wrote
in August to invite them to dinner with him at Stanway:

*My dear Tony,*
*It is delightful of you to send me that copy of the old cricket*
*booklet, which I see I was sent some time ago but only reached*
*me now. I am here again and trying to see you. Could you*
*both come out to dinner on Thursday (8-15)? I wish so much*
*you would, and there are others also wanting to greet you.*

Then the following year, in September, he wrote in a postscript to Mary that, 'Yes, I knew my hat trick would be a bitter
pill and nauseous draught for you.' This was a reprise of that
mock-combative relationship between the two which had begun
so many years earlier and had always found its purest expression
in battle by cricket. Yet in general Barrie is far more subdued in
his letters to the de Navarros than he had been twenty-five years
previously; he's also rather reflective and melancholic too as seen
in the body of the letter in which he writes about the hat-trick.
'You once read a little thing of mine (now lost) called "The Dead
Donkey". Grand. It was about myself.'

Asquith relates that in 1923 there was 'a complication' with the
Stanway summer due to the fact that 'to Barrie's embarrassment
and annoyance, his sometime wife, Mrs Cannan, who, according
to Elizabeth Lucas – deaf to the lesson of Dear Brutus – hankered
after a "Second Chance", had taken up for the summer a strat-
egical position at Broadway. Consequently, Broadway, which is only
five miles off, was put strictly out of bounds. In no circumstances,
Barrie adjured me, must anyone from Stanway ever go there.'

Mary's second marriage, to Gilbert Cannan, had fallen apart in
1917 when Cannan had first seduced their maid and then ran off
with another woman. He had been a promising novelist and was
friends with D. H. Lawrence among others. But he had also suffered
with mental problems for some time and in 1923 he was put in an
asylum where he remained for the rest of his life. Barrie did not

go back to Mary but he did give her an annual allowance. She lived most of the rest of her life in France and died in Biarritz in 1950.

Nico Llewelyn Davies recalled the story of Barrie's hat-trick, which took place on the picturesque cricket field just a short walk from the house, between an XI of Nico's old Eton friends (the youngest of the Llewelyn Davies boys, he was now twenty years old) and a local village side. Barrie was not even meant to be playing, according to Nico.

> The last match we played there I was fielding somewhere near to where Uncle Jim was sitting and he said 'I think I'd like to have a bowl'. 'Why not', I said. Of course he was in his Homburg hat and his brown suit and so on; we all had yellow caps which he gave us and so I gave him his yellow cap and he walked out on the field and believe it or not he took a hat-trick. He was a very very slow bowler – he said he was the only slow bowler – because he was the only one who bowled so slowly that if he didn't like the look of it he could go after it and get it back!

Asquith, perhaps rather unkindly, suggests that there may have been some co-operation 'from batsman, wicket-keeper and umpire'. But even so, cricket is such an elaborate game that batsmen can struggle to get out even when they try to; and it is certainly far harder to take three wickets in three balls with the opposition's help, than it is, for example, to score three goals in football. Umpires have historically been told to give the batsman the benefit of the doubt; we shall do the same with Barrie.

He enjoyed watching village cricket on this little ground sheltered by the Cotswolds and with the Malvern Hills in the distance, surrounded by green fields and the ancient trees on the Stanway estate: a place that perfectly captures the stereotype of England as a green and pleasant land. It fitted in with the surroundings that he had always wanted the Allahakbarries to play in: an unspoilt pastoral paradise which was a retreat from the modern world. The English countryside, though, is also a landscape which has its origins in feudal land ownership, nowhere more so than at Stanway, in fact, and Barrie's sentimental obsession with wanting everything to remain the same points as much to a rigid rural conservatism as to a love of nature.

Asquith remembered how 'Village cricket with all its drama and humour provided, as I had hoped, endless entertainment. Saturday after Saturday found Barrie perched, pipe in mouth, on an uncompromisingly hard bench, keenly scrutinising every ball, stroke, pick-up and throw-in, and always ready with a word of congratulation or commiseration for the returning batsman.'

He particularly enjoyed watching the innings of Harry Last, the gamekeeper, who true to his name was always the last man in and would soon after be out again too – either after some spectacular hitting or after he missed a mighty heave off his first ball and looked round to find his middle stump ripped from the ground. In a comic film, which Barrie made at Stanway in 1923 called *The Yellow Week at Stanway* ('A record of fair women and brainy men'), there is a close-up shot of Nico stumping the gamekeeper who has rushed forward impetuously to drive the ball. There was a disused railway carriage on the ground that had been acting as a pavilion but in 1925 Barrie paid for a new pavillion to be built, reputedly based on his own design. It is still standing: a thatched, wooden-framed structure that rests on saddlestones and has an extensive sheltered balcony. But Barrie, rather ironically, is said to have despised it, saying that it had ruined the charm of the ground.

He also said, in a speech in 1926, that village cricket summed up the true spirit of the game, in a way which is striking for the perceived timelessness that was such an integral part of his love for the game.

And let us not forget, especially at this time, that the great glory of cricket does not lie in Test Matches, nor county championships, nor Sheffield Shields, but rather on village greens, the cradle of cricket. The Tests are but the fevers of the game.

As the years roll on they become of small account . . . but long, long afterwards, I think, your far-off progeny will still of summer afternoons hear the crack of the bat, and the local champion calling for his ale on the same on bumpy wickets.

When Nico took his Eton friends to Stanway to play cricket during the annual cricket weeks which ran for a few seasons, he felt that Barrie 'obviously loved every single thing about it,' and remembered how on one occasion he invited all his friends to make after-dinner speeches. 'And he always ended up with a speech of his own which lasted for about ten minutes to quarter of an hour: out of this world . . . . And he was riddled with entertainment and pleasure by the whole thing.'

Barrie did increasingly more speaking and less writing after the First World War, despite the fact that he had once insisted that 'there is no surer sign of mediocrity than being accepted as a successful after-dinner speaker.' His most famous and memorable speech was his rectorial address at St Andrews University, called 'Courage', for which he had being making notes for almost three years. He was speaking immediately after the newly appointed chancellor of the university and the previous rector, Douglas Haig, another Scot, and the Commander-in-Chief of the British Expeditionary Force from 1915 onwards whose diaries had been an important part of Conan Doyle's six-volume history of the conflict (which received generally negative reviews). Whether Haig was also directly responsible for deliberately marching tens of thousands of soldiers to their certain deaths during the major battles of the war is a matter of intense historical debate. But the tag of the 'Butcher of the Somme' is one that has long been attached to Haig in the popular imagination. Certainly the undergraduates of St Andrews had little time for him in 1922. According to Denis Mackail, 'The students showed little or no respect for Lord Haig, whatever they may have felt, and he had to fight one of his less successful engagements to get through his own part of the proceedings at all.'

When Haig had made his rectorial address some three years previously, just a few months after the end of the war, he had wanted to reassert the old values of the British Empire, which had been so effectively translated to young men before the war through Newbolt's verses on cricket and battle.

We have won, and if my reading of history and current events is correct, we have won because our national character is sound; because it is founded in honesty and love of justice, inspired by comradeship and self-sacrifice, secured by a great capacity for common action in pursuit of high ideals. Let us do our utmost to keep it so and to hand it on strengthened to our children. So long as our national character remains unchanged we shall always win in all we undertake. It is the sword and buckler of our Empire.

But Barrie set out to strike a very different note with his address. He was nervous, pale as a ghost and looked smaller than ever as he started to speak having just seen Haig struggle against the 'yells, paper streamers – even *boots* – flying about' and although the students were quieter now his voice was still inaudible as he began. But then there was a shout from the audience that snapped him out of his mumbling nervousness and he spoke up, clearly and forcefully, for almost an hour and a half. It was a searing, emotive speech, utterly frank and serious, though there were also a few characteristic comic and sentimental touches, as well as the introduction for the first time of Barrie's latest alter ego M'Connachie. It was an address from one generation to the next; from age to youth.

. . . the war and other happenings have shown you that age is not necessarily another name for sapience; that our avoidance of frankness in life and in the arts is often, but not as often as you think, a cowardly shirking of unpalatable truths, and that you have taken us off our pedestals because we look more natural on the ground. You who are at the rash age even accuse your elders, sometimes not without justification, of being more rash than yourselves. 'If youth only knew,' we used to teach you to sing; but now, just because Youth has been to the war, it wants to change the next line into 'If Age had only to do.'

In so far as this attitude of yours is merely passive, sullen, negative, as it mainly is, despairing of our capacity and anticipating a future of gloom, it is no game for man or woman. It is certainly the opposite for that which I plead. Do not stand aloof, despising, disbelieving, but come in and help – insist on coming in and helping. After all we have shown a good deal of courage; and your part is to add a greater courage to it. There are glorious years lying ahead of you if you choose to make them glorious.

Indeed, he urged his young audience to have the courage to take control of their own destiny above all else: 'Courage is the thing. All goes if courage goes. . . . Be not merely courageous, but light-hearted and gay.'

This is what George had written in his last letter to Barrie from the Western Front: 'carry on with your job of keeping up your courage.' And Barrie urged them to show this courage now, rather than 'seeking cushions' or else they would merely end up being like his own generation.

Make haste, or you will become like us, with only the thing we proudly call experience to add to your stock, a poor exchange for the generous feelings that time will take away. We have no intention of giving you your share. Look around and see how much share Youth has now that the war is over. You got a handsome share while it lasted.

I expect we shall beat you; unless your fortitude be doubly girded by a desire to send a message of cheer to your brothers who fell, the only message, I believe, for which they crave. . . . They want to know if you have learned wisely from what befell them; if you have, they will be braced in the feeling that they did not die in vain. Some of them think that they did. They will not take our word for it that they did not. You are their living image; they know you could not lie to them, but they distrust our flattery and our cunning faces.

Barrie even suggested that youth should reconsider the notion of patriotism. 'You have more in common with the youth of other lands than Youth and Age can ever have with each other'.

And near the end of his address he made a joke, which united young and old together. 'Well, we have at last come to an end. Some of you may remember when I began this address; we are all older now.'

After he had finished there was long and thunderous applause from the students who had been inspired and moved by his speech.

He gave a number of other speeches while he was in Scotland, including one on 5 May at University College, Dundee, to mark the opening of the sports ground there, where he gave a far more funny and informal (and sometimes inaccurate) talk all about the Allahakbarries. Arriving at the ground he was borne aloft on the students' shoulders and a photograph of Barrie being held in the air is perhaps the most extraordinary of all photographs of Barrie for all around him there are a sea of youthful and exuberant faces yet he looks silent, still and solemn as he is raised above them, staring intently and morosely at the camera.

He described the team's first game at Shere and the games at Broadway against Mary de Navarro's team ('She was frightfully keen but could not learn the game'). He also mentioned the fact that she called it 'crickets' rather than cricket. De Navarro evidently heard that she had been mentioned in one of Barrie's speeches and wrote to him. This was Barrie's reply:

*My dear Mamie,*
*By the time I got to cricket I expect I didn't know what I was saying there were so many speeches, and I am so unused to them. However I feel sure I said lovely things about you as I am always thinking them. The students were very nice but I am glad to be back in the quietness of London.*

After his speech he picked up a cricket ball and bowled to Haig
out on the cricket pitch, wearing his grey Homburg hat with a
black band, and a flapping scarf around his neck, while the more
obviously manly Haig, with his bushy white military moustache,
took guard in full uniform which included black, almost knee-
high leather boots. It was Peter Pan bowling to Captain Hook all
over again; Haig the pirate captain who sent the lost boys to their
deaths on the Western Front, forcing them to walk the gang-
plank. Barrie bowled him out and Pan was victorious yet again.
Though in actual fact, Barrie liked Haig. He did not seem to
resent him at all, as others, including many junior officers who
served on the front, did, for the deaths of thousands of young
soldiers, despite Barrie's intimate connection with a number of
those who had died. They became friends and Barrie later arranged
a dinner in his honour at his Adelphi flat. In a letter to George
Bernard Shaw the actress Ellen Terry, who had heard Barrie's
speeches in Scotland and watched the improvised cricket, wrote
that 'Haig is a pet, and the two together [Barrie and Haig] are –
well, I'm glad I was there to see two such boys! They're fun!'

The following year he was awarded the Order of Merit, joining
two of his greatest heroes, Hardy and Meredith, in achieving the
accolade. And after his performance at St Andrews and the attention it brought him in the press, Barrie was in huge demand as a
public speaker. He was a beguiling talker with his Scotch drawl
and poker face providing a perfect means for expressing his dry,
sardonic humour. He usually puffed on a cigar throughout his
speeches and E. V. Lucas wrote that he conveyed the 'impression
of weary improvisation' as though the effort of making a speech
was all too much for him. On a number of occasions he was able
to combine public speaking with his love of cricket and these occasions brought out that same strain of gleeful and absurd fun that
had characterised the captaincy of his own team. In particular he
spoke to the Australian touring sides of the late 1920s and early
1930s with some of them, including Donald Bradman, becoming

personal friends. But despite these friendships he was firmly on the side of the English XI. When he spoke to the team at an Institute of Journalists' lunch on 20 April 1926, he told them that the England team this year had a few surprises up its sleeve.

> Our team is mostly new and is at present hidden away in cellars. Our fast bowler – I mention this in confidence – is W. K. Thunder, who has never been known to smile except when he hears Mr Gregory referred to as a *fast* bowler. Of our batsmen, I shall merely indicate their quality by saying that Hobbs is to be twelfth man.

Later that summer the entire Australian team went to Stanway where they were entertained by Barrie and the rest of the temporary residents at the house. They went out onto the cricket field so that each member of the party could have the privilege of being bowled out by Arthur Mailey, the Australian leg-spin bowler who had once taken nine wickets for 121 runs against England at Melbourne. Mailey, along with his captain, Herbie Collins, and Charlie Macartney, an unconventional, hard-hitting batsman who had averaged 94.6 in the test series that summer, all decided to stay the night. But Macartney had to finish a long letter to his wife so Barrie promised him that he would write it, which he did. Perhaps there was a tacit agreement between the two men on this point for in their knockabout cricket game, Barrie was able to take Macartney's wicket, clean bowled; something which the frustrated England bowlers that summer would have paid good money for, though England did win the series 1–0 in the last match after four successive draws.

Four years later on 7 June 1930, just a month after Barrie's seventieth birthday, Macartney and Mailey were on hand to play for a side which for the day was called the Allahakbarries: a final outing for the club in name only. The venue was a very special one in Barrie's personal cricketing history: it was where he first learnt to play the game. He was being awarded the freedom of his home town Kirriemuir, and he presented the cricket club there with a new pavilion and a *camera obscura*. In his speech he said that 'My love for cricket began as I sat on the hill cheering for the renowned Kirrie Club. I see them still, pausing at Charlie Wilkie's lodge to pick up their implements, sometimes even letting me help to carry the cricket bag.' In honour of the occasion the last team to call themselves the Allahakbarries, with Barrie himself as a nominal twelfth man, turned out to play the West of Scotland. Apart from Barrie's presence in the pavilion (he was too old to play himself) and out on the wicket tossing the coin, there were no other reminders of the Allahakbarries teams of the past. The lack of continuity with the sides of yesteryear was further emphasised by their clinical victory over Western Scotland. They first of all bowled them out with ease and then reached their target of 120 with the loss of just four wickets. Macartney made 101 not out and the *Kirriemuir Free Press* reported that he gave 'a stylish display with the bat, hitting freely all round and only once giving a hard chance.'

In that same summer of 1930 Donald Bradman, aged twenty-two, was on his first Ashes tour of England, and had a spectacular season scoring a century in the first test, a double century in the second and a triple century (334) in the third. He became the most successful batsman of all time and one of the most celebrated and famous cricketers ever to have played the game. After accumulating more than 3,000 runs in all matches during the tour he attended a farewell banquet on 8 September hosted by the president of the MCC Sir Kynaston Studd at the Merchant Taylor's Hall on Threadneedle Street where he met Barrie for the first time. The two men became friends. In September 1934, when Bradman was close to death in London following complications after an operation for acute appendicitis, Barrie was one of the first people to be allowed into his hospital room when he was making a recovery. In 1950, more than a decade after Barrie's death, his cricketing booklet from 1899 was republished with a foreword from Bradman ('My favourite [of Barrie's stories]', he wrote, 'was the one in which, describing his bowling, he told how, after delivering the ball, he would go and sit on the turf at mid-off, and wait for it to reach the other end – "which it sometimes did"'). But at the dinner in 1930, Bradman was one among many of the Australian players who was the butt of Barrie's benevolent jokes as he made use of the technique of 'running through the order', which he had crafted to perfection long ago with the Allahakbarries.

> The next man is . . . Sir Kynaston made me out a list of the various combatants, and he told me that when I mentioned this name it would be received with hearty but hollow cheers. The name, so far as I can make it out, is Mr Badman. I feel very sorry for Mr Badman. I do not doubt that he meant to do better. When the Australian team return home they will be met, as we can well imagine, by countless thousands of Australians all straining at the leash to hear from Mr Woodfull [the Australian captain] which side won, and when they hear there will be tremendous rejoicings. The team will be taken to hotels and public places and feasted – all with the exception of Mr Badman. He has carried this plan of his not knowing how to get out to such an extent that he now cannot get out of anything. He won't be even able to get out of the ship when all the others are merry and bright. We now leave him pacing the deck, a gloomy figure.

In a sense Barrie was more accurate than he probably could have known, for it was true that Bradman could not 'get out' of the fame that his herculean scoring had given him: he was a reluctant hero. He also could not 'get out' of the fact that many of his team-mates seemed to resent his singular and remarkable ability and found him aloof, which no doubt left him on occasion the 'gloomy figure' which Barrie describes.

When in 1934 the Australians were back in England after the fractious bodyline tour of 1932/3 ('What warfare in Australia!'

Barrie had written in one of his many cricket-related letters to Charles Turley Smith) Barrie was entertaining them again with what was his penultimate public speech. At a dinner at Carpenter's Hall on Throgmorton Avenue in the City of London on 31 May, hosted by Surrey County Cricket Club, Barrie made reference to an innings of Bradman's he had made just three days earlier against Middlesex at Lord's when he had scored 160 in 124 minutes including seventy-seven fours and one six. It was a piece of bravura batting, in contrast to the more scientific approach he had demonstrated four years previously.

'Bradman,' said Barrie: 'when you were here before, we knew that another prodigy had arisen in the land of cricket; you won every garland batting can claim except one only, yours did not seem to issue sufficiently out of excess of joy and gaiety to win the love of greybeards, but the other day at Lord's you did enter into our love.'

Barrie made some more general observations about cricket in this speech as well which perhaps demonstrates his natural affinity as a Scot for the Australian team – both outsiders in England.

How can I, a Scot, dare to talk about the game in this den of cricketers? No Scot really knows anything about cricket.

You English and your games! It is many years agone since I left my kilted fastness and came to reside among you queer ones. Yet in a sense your cricket has got to me. I too have fallen, O Lucifer!

And he went on to elaborate on his love for the game, instilling it with a previously unsuspected pantheistic divinity.

May I venture, before I sit down, to say what I think cricket is? Cricket is an idea. It was an idea of the gods. They looked down at poor humanity and its often tragic efforts, and though we made them wince we occasionally found favour in their eyes, and they sent us gifts – a little fortitude, a sense of fairness, an unconquerable gaiety of heart, and perhaps an aphorism about the wisdom of sometimes forgetting. They did not send those gifts down to us one at a time, they rolled them up into quite a little ball and tossed it down to us. The name cricket is ours. Any genius could have invented it. But its meaning is theirs. The ball does not, as is generally supposed, contain ashes, it contains a living thing, a winged word about 'playing the game'. The immortals left it at that, for cricket is the only game they play themselves.

The elevation of cricket to the game of the gods is perhaps out of the Neville Cardus school of hyperbole, and he and Barrie were cricketing friends, occasionally meeting at Lord's to watch games together. In the widespread atmosphere of nostalgia about the pre-war years during the 1920s, Cardus focused on Edwardian cricket. His memory of Jessop's famous innings at the Oval in 1902, for example, which P. G. Wodehouse had missed because he had to return to his office, is a great example of this romanticism. 'This innings by Jessop had immortal longings; it will never be forgotten. The vision, the undying chivalry of it, belong not only to cricket, but to the unwritten saga of the English people.'

This sounds very much like Haig, emphasising the continuity of the values of the British Empire. Barrie contributed to this myth in his way too, with the story of the exploits of his team: there is no doubt that the Allahakbarries became a minor but significant part of that history of the golden age of cricket and testament to a very English type of eccentricity and individualism. Barrie was also not averse to some nostalgia himself, signalling the onset of such episodes in conversation by 'lolling back in his chair with one leg tucked under the other' and asking 'D'you remember'? These reminiscences were eventually written down in his book *The Greenwood Hat*, published in 1930, which combined memories along with articles from his early days as a journalist. Yet his speech about courage had also shown that he felt myths about the past alone could not sustain the generations of the future.

In the twenties and thirties it was Barrie's own generation, and members of the Allahakbarries, who began to fall away in significant numbers after many of their juniors had already died. Hesketh Prichard had been struggling with an illness for some time at the end of the war but still managed to write an account of his time as an expert sniper on the front line, called *Sniping in France*, and another about game hunting called *Sport in Wildest Britain*. He died on 14 June 1922 of what at the time was thought to be the side-effects from German gas attacks during the war, but what was probably actually malaria picked up on his travels. His final book was published in 1921 by W. Heinemann, who at the time was run by another ex-Allahakbarrie Sidney Pawling, who died in Eastbourne in December that same year.

The previous year Hornung had died of pneumonia in St-Jean-de-Luz in the south of France, aged fifty-four and was buried there in the same cemetery as George Gissing. Bernard Partridge was knighted in 1925 but in 1927 Jerome died soon after the publication of his autobiography, and in 1928 so did two more of Barrie's friends, Thomas Hardy and Douglas Haig. Barrie joined Kipling, Stanley Baldwin, Ramsay MacDonald, George Bernard Shaw, John Galsworthy and A. E. Housman as a pallbearer at Westminster Abbey for Hardy's coffin. Conan Doyle believed that he had a message from Douglas Haig 'on the other side' a few days after his death and sent a letter to his widow asking whether she would like him to relay it to her. Two years later, on 7 July, he too was dead, aged seventy-one. The novelist Hugh Walpole wrote in his diary the following day: 'Conan Doyle dead. A brave simple, childish man. How hard he tried to make me a spiritualist! Very conscious of him – tonight.'

Charles Whibley also died that year and there were few of the team left standing by the end of 1930. Owen Seaman was made a baronet in 1933, a year after his retirement from *Punch*, and he thanked well-wishers with a couplet:

> I thank you from a swelling heart
> For being glad that I'm a Bart.

In the summer of 1933 Barrie had been taken ill at Stanway and the summer residency was never repeated. Cynthia Asquith remembered how she had suddenly realised that Barrie's own cricketing career had come to an end.

> Those long-ago Augusts at Stanway have blurred in my memory. Looked back upon from this distance of time, they fuse into one summer – a single summer; but a mysterious one; in whose slow, unbroken course, babies surreptitiously turn into children; children into boys; the muzzles of young dogs whiten; and, almost imperceptibly, Barrie's step grows slower, until, all of a sudden, I realise with a pang that instead of joining in the lawn-cricket he sits beneath the tulip tree and watches others play.

Birrell died that same year, followed by Gerald du Maurier, another of the Allahakbarries to have received a knighthood, in 1935. Then in 1936 Seaman himself, and Barrie's most faithful friend Gilmour, both passed away.

Alongside Barrie now there were only Turley, Mason, Ives, Lucas and Partridge left from his own generation, and Mackail, Wodehouse and Milne among the prominent younger members of the Allahakbarries who were still alive: a little way off an eleven. In December 1936 Barrie's last play *The Boy David* was performed, soon after the abdication of King Edward VIII, though it wasn't a success and closed soon after. Barrie's life, too, was coming to a close: mortality had finally caught up with the eternal boy.

He died six months later on 19 June 1937, aged seventy-seven, and was buried alongside his family on the hill in Kirriemuir, his name added to the foot of the plain granite gravestone with those of his parents, brothers and sisters above his, as he had wanted. Not far away was the cricket pitch where he had learnt to play the game and where the pavilion stood which he had given to the town in 1930. His body lay in ground guarded by the same gates he had used as wickets when he played there as a child. It was the place where he had watched boyhood heroes and heroes of his adult life too, such as the Australian batsman Charlie Macartney, who had scored a century on the ground seven years previously. Barrie's own innings had been a distinguished one, full of incident, quirkiness, some big hits, and all played with resolute and determined courage.

The Allahakbarries were for a short period the literary establishment in Britain yet many of them, taking their cue from their captain, were unconventional spirits and outsiders. After the First World War they retreated to their writer's studies and their other private spaces as though the idea of notoriously individualistic authors all playing games on a field together had been an aberration. 'To be born is to be wrecked on an island', Barrie once wrote, but cricket, along with his writing, was one of the main things in his life which helped him to express his personality; to enable the distance between the islands to become more bearable. He played games all his life and he inspired his grown-up friends to shrug off the pompous conservatism of the Victorian age and join in with him in a way which was not just a throwback to childhood, but a memory of what he saw as a pastoral age when games had been an integral part of the more harmonious relationship between man and nature. The Allahakbarries were not just a celebration of cricket but of the green fields where they played. Barrie led them from the city like Pan with his pipes and took them to Neverland, the island where time stood still, where there was no death; an idealised, romanticised England of peaceful meadows and figures on reasonable terms playing cricket and laughing together, where Michael and George will always be playing at pirates with their brothers on the boundary-edge.

# EPILOGUE:
# WHAT HAPPENED TO THE
# OTHER ALLAHAKBARRIES?

AUGUSTINE BIRRELL

Birrell, that 'engaging fancy cricketer', became chief secretary for Ireland in 1907 and was forced to resign in 1916 after the Easter uprising, which also ruined his political reputation and legacy. He had actually tried to resign much earlier after he had helped to pass the Home Rule Bill in 1912. Had he done so he would probably have been remembered for a number of significant achievements that paved the way for self-government by Ireland. But his offer of resignation on that occasion, and a number of times afterwards, was not accepted by the prime minister, Herbert Asquith.

Birrell's judgement became increasingly impaired as his wife slowly died of a brain tumour, diagnosed in 1911. He kept her condition a family secret, though it severely affected his work. She finally died in 1915. The following year, in 1916, a serious error of judgement by Birrell made his position untenable. Birrell felt that the danger of a bomb from the extreme nationalists was greater than that of an uprising. He was proved wrong. The Easter Rising began on Easter Monday, 24 April 1916. He had spent Easter in London and answered questions in parliament on Tuesday and Wednesday, then travelled to Dublin, arriving on Thursday morning. He wrote to the prime minister from the city and gave him his assessment of the situation there. Soon after he offered his resignation, which Asquith accepted on 1 May, 'with infinite regret', and made his resignation speech in the House of Commons on 3 May. 'One circumstance and one alone about this Easter Rebellion gave me a certain savage satisfaction,' he later wrote in his memoirs, 'for before it happened my wife was dead'.

It was the start of his retirement, at the age of sixty-six, and he spent the rest of his life at home in Chelsea, where he wrote two volumes of published essays and an autobiography called *Things Past Redress*. He died in 1933.

### E. W. HORNUNG

Hornung wanted to play a part in the war and volunteered for the YMCA, at first doing work for troops on leave at home in London, and then serving at a canteen just behind the front lines in Arras. He set up a lending library for the soldiers, where he noted with some disappointment that Sherlock Holmes was far more popular than Raffles, though he still received some attention from the soldiers when they found out that he was the creator of the amateur cracksman. He published a number of poems both during and immediately after the war but died of pneumonia in St Jean-de-Luz in the south of France, aged fifty-four, in 1921.

### JEROME K. JEROME

Jerome K. Jerome was fifty-five at the start of the First World War. It meant that he was far too old to enlist. Instead he volunteered to drive an ambulance for the French Army. He was distraught by what he saw in France and by 1916 he wanted to return home. When he did he was told that the stress of his work in France had weakened his heart. His secretary wrote that 'the old Jerome had gone. In his place was a stranger. He was a broken man.' He campaigned for peace in England but it was an unpopular cause. He died from a stroke in 1927 a year after publishing his autobiography *My Life and Times*.

## PETER LLEWELYN DAVIES

Peter Llewelyn Davies became a book publisher, setting up his own firm Peter Davies Limited in 1926. He married and had three sons but committed suicide in 1960 by throwing himself from the platform under an oncoming London Underground train at Sloane Square station.

## E. V. LUCAS

Lucas continued to write for *Punch* but became estranged from his family at the end of the First World War. He saw his daughter Audrey very infrequently during the 1920s and she reported that 'In 1931, when I began to see him again, he was physically much altered. He had been very ill; he was greyer; heavier in build; more florid in complexion. That he was older is obvious, but the ageing did not show in his mind or in his outlook.' He was an alcoholic and Audrey wrote that he 'gave his friends champagne because he hoped they would enjoy it; he drank it himself because he had to'. But he was also chairman of the publishing firm Methuen from 1924. He introduced A. A. Milne to the artist E. H. Shepherd, and the Winnie-the-Pooh books that this successful partnership produced were published by Methuen and were highly profitable for the firm. He died a year after Barrie in 1938.

## DENIS MACKAIL

Denis Mackail suffered from poor health and was not eligible to fight in the First World War, but did work as a civil servant for the War Office. After the war he began writing novels and produced a prodigious number over the next twenty years, none of which were hugely successful, but nonetheless enabled him to provide for his family. He also wrote a biography of Barrie, *The Story of J. M. B.* which was published in 1941 by Peter Davies Ltd. He died in 1971.

## A. E. W. MASON

Mason, like Hesketh Prichard, was promoted from captain to major during the First World War, serving first in the Manchester regiment and then in the Royal Marine light infantry. He ended the war working as a naval intelligence officer in Spain, Morocco and Mexico. He afterwards resumed his writing career and during the 1920s published three more novels in a series about a French detective called Inspector Hanaud, which had begun in 1910 with the publication of *At the Villa Rose*. He wrote a number of other novels in the twenties and thirties, remained a bachelor all his life and turned down a knighthood. He died at his home in Mayfair in 1948, aged eighty-three.

## BERNARD PARTRIDGE

Partridge remained a cartoonist for *Punch* until just a few months before his death in August 1945, which meant that he had contributed fifty-four years of service to the publication in all between the ages of thirty and eighty-four.

## A. A. MILNE AND P. G. WODEHOUSE

Wodehouse flitted between living in England and writing for films in Hollywood during the twenties and early thirties. He had significant problems with the tax authorities in England and America and so set up a third base in France, buying a house in Le Touquet, Normandy.

Milne tried to go back to *Punch* after the First World War. But Seaman did not want him back. So he continued with his career as a playwright and for a short time became one of the most successful dramatists in England, his first real success being *Mr Pim Passes By*, which opened in 1920. Milne's son, Christopher Robin, was born the same year.

Milne's first children's book, a book of poems called *When We Were Very Young*, was published in 1924 by Methuen. It was extremely successful in Britain and America and it marked the first appearance of the character with whom Milne has been associated with ever since: Winnie-the-Pooh. The honey-loving bear appeared in an eponymous book in 1926 and later in *The House at Pooh Corner* in 1928.

The Germans invaded France in 1940, where Wodehouse and his wife were still living. They remained there after the declaration of war and made no real effort to escape. P. G. was interred in a relatively relaxed camp. He kept a camp journal, which is mostly a description of the food situation in the camp, as well as some of the people and the regime they lived under. He played cricket in the camp in March 1941; the first time he had played for twenty-seven years.

One of the camp commanders allowed him to use a typewriter and suggested that he should think about doing some radio broadcasts. In June 1941, Wodehouse was moved under guard to the Hotel Adlon in Berlin. He gave five talks, which were recorded on wax and broadcast, the first on 27 June 1941. They were mildly subversive in that he laughed at his captors: 'Our Kommandant was a careful man. I think he must once have missed an important train, and it preyed on his mind.' But the mood in Britain had become far too serious and determined to appreciate this kind of flippancy, broadcast on enemy radio. There was outrage.

A. A. Milne delivered the strongest attack of Wodehouse from a fellow author: 'Irresponsibility in what the papers call "a licensed humorist" can be carried too far; naïveté can be carried too far. Wodehouse has been given a good deal of license in the past, but I fancy that now his license will be withdrawn.'

Milne claimed that Wodehouse had confessed to him that he wished he'd fathered a son, 'But he would have to be born at the age of fifteen, when he was just getting into his House Eleven.' This, Milne alleged, was a further sign of irresponsibility.

Wodehouse and his wife were moved from Berlin to Paris by 1944, and soon after the liberation Major Malcolm Muggeridge (later an editor of *Punch* who got Wodehouse writing for the magazine again after a fifty-year hiatus) investigated the case. The verdict was that Wodehouse was naïve and foolish, maybe, but not a traitor.

Yet Wodehouse was firmly established in the public mind as exactly that. Sales of his books dropped sharply. Wodehouse spent most of the rest of his life living in New York, though he was also the final member of the Allahakbarries to be knighted, shortly before he died in 1975.

The relationship between Milne and his son also soured towards the end of Milne's life, most notably when Christopher gave a newspaper interview to the *Sunday Dispatch* in 1952 when Milne was recovering from a stroke in hospital. A.A. Milne died in 1956.

# ACKNOWLEDGEMENTS

The experience of the author, just like that of the batsman, can be a lonely one, but fortunately many other people have also contributed to producing this book. However, any 'loose shots' in the form of errors or omissions are of course my own.

My literary agent, Andrew Gordon, gave me excellent advice at the start of the project, which has hopefully helped to make a fascinating-sounding story become an entertaining and engaging book. I'd like to thank him for his ideas and for his infectious enthusiasm for the material.

My greatest thanks, though, go to Michael de Navarro QC, the grandson of Mary de Navarro, who lives in the same house, Court Farm, as his grandmother did when she captained her team against the Allahakbarries in the late 1890s. He is also a cricketing enthusiast and he very generously showed me and my wife around Court Farm and liberally treated us to refreshments. But most kindly of all, I think, and certainly most significantly for me, he uncovered a treasure trove of letters from Barrie to his grandparents and trustingly handed them over to me with the instruction, 'please return them to my chambers in London when you've finished with them'. They are packed full of useful information, but, more importantly still, they gave me a great insight into the personality that Barrie became when cricket was on his mind – for many of the letters are solely on that subject. The book would be poorer without them.

Thanks also to Michael's wife, Jill, for her hospitality. And to Neil Hilton, too, a resident of Broadway who kindly provided the introduction with Michael de Navarro and took the time to talk to me about the history of the village.

Similarly, Elizabeth Rich, the curator at Shere Museum, spent a significant amount of time talking to me about people who lived in the village at the time when the Allahakbarries were playing there. She also unearthed a hitherto unpublished photograph containing Barrie, along with some other great pictures from Shere's very own golden age of cricket. These materials, and Elizabeth's knowledge of Shere, have been extremely important to my research, and I appreciate her efforts all the more because she was undertaking the laborious task of moving the entire museum from one end of the village to the other, where it is now in its new home – right next to the cricket pitch. Thanks also to Barbara Karlsson at the Shere, Gomshall and Peaslake Local History Society, who provided me with the introduction to Elizabeth. And to John Askew from Shere, who spoke to me about his great-grandfather, Dickie Askew.

Brian Jermyn very kindly showed me around the grounds of Barrie's old country retreat, Black Lake Cottage near Farnham, where he lives and which is now divided into three separate homes and has been renamed.

The eminent authors Andrew Birkin, Andrew Lycett, Ann Thwaite, and David Frith have all been extremely helpful to me and provided me with some useful information. Andrew Birkin's website devoted to J. M. Barrie, www.jmbarrie.co.uk, has been especially helpful and David Frith's extensive cricketing archives have been the source of some brilliant photographs. I am particularly indebted to the following works: Andrew Birkin's *J. M. Barrie and the Lost Boys*, Andrew Lycett's *Conan Doyle: The Man Who Created Sherlock Holmes*, Denis Mackail's *The Story of J.M.B.* and Ann Thwaite's *A. A. Milne: His Life*. David Rayvern Allen's anthology of Barrie's cricket writings and speeches, *Peter Pan and Cricket*, has clearly been essential

ACKNOWLEDGEMENTS

reading. The details of all these sources can be found in the Note on Sources section.

Neil Robinson at the MCC Library at Lord's Cricket Ground, has been very obliging in helping me to sniff out obscure cricket books and pictures, and Peter Wynne-Thomas at Nottinghamshire County Cricket Club helped me to locate some relevant articles in *The Cricketer* magazine.

Christine de Poortere, Nicholas Baldwin and Dr Andrea Tanner from Great Ormond Street Hospital have all helped me in various ways relating to Barrie and *Peter Pan*. Paula Borton, who was my editor at Simon & Schuster for my book on Great Ormond Street Hospital, was also my first sounding board for the idea of a story about the Allahakbarries. Without her help, kindness and encouragement this book may never have been published.

I would also like to thank Nick Swan and Dian Mordin from Aldro School in Shackleford, Jennifer Kingsland, the archivist at Downe House School, Molly Schwartzburg and Jean Cannon at the University of Texas, Naomi Saito, Eva Guggemos, Timothy Young and Ellen Doon at Yale University, Rachel Foss at the British Library, Dr Carolyn Hares-Stryker, McCoy Professor of English at Marietta College, Ohio, Bob Holden from Downe Cricket Club, Martin Goffe and Simon Davies.

The British Library, BFI and Colindale Newspaper Library have all been vital for my research, and the British Library in particular has provided me with an ideal environment for research and writing. I am also thankful to the University of Dundee, the University of St Andrews and Cheltenham College.

The team at Hodder have been enthusiastic, professional and efficient. I was lucky to have Rupert Lancaster as my editor, who is both a serious cricket-lover and an experienced editor of many great cricket (and other) books. My copy-editor, Justine Taylor, made a number of judicious recommendations that greatly improved the manuscript. Thanks are also due to Juliet Brightmore and Laura Macaulay.

Last, but a thousand runs away from being least, I want to thank my family and friends who have supported and inspired me along the way, as well as enduring what must have felt like endless talk of Edwardian cricket and Barrie-ana over many months. I am particularly grateful to my wife, Bridget, to my mum and dad, my brother Simon, and to Ant Green, Helen and Chris Davis, Dr Zigmund Rogoff, Gerrie Villon, Graeme Rodrigo, and to Lidia Oshlyansky, who made me understand, the hard way, what Barrie must have felt like when he lost to a cricket team captained by a female American.

## SOURCES OF PHOTOGRAPHS AND ILLUSTRATIONS

Insets pages 1 – 16
Eleanor Adlard (Ed), *Dear Turley*, Frederick Muller Ltd., 1942: 9 bottom left and right (photograph by F. Muller). *The Allahakbarrie Book of Broadway Cricket for 1899*, illustration by Bernard Partridge: 1. J.M. Barrie, *The Greenwood Hat*, Peter Davies Ltd., London 1937: 4 top, 6 top left. Mary Evans Picture Library/Graham Hales Collection: 10 top left. Courtesy of David Frith: 3, 4 middle and bottom, 10 top right, 12 bottom, 13 bottom. Photographs reproduced by courtesy of Great Ormond Street Hospital for Children, London: 2 top left and right, 6 top right and bottom, 7, 11, 12 top left, right and middle. Audrey Lucas, *E.V. Lucas, A Portrait*, Methuen, 1939: 16. Marylebone Cricket Club, London: 2 bottom left (photo Bridgeman Art Library), 8. Eric Parker, *Hesketh Prichard ... A Memoir*, T. Fisher Unwin Ltd., London, 1924: 10 bottom. Private Collections: 9 top, 13 top, 14, 15. Courtesy of Shere Museum/Elizabeth Rich: 5. *Sunday Mail* 8th June, 1930: 13 middle.

Illustrations within text
*The Allahakbarrie Book of Broadway Cricket for 1899*: 40 illustration by E.T. Reed, 93, 111 illustration by Herman Herkomer, 119, 127

illustration by Henry Ford, 152, 166. J. M. Barrie, *The Greenwood Hat*, Peter Davies Ltd., London 1937: 30 illustration by T. L Gilmour. J. M. Barrie, *The Little White Bird*, Hodder & Stoughton, 1902: 41 illustration by Henry Ford. Courtesy of David Frith: 272. National Portrait Gallery, London: 45. Courtesy of Michael de Navarro: 106. *Punch*: 68 (May 1888) illustration by G.D. Armour, 79 (February 1910) illustration by Lewis Baumer, 59 (August 1896) illustration by George du Maurier, 164 (December 1902) illustrations by G. R. Halkett, 250 (July 1910) illustration by A. Wallis Mills, 35 (June 1891), 182 (May 1901), 220 (February 1906), 294 (May 1926) illustrations by Bernard Partridge, 207 (February 1912) illustration by L. Raven-Hill, 71 (April 1898), 75 (July 1891), 115 (April 1906), illustrations by E. T. Reed, 19 (August 1889), 157 (September 1896), 132 (July 1898), 168 (June 1903), illustrations by H. Linley Sambourne, 145 (July 1912) illustration by G. Hillyard Swinstead. Royal Geographical Society, London: 37.

# NOTES ON SOURCES

## Unpublished source material

The only known scorebook of the Allahakbarries is held in the archives at the MCC Library at Lord's Cricket Ground. This has been invaluable in helping me to piece together what happened in the Allahakbarries games that it covers. The MCC's own scorebooks, held in the same library, which record every match played by Middlesex and the various MCC teams, as well as every match played at Lord's, were also vital in providing a wide range of information about many cricket matches that were of interest to me.

Thanks to Michael de Navarro, I was fortunate to have access to a large collection of letters from Barrie to Mary and Antonio de Navarro, written between 1897 and 1936, most of which are previously unpublished and many of which are on the subject of cricket matches at Broadway and elsewhere. I was able to look at other letters both from Barrie and other members of the Allahakbarries courtesy of the Walter Beinecke Jnr. Collection at Yale University, the Harry Ransom Center at the University of Texas and the British Library. I was also able to view a variety of material related to Arthur Conan Doyle at the British Library, including his diaries, photographs of the Allahakbarries, and his 'dream book'.

The website www.jmbarrie.co.uk which is run by Andrew Birkin, author of *J. M. Barrie and the Lost Boys*, has been of inestimable value in my research. Not only does it make available an enormous amount of Barrie-related archive material including photographs, notebook entries, sound and video recordings and letters, but it also hosts a forum which serves as an online community for a number of Barrie enthusiasts.

I was able to watch Barrie's silent film from 1923, the *Yellow Week at Stanway*, courtesy of the Mediateque centre at the British Film Institute in London.

And Elizabeth Rich at Shere Museum in Surrey allowed me to look at a variety of unpublished material relating to life, and cricket, in the village in the late-nineteenth and early twentieth centuries.

## CONTEMPORARY NEWSPAPERS, MAGAZINES AND ALMANACS

*British Weekly*
*Cricket*
*Daily Chronicle*
*Daily Express*
*Daily Mail*
*Dundee Advertiser*
*Edinburgh Evening Dispatch*
*Evesham Journal and Four Shires Advertiser*
*Farnham, Haslemere and Hindhead Herald*
*Fife Herald and Journal*
*Home Chimes*

*Idler*
*Kirriemuir Observer*
*National Observer*
*New York Times*
*Nottingham Journal*
*Pall Mall Gazette*
*Punch*
*St James's Gazette*
*Sporting Times*
*Strand Magazine*
*The Times*
*Wisden*

## SELECTED WORKS OF THE ALLAHAKBARRIES

Barrie, J. M., *Auld Licht Idylls*, Hodder & Stoughton, London, 1888

Barrie, J. M., *The Allahakbarrie Book of Broadway Cricket for 1899*, privately printed, 1899

Barrie, J. M., *The Little White Bird*, Hodder & Stoughton, London, 1902

Barrie, J. M., *Courage*, Hodder & Stoughton, London, 1922

Barrie, J. M., *The Greenwood Hat*, Peter Davies, London, 1937 (a first edition of fifty copies was published privately in 1930)

Barrie, J. M., *The Definitive Edition of the Plays of J. M. Barrie*, Hodder & Stoughton, London, 1942

Barrie, J. M., *Allahakbarries C. C.*, J. Barrie Publishers, London, 1950

Birrell, Augustine, *Things Past Redress*, Faber and Faber Limited, London, 1937

Doyle, Sir Arthur Conan, *The Adventures of Sherlock Holmes*, G. Newnes, London, 1892

Doyle, Sir Arthur Conan, *The Memoirs of Sherlock Holmes*, G. Newnes, London, 1893

Doyle, Sir Arthur Conan, *The Great Boer War*, Bernhard Tauchnitz, Leipzig, 1900

Doyle, Sir Arthur Conan, *The Hound of the Baskervilles*, G. Newnes, London, 1902

Doyle, Sir Arthur Conan, *The Return of Sherlock Holmes*, G. Newnes, London, 1905

Doyle, Sir Arthur Conan, *Memories and Adventures*, Hodder & Stoughton, London, 1924

Doyle, Sir Arthur Conan, *The Casebook of Sherlock Holmes*, John Murray, London, 1927

Hornung, E. W., *The Amateur Cracksman*, Methuen & Co., London, 1899

Hornung, E. W., *The Black Mask*, Grant Richards, London, 1901

Hornung, E. W., *A Thief in the Night*, Chatto & Windus, London, 1905

Hornung, E. W., *Justice Raffles*, Smith, Elder & Co., London, 1909

Ives, George, *The Graeco-Roman View of Youth*, Philip Sainsbury, London, 1926

Jerome, Jerome K., *The Idle Thoughts of an Idle Fellow*, Field & Tuer, London, 1886

Jerome, Jerome K., *Three Men in a Boat*, J. W. Arrowsmith, Bristol, 1889

Jerome, Jerome, K., *Three Men in a Boat: (to say nothing of the dog)*, annotated and introduced by Christopher Matthew and Benny Green, Pavilion, London, 1982

Jerome, Jerome K., *My Life and Times*, Allan Sutton, Gloucester, 1984

Lucas, E. V. (Ed.), *The Hambledon Men: being a new edition of John Nyren's 'Young Cricketer's Tutor'*, Henry Frowde, London, 1907

Lucas, E. V., *Reading, Writing and Remembering*, Methuen, London, 1932

Lucas, E.V., *Cricket all his life*, Hart-Davis, London 1950

Mason, A. E. W., *A Romance of Wastdale*, E. Mathews, London, 1895

Mason, A. E. W., *The Four Feathers*, Smith, Elder & Co., London, 1902

Milne, A. A., *The Day's Play*, Methuen, London, 1910

Milne, A. A., *First Plays (Wurzel-Flummery; The Luck One; The Boy Comes Home; Belinda, The Red Feathers)*, Chatto & Windus, London, 1919

Milne, A. A., *Winnie-the-Pooh*, Methuen, London, 1926

Milne, A. A., *The House at Pooh Corner*, Methuen, London, 1928

Milne, A. A. *Those were the Days*, Methuen, London, 1929

Milne, A. A., *It's Too Late Now*, Methuen, London, 1939

Snaith, J. C., *Willow The King*, Ward, Lock & Co., London, 1899

Trevor, Captain Philip, *The Lighter Side of Cricket*, Methuen, London, 1901

Trevor, Major Philip, *The Problems of Cricket*, Sampson, Low and Marston, London, 1907

Turley, Charles, *The Left Hander*, Oxford University Press, 1930

Wodehouse, P. G., *Mike, A Public School Story*, Adam & Charles Black, London, 1909

Wodehouse, P. G., *Nothing Serious*, Herbert Jenkins Limited, London, 1950

Wodehouse, P. G., *The Mating Season*, Penguin, London, 1957

Wodehouse, P. G., *Jeeves and Wooster Omnibus*, Penguin, London, 2001

## SELECT BIBLIOGRAPHY OF OTHER AUTHORS

Adlard, Eleanor, ed., *Dear Turley*, Frederick Muller, London, 1942

Adlard, John, *Owen Seaman: His Life and Work*, The Eighteen Nineties Society, London, 1977

Anderson, Mary (Mary de Navarro), *A Few More Memories*, Hutchinson & Co., London, 1936

Ansell, Mary, *The Happy Garden*, Cassell and Co. Ltd. London, 1912

Ansell, Mary, *Dogs and Men*, Duckworth and Co., London, 1924

Aries, Philippe, *Centuries of Childhood*, New York, 1962

Asquith, Cynthia, *Portrait of Barrie*, Barrie, London, 1954

Berkmann, Marcus, *Rain Men: The Madness of Cricket*, Little, Brown and Co., London, 1995

Binyon, Laurence, *For the Fallen, and other poems*, Hodder & Stoughton, London, 1917

Birkin, Andrew, *J. M. Barrie and the Lost Boys*, Constable, 1979, and Yale University Press, 2003

Birley, Derek, *A Social History of English Cricket*, Aurum, 2003

Blanchard, Kendall, *The Anthropology of Sport: An Introduction*, Bergin & Garvey, Connecticut, 1995

Bond, Brian, *The Unquiet Western Front: Britain's Role in Literature and History*, Cambridge University Press, 2002

Bongie, Chris, *Exotic memories: Literature, colonialism and the Fin de Siècle*, Stanford University Press, 1991

Buchan, John, *The Thirty-Nine Steps*, W. Blackwood & Sons, Edinburgh and London, 1915

Buitenhuis, Peter, The *Great War of Words: Literature as Propaganda 1914–18 and after*, B. T. Batsford Ltd, London 1989

Cardus, Neville, *Days in the Sun*, Grant Richards, London, 1924

Cardus, Neville, *Cricket*, London, Longmans & Co., London, 1930

Cardus, Neville, *English Cricket*, Collins, London, 1945

Cardus, Neville, *Autobiography*, Collins, London, 1947

Carr, John Dickson, *The Life of Sir Arthur Conan Doyle*, John Murray, London, 1949

Chaney, Lisa, *Hide-and-Seek with Angels: A Life of J. M. Barrie*, Hutchinson, London, 2005

Chase, Pauline, *Peter Pan's Postbag: Letters to Pauline Chase*, William Heinemann, London, 1909

Connolly, Joseph, *Jerome K Jerome – A Critical biography*, Orbis Publishing, London, 1982

Crane, David, *Scott of the Antarctic, A Life of Courage and Tragedy in the Extreme South*, HarperCollins, London, 2005

Darlington, W. A., *J. M. Barrie*, Blackie & Son Limited, 1938

Davis, S. E., *The Visitor's Guide to Broadway*, W. & H. Smith, Evesham, 1906

Dobbs, Brian, *Edwardians at Play*, Pelham Books Ltd., London, 1973

Donaldson, Francis, *P.G. Wodehouse, a Biography*, Weidenfeld and Nicolson, 1982

Du Maurier, Daphne, *Gerald, A Portrait*, London, 1934

Dunbar, Janet, *J. M. Barrie: The Man Behind the Image*, Collins, London, 1970

Easdale, Roderick, *The Novel Life of P.G. Wodehouse*, Superscript, 2003

Foot, Michael, *H. G., The History of Mr Wells*, Doubleday, 1995

Frith, David, *My Dear Victorious Stod*, New Malden, 1970

Frith, David, *The Golden Age of Cricket: 1890–1914*, Lutterworth Press, London, 1978

Fry, C. B., *Life Worth Living: Some Phases of an Englishman*, Eyre & Spotiswoode, London, 1939

Grahame, Kenneth, *Pagan Papers*, E. Mathews & J. Lane, London, 1893

Grahame, Kenneth, *The Golden Age*, John Lane, London, 1895

Hedgcock, Murray (Ed.), *Wodehouse at the Wicket*, Hutchinson, London, 1997

Holt, Richard, *Sport and the British: A Modern History*, Oxford University Press, 1990

Holt, Richard, Mangan, J. A., & Lafranchi, Pierre (Eds.), *European Heroes: Myth, Identity and Sport*, Frank Cass, London, 1996

Jeal, Tim, *Baden-Powell: Founder of the Boy Scouts*, Hutchinson, London, 1989

Kinross, Albert, *An Unconventional Cricketer*, Harold Shaylor, London 1930

Lancelyn Green, Roger, *A. E. W. Mason*, Max Parrish, London, 1952

Lancelyn Green, Roger, *Fifty Years of Peter Pan*, Peter Davies, London, 1954

Lancelyn Green, Roger, *J. M. Barrie*, Bodley Head, 1960

Lellenberg, Stashower and Foley (Eds), *Arthur Conan Doyle, A Life in Letters*, HarperPress 2007

Lucas, Audrey, *E.V. Lucas, A Portrait*, Methuen, 1939

Lycett, Andrew, *Conan Doyle: The Man Who Created Sherlock Holmes*, Weidenfeld and Nicolson, London, 2007

Mackail, Denis, *The story of J.M.B.*, Peter Davies, London, 1941

Mackail, Denis, *Life with Topsy*, William Heinemann, London 1942

Major, John, *More than a Game: The Story of Cricket's Early Years*, HarperPress, London, 2007

Mangan, J. A., *Athleticism in the Victorian and Edwardian Public School*, Cambridge University Press, 1981

Mangan, J. A., *The Games Ethic and Imperialism: Aspects of the diffusion of an ideal*, Viking, 1986

Marcossin, I. and Frohman, Daniel, *Charles Frohman: Manager and Man*, Bodley Head, New York, 1915

McConkey, Kenneth, *Edwardian Portraits: Images of an age of Opulence*, Suffolk, 1987

McCrum, Robert, *Wodehouse: A Life*, Penguin, London, 2005

McKinstry, Leo, *Rosebery: Statesman in Turmoil*, John Murray, London, 2005

Mead, Gary, *The Good Soldier: The Biography of Douglas Haig*, Atlantic Books, London, 2007

Meredith, George, *Letters of George Meredith, edited by his son*, Constable, London, 1912

Merivale, Patricia, *Pan the Goat-God: His Myth in Modern Times*, Harvard University Press, 1969

Meynell, Viola (Ed.), *The Letters of J. M. Barrie*, Peter Davies, London, 1942

Midwinter, Eric, *Quill on Willow*, Aneas Press, 2001

Moore, Decima and Guggisberg, Major F. G., *We Two in West Africa*, William Heinemann, 1909

Morrah, Patrick, *The Golden Age of Cricket*, Eyre & Spottiswoode, London, 1967

Neubauer, John, *The Fin-de-Siècle Culture of Adolescence*, London, 1992

Newbolt, Henry, *Selected Poems of Henry Newbolt*, Hodder & Stoughton, London, 1981

Nicoll, Catherine Robertson, *Under the Bay Tree*, privately printed, London, 1934

Owen, Wilfred, *The Complete Poems and Fragments*, Chatto & Windus, London, 1983

Parker, Eric, *Hesketh Prichard: A Memoir*, T. Fisher Unwin Ltd., London, 1924

Paxman, Jeremy, *The English*, Michael Joseph, London, 1998

Plumtre, George, *The Golden Age of Cricket*, London, 1990

Priestley, J. B., *George Meredith*, Macmillan, London, 1926

Price, R. G. G., *A History of Punch*, London, 1956

Rae, Simon, *W. G. Grace: A Life*, Faber and Faber, London, 1998

Ranjitsinhji, K. S., *The Jubilee Book of Cricket*, William Blackwood, Edinburgh, 1897

Rayvern Allen, David, *Sir Aubrey*, Elm Tree Press, London, 1982

Rayvern Allen, David, *Peter Pan and Cricket*, Constable, London, 1988

Rayvern Allen, David (Ed.), *A Breathless Hush, The MCC Anthology of Cricket Verse*, Methuen, London, 2004

Rayvern Allen, David, *Cricket through the pages: An illustrated anthology spanning 200 years of cricket*, Andre Deutsch, London, 2002

Rose, Jacqueline, *The Case of Peter Pan, or The Impossibility of Children's Fiction*, Macmillan, London, 1984

Rosenwater, Irving, *Sir Donald Bradman, a biography*, Batsford, London, 1978

Rowland, Peter, *Raffles and his Creator, The Life and Works of E. W. Hornung*, Nekta, London, 1999

Sassoon, Siegfried, *The War Poems of Siegfried Sassoon*, Faber, London, 1983

Schur, Owen, *Victorian Pastoral: Tennyson, Hardy, and the Subversion of Forms*, Ohio State University Press, Columbus 1989

Scott, Peter, *The Eye of the Wind*, Hodder & Stoughton, London,1966

Shere, Gomshall & Peaslake Local History Society, *Shere, Gomshall and Peaslake, A Short History*, Jamaica Press, Devon, 2008

Smart, John Blythe, *The Real Colin Blythe*, Blythe Smart Publications, Kent, 2009

Squires, Michael, *The Pastoral Novel: Studies in George Eliot, Thomas Hardy, and D. H. Lawrence*, University Press of Virginia, Charlottesville, 1974

Terry, Ellen, *Memoirs*, Gollancz, 1933

Thwaite, Ann, *A. A. Milne: His Life*, Faber and Faber, London, 1990

Titchener-Barrett, Robert, *Eton and Harrow at Lord's*, Quiller Press, 1996

Warner, P. F., *How We Recovered the Ashes*, Chapman and Hall, London, 1904

Warner, P. F., *My Cricketing Life*, Hodder & Stoughton, London, 1921

Williams, Jack, *Cricket and England: A Cultural and Social History of the Inter-war Years*, Frank Cass, London & Portland, Oregon,1999

Wilton, Iain, *C. B. Fry*, Richard Cohen Books, London, 1999

Wullschläger, Jackie, *Inventing Wonderland: The Lives of Lewis Carroll, Edward Lear, J.M. Barrie, Kenneth Grahame and A.A. Milne*, Methuen, London, 1995

# INDEX

The initials J. M. B. and the name Barrie,
used without initials, both designate J. M. Barrie.

Abbey, Edwin 100–1, 122, 189
Adams, Maude, letter from Barrie
    to 289
Allahakbarries Cricket Club 1–2,
    3, 145–6, 193, 249, 314; Artists
    v. Writers 94, 97–130, 146–7,
    165–6, 179–81, 218; Authors v.
    Esher (recorded in Allahakbar-
    ries' scorebook) 169–70;
    Barrie's centrality to 7–11;
    Barrie's speech about 305;
    Barrie's writings about them as
    'Celebrities at Home' 67–70;
    birth of 29–62; at Broadway
    97–130; 'Duffer's Match' 148–9;
    embezzled by Bright 222; first
    games 47–9, 50–3, 63–94;
    naming of 48–9; *Peter Pan*
    and 204–5; significance in
    English cricket 311; staging of
    *The Greedy Dwarf* 158–9; as
    true amateurs 56–7; v. E. V.
    Lucas's XI 262–5; v. Edgar
    Horne's XI (Shackleford team)
    151–2, 172, 174, 194, 209,
    218; v. Pasture Wood 193; v.
    *Punch* Bowl Cricket Club 162,
    170–2; v. Royal Engineers
    181; v. Shere 47–9, 50–3, 74,
    85–91, 94; v. Western Scotland

(Allahakbarries in name only)
    307–8; *see also individual team
    members*
Allen, David Rayvern 116
Alletson, Ted 250
Amundsen, Roald 251, 252
Anderson, Mary (Madame de
    Navarro) 8, 47, 99, 298–9, 305;
    Artists v. Writers games 101–9,
    112, 114, 116, 120–1, 129–30;
    on Barrie 111; bickerings with
    Barrie in their memoirs 113–14
Anon, James (pseudonym of J. M.
    Barrie) 12, 24–5, 31, 63–4; *see
    also* Barrie, J. M.: *The Greenwood
    Hat* memoirs
Ansell, Mary (later Mary Ansell
    Barrie) 83, 92; *see also* Barrie,
    Mary, née Ansell
Arlott, John 178
Arnold, Ted 212
Arthur Conan Doyle's XI 149–50
Artists v. Writers cricket games
    94, 97–130, 146–7, 165–6,
    179–81, 218
Ashes: (1882) 88–9; (1894/5) 92;
    (1897/8) 156; (1902) 184–5;
    (1904) 206; (1930) 308
Askew, Dickie 50–1, 52, 67
Asquith, Cynthia 25, 30, 48, 202–3,

335